Religion, Art, and Money

PETER W. WILLIAMS

Religion, Art, and Money

Episcopalians and American Culture from
the Civil War to the Great Depression

The University of North Carolina Press *Chapel Hill*

This book was published with the assistance of the William R. Kenan Jr. Fund of the University of North Carolina Press.

The paper in this book meets the guidelines for permanence and durability of the Committee on Production Guidelines for Book Longevity of the Council on Library Resources.

The University of North Carolina Press has been a member of the Green Press Initiative since 2003.

Cover illustration: reredos, Saint Thomas Church Fifth Avenue, New York, N.Y.

Library of Congress Cataloging-in-Publication Data
Williams, Peter W.
Religion, art, and money : Episcopalians and American culture from the Civil War to the Great Depression / Peter W. Williams.
    pages cm
Includes bibliographical references and index.
ISBN 978-1-4696-2697-0 (cloth : alk. paper)—ISBN 978-1-4696-2698-7 (ebook)
1. Episcopal Church—History—19th century. 2. Episcopal Church—History—20th century. 3. Episcopal Church—Influence. 4. Episcopalians—United States—History—19th century. 5. Episcopalians—United States—History—20th century. 6. United States—Church history—19th century. 7. United States—Church history—20th century. I. Title.
BX5882.W55   2016   283'.7309034—dc23
2015028003

Chapter 6 originally appeared in slightly different form as "The Gospel of Wealth and the Gospel of Art: Episcopalians and Cultural Philanthropy from the Gilded Age to the Depression," *Anglican and Episcopal History* 75, no. 2 (June 2006): 170–223. Used with permission.

For Dana and Jonathan,

as well as

Alban, Bailey, Clara, Macy, and Remington

Contents

Illustrations

Preface

In the improbable event that my grandparents, newly off the boat from the southern Baltic in the years after the Civil War, had presented themselves for worship at an Episcopal church one Sunday morning, the result would most likely have been mutual incomprehension. They would have found the English being spoken unintelligible, and would have been immediately branded as foreigners. In a few churches they might have found a familiar crucifix and some images of saints, but even there the décor would have seemed unwelcomingly austere. In some cases an usher might have directed them to a mission where they would find their own language spoken. Or perhaps another usher might, with just a hint of distaste, have shown them to a pew in the rear, far from those rented by and reserved for regular communicants. Most likely they would not have repeated their mistake and would have sought out instead a more gemütlich parish that would recreate the familiar sights, sounds, and smells of north central Europe.

The Episcopal Church in the era of massive European immigration was growing rapidly, but only in a few urban neighborhoods did its new membership come from recent immigrants. It was becoming *the* "Anglo" church at a time when the terms "English" and "Anglo-Saxon" were code for a fashionable aesthetic, a favored genetic lineage, and an ideology of racial superiority. New members were attracted in some cases by a traditional, euphonious liturgy, and they could pick and choose among a wide variety of theological options. Others perceived, at some level of consciousness, an opportunity to acquire a marker of enhanced social status and opportunities for business, professional, and political networking. The church might also have given their children entrée into the new educational world of the private boarding school, where they would find a fast track to an Ivy League college and a circle of acquaintance that would prove advantageous in later life on Wall Street or the higher reaches of government. It might have inspired them with a socially desirable (or even genuine) appreciation for the arts and have led them to become patrons of the museums and symphonies that every city aiming at respectability was striving to acquire. It might also have exposed them to a critique of laissez-faire capitalism, drawn them into movements of political reform, and provided opportunities for social service to their new—but probably not next-door—immigrant neighbors. Or, perhaps, these Episcopalian churchgoers experienced all of the above.

The following chapters examine the ways in which Episcopalians between the historical benchmarks of the Civil War and the Great Depression participated in social and cultural movements, on which they put their own stamp. They rarely did this in isolation, but in many cases they were leaders rather than followers. By leading these movements, they left a lasting mark on the American scene—most visibly in the churches and cathedrals that can still be found in most cities and in the elite boarding schools that flourish, especially in the northeast. More subtly, they made major contributions to urban "highbrow" culture and arguably helped smooth the way for a widespread acceptance of the visual and material as means of religious and cultural expression in a society where an iconoclastic Puritanism had shaped a dominant aesthetic. They were also pioneers in the application of Christian principles to social amelioration and political reform in that broader movement that came to be known as the "Social Gospel."

This history of Episcopalians' relationship to the broader American society does not aim to serve as a comprehensive history of the Episcopal Church during these decades. Rather, it is focused on analyzing how the members of this religious denomination participated in and helped bring about change in the wider American culture. The story emanates from the American Northeast, with occasional forays into cities such as San Francisco, which had been shaped by the culture of Yankeedom. Episcopalians were also influential in the American South, but that is a story for another time and place. The national Protestant Episcopal Church, which was growing and changing during these years, makes only occasional and fleeting appearances, as do some of its significant activities, such as missionary work. Laypeople—mostly, but not entirely, well-to-do white males—as well as clergy and bishops, all play roles in a collective biography that traces their interaction with buildings, ideas, institutions, and social forces. Their efforts helped to create a loosely bounded but nevertheless distinctive social and cultural nexus within the broader society, as well as an enduring legacy of a built environment that has continued to shape the ways in which Americans experience religion as a material as well as a spiritual phenomenon. Their story, unfolded at some length, should give balance and nuance to accounts of the Gilded Age and Progressive Era, which treat these Episcopalians, if at all, simply as plutocrats for whom churchgoing was a matter of providentially endorsed conspicuous consumption.[1]

THIS BOOK, WHICH COMES at the end of my active academic career, had its remote origins in the final chapter—"Anglicans and Aesthetes"—of my Yale doctoral dissertation of nearly half a century ago.[2] My two advisors, the late Sydney E. Ahlstrom and the very much alive Daniel Walker Howe, provided exemplary guidance in my first attempt at serious scholarship, and Dan has provided valuable input into this present work all these many years later. In addition to Dan Howe, other scholarly friends who have read and commented on individual chapters include Mary Kupiec Cayton, Jeanne Halgren Kilde, and Eugene Y. Lowe Jr. Special thanks are due to Charles H. Lippy, Anne C. Rose, and Thomas Rzeznik, who heroically read through the entire manuscript and offered many useful insights and suggestions. Archivists who generously made institutional materials available to me include Douglas Brown and Gail Friedman of Groton; Peggy Dahlberg at Christ Church, Cranbrook; Mary Davis and Patricia Hurley at Trinity Church, Boston; Judy Donald of Choate Rosemary Hall; Richard Greening Hewlett and Diane Ney of the National Cathedral; the Isabella Stewart Gardner Museum and Bridgman Images; Avery Griffin of St. Thomas Church, New York; Esslie Hughes, Jennifer Hull, and Gillian Kopenig, St. Bartholomew's Church, New York; Wayne Kempton at the Cathedral Church of St. John the Divine; Michael Lampen of Grace Cathedral, San Francisco; David Levesque of St. Paul's School; Bruce McLay of All Saints Ashmont; Matthew P. Payne of the diocese of Fond du Lac; Don Prout of "Cincinnativiews" website; Marel Rogers of the Kent School; Mark Tenniswood of St. George's Church, New York; and Julianne Ture of the Church of the Advent. Other scholars deserving an appreciative nod are David Bains, Robert A. Benson, John Schmalzbauer, and Susan Stonesifer. Thanks are also in order to the National Endowment of the Humanities, grants from which helped to lay the early foundations for this study; Amy Ansorg and James Constantine Hanges of the Department of Comparative Religion at Miami University, who aided significantly in its production; and the staff of the interlibrary loan division and the CIM laboratory at Miami's King Library.

Special thanks are also due to Elaine Maisner of the University of North Carolina Press, who patiently waited for an extraordinary number of years from our initial discussions to the culmination of this work. She and her staff, especially Alison Shay, have been instrumental in this project's ultimate realization. Victoria G. Pryor of Arcadia Literary Agency has also provided friendship, encouragement, tact, and professional expertise in negotiating final arrangements for publication.

By way of disclosure, I should say that I have been an active member of the Episcopal Church for most of my adult life. David L. Holmes and the late John Woolverton helped initiate me into the at times arcane world of Episcopal Church history. Over a number of years I have served as a member of several of its national agencies: the Historical Society, NEHA (National Episcopal Historians and Archivists), the Guild of Scholars, and the General Board of Examining Chaplains. In these capacities I have come to learn much of the denomination's lore and foibles, getting to know many remarkable bishops, clergy, seminary faculty, and laymen and women. I have also benefitted greatly from many decades of life in my home parish of Holy Trinity in Oxford, Ohio, whose rectors have ranged from a direct descendant and namesake of one of the Connecticut clergy who selected the first Episcopal bishop in Revolutionary times to the granddaughter of Greek immigrants. Fellow parishioners have included folk not only of British but also of African, Arab, Armenian, Bulgarian, German, Greek, Irish, Italian, Jewish, Mexican, Polish, Russian, and Scandinavian descent. Its multicultural character is further attested by the fact that it is also almost certainly the only Anglican parish in Christendom at which Dean Martin's "That's Amore" is ritually sung at its annual Christmas dinner. If my forebears would have been bewildered and quite likely turned away by the Episcopal Church of their day, I have been embraced by that of mine.

Finally, I wish to acknowledge the companionship and support of my late wife, Ruth Ann Alban Williams, who lived to see this project's completion but not, alas, its final publication. *Dona ei requiem.*

Religion, Art, and Money

Introduction

Three Ways of Looking at an Episcopalian

SHE IS NOW A DUCHESS

Miss Consuelo Vanderbilt's Marriage to the Duke of Marlborough

GREAT CROWDS CHEER THE BRIDE

Thousands of Women Besiege the Young Woman's Home and
St. Thomas's Church

GIVEN AWAY BY W. K. VANDERBILT

Guests at the Wedding Breakfast—

Departure of Bride and Bridegroom for Oakdale, L.I.

Thus read the lead-in to the elaborate coverage of the celebrity event of
the year in the *New York Times* for November 5, 1895. On the previous day, the
heiress Consuelo Vanderbilt had been forced by her mother into marriage
to the Ninth Duke of Marlborough, a cash-strapped English nobleman whom
she loathed. (The story was told that she had been locked in her hotel room
until she relented.)[1] Henry Codman Potter, the Episcopal bishop of New
York, who, with a cadre of other bishops and clergy, officiated at this notorious event, could easily be caricatured as a panderer to the rich—anciennes
and nouveaux—who made up his constituency. While there is an element of
truth in such a caricature, the reality of Potter's career is considerably more
complex. A genuine celebrity in New York, he was known not only as an
abettor of the follies of the wealthy, but also as a trusted ally by the working-
class community, few of whom were Episcopalian, and as a fair-minded ar-
bitrator of labor disputes.[2]

In truth, the world of the Episcopal Church between the Civil War and
the Great Depression was one of considerable complexity and ferment, with
consequences far beyond the internecine struggles among High, Low, and
Broad Church factions that make up much of the stuff of traditional institutional history. Episcopalians were also emerging at this time as a distinctive
social configuration, that is, a national elite. While by no means all numbered

themselves among "the rich, the well-born, and the able"—a phrase coined by a notable Episcopalian of an earlier time, Alexander Hamilton—enough did so that their denomination acquired a reputation that continued to attract many who aspired to high social status as well as retain those who had already achieved such status. Finally, many among the Episcopal Church's rapidly growing membership were involved in a variety of discourses and activities that helped shape an emergent, distinctively American, urban culture, just as they were in turn shaped by many of the broader forces in that culture.

To chronicle the history of the Episcopal Church as that of one denomination parallel to similar brands of Protestant Christianity has been done ably enough many times, but it is an approach that omits a good deal of what it meant to live as an Episcopalian during this era and what impact Episcopalians collectively exerted on the broader culture.* A tripartite analysis suggests itself, involving somewhat porous, but nonetheless useful, distinctions between religious, social, and cultural history. The first of these, which has been traced many times, can be brief. The second, which has never been treated very systematically, can be sketched from a variety of sources, but still awaits more definitive treatment by historians versed in the methods of social history. The third is the focus of this study, and includes such themes as philanthropy, the arts, education, and social criticism and reform.[3]

Religion

The Episcopal Church emerged from the Civil War reasonably unscathed. It avoided the antebellum divisions that had rent the national Baptist, Methodist, and Presbyterian denominations, in part because much of its leadership had made a policy of avoiding political involvement as beyond the scope of the church. It had been well established in the South during colonial times

---

*In American usage, "Episcopal" is an adjective, capitalized when used in the name of the denomination and, in lowercase, referring to governance by or the authority of bishops. "Episcopalian" is a proper noun designating a member of the Episcopal Church. "Anglican" refers to the international community of churches that began with the Church of England, spread through the British Empire, and took independent national form as that empire began to disintegrate. The (Protestant) Episcopal Church, which was organized in the 1780s in the wake of American independence, was the first independent Anglican church outside the British Isles, having been preceded by the Episcopal Church of Scotland. The use of some form of the *Book of Common Prayer* in worship and, since the mid-nineteenth century, attendance of bishops at the decennial Lambeth Conference convened by the archbishop of Canterbury, have been hallmarks of Anglican identity.

as the church of the elite, and that elite—including a number of clergy and bishops—continued to hold slaves after independence. Northern Episcopalians were not of one mind on the matter: Some actively defended the "peculiar institution," and only a few flocked to join the movement for abolition. The Southern dioceses seceded during the "late unpleasantness" to form the short-lived Protestant Episcopal Church in the Confederate States of America, but their bishops began to straggle back into the 1865 General Convention—the triennial assemblage by which the church is governed—and the *status quo ante* was restored with little fanfare or controversy.

The only enduring schism in the Episcopal Church during the nineteenth century arose out of a division not over social policy but rather over matters of doctrine and liturgical practice. Almost since its inception, the (Protestant) Episcopal Church found itself divided into two parties, which inherited from their English predecessors the labels "Low Church" and "High Church." In the United States, "Low Church" was code for "Evangelical"; its adherents, who were based in the vicinity of the nation's capital, saw themselves as Reformed Christians who followed a distinctive liturgy—the *Book of Common Prayer*—and were governed by bishops. However, they regarded these particulars as less important than the universal marks of Evangelical Protestantism: the authority of scripture, the need for a personal experience of regeneration, the doctrine of the vicarious atonement, and the imperative to spread the faith aggressively. "High Church" Episcopalians, based in New York City, stressed instead the centrality of Episcopal polity—that is, the necessity that its bishops be firmly planted in the "historic episcopate," or apostolic succession of bishops—and of sacramental worship, focused on the "dominically instituted" rites of baptism and the Holy Eucharist, which were believed to have been mandated personally by Jesus. Much of the antebellum history of the Episcopal Church consisted of sniping and jockeying between these two factions as they vied for control of the denomination and its agencies.

The question of whether Episcopalians were essentially Evangelical Protestants or Reformed Catholics reemerged after the Civil War, as each of these parties began to mutate and factionalize internally with changes in generational leadership. The more extreme Evangelicals grew increasingly restive with what they saw as insufficiently Reformed language concerning regeneration in the prayer book's baptismal service, and unsuccessfully petitioned the General Convention of the Episcopal Church to change the wording. This did not happen, and those clergy who substituted their own wording without Episcopal authorization sometimes found themselves facing disciplinary action. The more militant Dissenters left to organize the Reformed Episcopal Church in 1871. Although this schismatic group, which still exists, has never flourished numerically, it drained enough of the younger leadership from the Low Church community that the latter's influence was thereafter minimized within the parent denomination. In the following account, they play only a marginal role.

One of the reasons for the drastic action taken by the more militant Evangelicals was their growing alarm over developments within the High Church community. The latter had been energized in the 1840s by the emergence in England of the Oxford, or Tractarian, movement, led by university dons John Henry Newman, John Keble, and Edward Bouvier Pusey. These "Oxford Apostles" argued that the apostolically rooted and historically continuous character of the church as the repository of sacramental worship was essential to authentic Christian life and practice. Tractarianism rapidly took root in the United States in the old High Church hotbeds of New York and New Jersey especially, and was accompanied by its Cambridge-based counterpart, known as the Ecclesiological movement. English and American Ecclesiologists argued that proper Christian worship along Tractarian lines could be conducted only in churches designed on the medieval Gothic model, every detail of which was believed to have symbolic and sacramental significance. (This doubtful assertion was based on the Ecclesiologists' reading of a late medieval text by Durandus, who delighted in finding symbolism where the builders had most likely intended practicality or ornament.)[4] The results were embodied in a wave of new church designs, beginning with St. James the Less in what is now Philadelphia, and continuing with the prolific work of English-born architect Richard Upjohn, whose 1845 Trinity Church in lower Manhattan is still a monument to the Gothic revival in the United States.[5] These churches were designed not as preaching halls but as sacramental centers, and featured such elements as a sanctuary clearly delineated from the nave, where the congregation was seated, in which the *altar—not* the "Communion table"—was the visual and spiritual center of the structure.

Following the Civil War, a new emphasis developed among the heirs of the Oxford movement that also derived from English precedent, namely, "Ritualism" (a term more or less interchangeable with "Anglo-Catholicism.") Ritualists embraced what their opponents saw as an extreme Roman version of liturgical observance, a practice made all the more alarming because of the defection of a number of prominent Episcopalians, including one bishop, to Roman Catholicism prior to the Civil War.[6] They advocated such practices as auricular confession (that is, made orally and individually to a priest) and absolution; veneration of the saints; belief in the Real Presence of Jesus in the Eucharist; and adoration of the exposed Eucharistic host. Ritualists were also fond of the use of incense and of bells during services, which gained their churches the enduring nickname of "smells and bells." In major eastern cities, such as Boston, New York, and Philadelphia, they were represented particularly by one of the new religious orders, recently revived in and imported from England, the Cowley Fathers, who periodically encountered resistance both from local bishops and their superiors back in England.[7] These religious orders, for both men and women, would play an instrumental role both in the promotion of educational and social projects as well as in the introduction of a new kind of spirituality for clergy and laity alike.

It was in the Great Lakes area, however, where American Ritualism particularly flourished under the leadership of bishops such as Charles Grafton of Fond du Lac, Wisconsin, and James DeKoven of Illinois. This area was nicknamed the "Biretta Belt," after a piece of headgear worn by Roman Catholic clerics and favored by Ritualists, and the flavor of the community there was captured in a 1900 photograph of an assemblage of Anglo-Catholic bishops colorfully arrayed in a variety of Episcopal regalia, some apparently borrowed from the Eastern Orthodox Church, which earned the assemblage the derogatory label "the Fond du Lac Circus." Nashotah House, a seminary founded in Wisconsin in 1842, became the center for training clergy in this tradition. New York City's General Theological Seminary, the first Episcopal theological school in the nation, was founded in 1817 as a focus for the older High Church party led by New York bishop John Henry Hobart. Its Low Church counterpart historically was Virginia Theological Seminary in Alexandria (1823), now a suburb of Washington, D.C.

Though Ritualism had to struggle against Low Church opposition during its early years and never gained ascendancy within the denomination, many of its less extreme liturgical innovations eventually gained wide acceptance, and the educational and social work of its religious orders was a major contribution to Episcopal outreach efforts. The wave of the immediate future, however, was to be neither High nor Low, but rather lay in a new movement, also English-inspired, that began to take shape during the decades that followed the Civil War. The "Broad Church" movement, as it came to be called, was never an organized faction, but rather a climate of opinion that rapidly spread among some of the most influential church leaders of the era such as Boston's Phillips Brooks and New York's William Reed Huntington.

"The Fond du Lac Circus" is the nickname given to this photograph of Anglo-Catholic bishops clad in Catholic vestments assembled for the consecration of Reginald Heber Weller as Bishop Coadjutor of the diocese of Fond du Lac, Wisconsin, in 1900. Also present were bishops of the Russian Orthodox and Polish National Catholic Churches. (Courtesy of the Diocese of Fond du Lac archives. The negative is held at the Wisconsin Historical Society, Key Number (X3)40940.)

The Broad Church movement essentially was an attempt to adapt the best from modern thought and culture to the purposes of the church. Its origins can be traced to the publication in England in 1860 of a collection of articles by several scholars entitled *Essays and Reviews,* which were intended to intro-duce an Anglican audience to the fruits of the new, critical biblical scholarship that had been developing in Germany. Subsequent English theologians such as Charles Gore published in 1889 another collection entitled *Lux Mundi* ("The Light of the World"), which built on this earlier recognition of the value of modern scientific and historical thought to religion. The authors of *Lux Mundi* stressed especially the centrality of the traditional Christian doctrine of the Incarnation, thereby legitimizing a focus of Christian concern away from the ecclesiastical and supernatural and toward the contempo-rary world and its opportunities and challenges. Among the latter were the traumatic results of industrialization and urbanization in Britain, issues that prompted Anglican writers such as Frederick Denison Maurice and Charles

Kingsley to mobilize Anglican theology as a basis for a rigorous critique of laissez-faire capitalism. Another representative of British Broad Church concerns was Thomas Arnold, whose literary son Matthew is better remembered today. Arnold was an educational reformer—he transformed Rugby School according to his version of Christian principles—and advocate of church reform, as well as the inspiration for the popular English novel *Tom Brown's Schooldays*.[8] Arnold's role as an embodiment of the movement's principles is captured in a contemporary's observation that "he awoke every morning with the conviction that everything was an open question."[9]

The American Broad Church movement absorbed much from its British antecedents and contemporaries, and set about applying these lessons not only to the Episcopal Church but to contemporary society more broadly, which they saw as the ultimate object of their ministry. Phillips Brooks, for example, organized groups of local clergy, first in Philadelphia and then in Boston, for ecumenical discussion of current topics of all sorts. He and like-minded Episcopal clergy in 1874 expanded the scope of these meetings into the American Church Congress, a forum open to Episcopal clergy of all stripes that also entertained visiting speakers of a variety of persuasions, such as the tax reformer Henry George.[10] The idea here was to engage the world on its own terms rather than distancing oneself in an ecclesiastical ghetto.

Broad Church advocates were by-and-large committed Episcopalians, although a few, such as William S. Rainsford at St. George's in New York, eventually found that even the minimal creedal requirements of the church were more than they could in good conscience accept. Where Low Churchmen felt kinship with fellow Evangelicals in Reformed denominations, and Anglo-Catholics sometimes went the whole distance to Rome, those of the Broad persuasion felt themselves to be kindred spirits with other liberal Protestants. One arena in which this collaboration played itself out was the Social Gospel movement, which marshaled the resources of German-derived theology and biblical scholarship to reinterpret the Christian message as aimed at the redemption not only of the individual but of society as a whole. Its most visible publicists were not Episcopalians: Walter Rauschenbusch was a Baptist and Washington Gladden a Congregationalist. However, as will become clearer in a later chapter, Episcopalians played an early and especially creative role in applying the movement's teachings to the social realities of the contemporary American urban scene.

A few other developments within the Episcopal Church during these decades are worth noting by way of background. One was negative. The furor raised within the Reformed denominations, especially Baptists and Presbyterians, by the twin challenges of Darwinian evolution and German biblical criticism—both posited on the assumption of dynamic development over time rather than stasis, whether of species or revelation—were nonstarters among Episcopalians. Charles Briggs, for example, the controversial professor of biblical studies at New York's Union Theological Seminary, was deposed from his status as a Presbyterian minister, but was shortly afterward ordained as an Episcopal priest. Although by no means all Episcopalians accepted these developments with equanimity, these issues never rose to such a point of contentiousness as to threaten denominational unity or the good standing of individual clergy.

A very different sort of development reflected the impact of the broader culture on the church's polity. Although the establishment of the Protestant Episcopal Church in 1789 as an American denomination independent of the Church of England provided for Episcopal polity—that is, governance by bishops—its canon law did not empower bishops with a great deal of authority within their dioceses. There was a presiding bishop, but this was more of an honorific for the senior bishop than a post carrying real power. This latter office was made elective and upgraded to carry with it real executive status by acts of General Convention in 1901 and 1919, reflecting the themes of consolidation, centralization, and professionalization that characterized business and other secular institutions during the Progressive Era. Similarly, individual bishops sought consolidation of their diocesan authority, in part through the movement begun in the mid-1860s to establish cathedrals as symbols of Episcopal presence and centralized agencies of administration. Although early cathedrals were usually urban churches with enhanced status, the desire for such structures soon gave rise to such architectural marvels as St. John the Divine in New York, Grace Cathedral in San Francisco, and the National Cathedral in Washington, D.C. The potential of such cathedrals for artistic and symbolic expression is a major theme of this study.

Society

One of the most remarkable figures of mid-nineteenth century Manhattan was Isaac Hull Brown, who served as sexton of Grace Church from 1845 until his death in 1880. Weighing in at some four hundred pounds, "Brown," as he was invariably known, began his career as a carpenter, and, in a very American story of (ambiguously) upward mobility, he parleyed his position as church caretaker into one of unrivalled influence in the highest circles of New York society. Described as "the leading clerical factotum for the city's rich and famous Episcopalians," Brown served not only as pew-rent collector, plant manager, and undertaker for his parish, but also as a sort of free-lance, entrepreneurial concierge for the parish's members, who came to rely on him as someone who could make social events happen properly by knowing where to obtain every necessary service and commodity. These services included "Brown's Brigade," a cadre of well-dressed and mannered young men who could serve as suitable escorts for the daughters of the elite on particular occasions while knowing their proper place at other times. Although never rising above working-class status himself, Brown acquired the position of a social arbiter upon whom the elite relied to be an impeccable judge as to who possessed "correct form."[11]

Grace Church, designed in its most recent incarnation by James Renwick Jr. in the mid-1840s, has been described as "a handsome venue for a collective social display of the city's most privileged citizens, and a place dedicated to secular affirmation of class solidarity."[12] Renwick, an Episcopalian, was also the architect for St. Patrick's Roman Catholic Cathedral on Fifth Avenue as well as the Smithsonian Institution's "Castle." As at most such churches, pews were not open to the general public, but were rented or sold at auction to raise funds for the church and to guarantee a literal and figurative position for the pew holder. Pews were thus real property, subject to being passed down as part of an estate and subdivided among heirs and even being sold to third parties.[13] At Boston's Trinity Church, the story goes, an entrepreneurial vestryman regularly rented a number of prime pews, sublet them profitably, and dutifully returned 10 percent of his yield to the parish.[14]

Although Grace Church has retained its fashionable cachet to the present day, it would be both unfair and inaccurate to dismiss it as the preserve of the well-to-do. Under a series of remarkable rectors in the late nineteenth and early twentieth centuries, Grace Church, like many of its urban counterparts, invested its funds not only in architectural enhancement and musical programming but also in outreach to the community. Henry Codman Potter, who served as rector from 1868 until his election as bishop in 1883, instituted a parish yearbook in order to publicize the parish's outreach work, and transformed the once complacent parish into the prototype of one of the Episcopal Church's major contributions to social Christianity: the institutional church.

(The phenomenon of the institutional church—usually a vast urban plant including all manner of recreational, educational, and even medical facilities as well as worship space—will be revisited at some length in chapter 4.)[15]

Potter was followed as rector by William Reed Huntington (1884–1909), the ecumenicist responsible for that formative statement of faith, the Chicago-Lambeth Quadrilateral. Huntington was not only an ecumenist but also a Broad Church promoter of the church as a vehicle for social amelioration. During his rectorship, a Great Mission House was established that, among other things, provided a place for poor women and girls from the immigrant community to work. This center encroached upon what had been the fashionable neighborhood of Broadway and Tenth Street.[16] Huntington prided Grace Church on resisting the temptation to become part of the "spoor of the rich," as Episcopal churches had been called as their constituencies migrated further and further uptown.[17] In the early 1890s, Grace became the employer of the first three graduates of the New York Training School for Deaconesses, "deaconess" being a new vocational category that allowed unmarried women to pursue a career of social service without the taint carried by the terms "nun" or "sister," which smacked of Romanism. Grace, like other downtown churches, opened a chapel that the poor might attend, presumably to avoid social discomfort both to themselves and their more affluent counterparts. Huntington also kept the church open on weekdays for the benefit of passersby and opened its reserved pews for general attendance at Sunday evening services. Grace eventually abolished pew rents in the 1930s.[18]

Although Grace was hardly on the cutting edge in its program of outreach to the poor—St. George's in Stuyvesant Square, of which financier J. P. Morgan was the longtime senior warden, was far more energetic in its outreach programs and abolished pew rents earlier than many others—it does nicely illustrate the fact that wealthy and fashionable congregations often felt compelled to utilize their wealth on behalf of the poor, who were not yet rendered invisible by suburbanization.[19] In Manhattan, however, it is safe to say that Episcopal churches were in fact places where the wealthy and fashionable—or the newly wealthy and would-be fashionable—tended to congregate. The Episcopal Church was well established as the church of what passed for an aristocracy in New York well before the Civil War. Columbia University had its origins as King's College under Anglican aegis, and Trinity Church at Wall Street and Broadway continues to this day to own acres of land in the most expensive part of the nation's richest city. However, New York's "masters of the universe," as Tom Wolfe would later style them, were a notoriously unstable community, and the city's Episcopal churches served as a vehicle through which the mores of the Knickerbockers—the old families of English and Dutch descent—could be passed along to the nouveaux riches "auslanders" who have endlessly replenished the city's economic leadership.[20]

In other cities, the situation was somewhat different. Chicago, at one end of the spectrum, was a creature of the postbellum era, and had no established aristocracy—all its *riches* were equally *nouveaux*. Although the Episcopal Church had no historic boundaries, it was brought to the city with the earliest entrepreneurs from "back East," and churches such as St. James—today its cathedral—vied with First Congregational and First, Second, and Fourth Presbyterian as places where business and dynastic alliances could be consummated, just as they could later be at urban and country clubs.[21] Much the same might be said of Detroit and other newly flourishing cities of the time.

At the other end of the American urban historical spectrum were Boston, Philadelphia, and even Pittsburgh, in which Unitarians, Quakers, and Presbyterians had the advantage of colonial or at least antebellum beginnings. Boston had, by the early nineteenth century, shed most traces of its Puritan origins, and the liberal Congregationalists—by 1825 officially organized as Unitarians—were universally, if sometimes ruefully, recognized as dominating the city's educational, cultural, and financial as well as religious institutions.[22] Harriet Beecher Stowe (a convert to the Episcopal Church) wrote in the autobiography of her father, the redoubtable evangelist Lyman Beecher: "All the literary men of Massachusetts were Unitarians. All the trustees and professors of Harvard College were Unitarians. All the elite of wealth and fashion crowded Unitarian churches."[23]

By the 1870s, however, the situation was shifting. Cleveland Amory, the chronicler of *The Proper Bostonians*, wrote of this transition:

> Little by little, however, a practical low-church Episcopalianism began to make severe inroads on Boston's home-grown Unitarianism. Many a First Family woman turned with joy to the more definite ritual of Episcopalianism, which included kneeling for prayer—Unitarians bend and make "slight obeisance" but do not kneel—and belief in the divinity of Christ. Sometimes she brought her husband along with her; sometimes First Families were split on the question. When the handsome young bachelor Phillips Brooks came to Boston in 1869 from Philadelphia, it was the Boston woman who soon made a social as well as an ecclesiastical lion out of him. With ringing rhetoric from his

Trinity Church pulpit Brooks soon had even such staunch Unitarian feminists as the daughters of James Russell Lowell and Dr. Oliver Wendell Holmes proudly referring to him as "our bishop"; since Brooks had been born a Unitarian, his success was singularly important in placing Episcopalianism on a par with Unitarianism in the fight for the No. 1 religion of Boston's best.[24]

Philadelphia was a somewhat different situation. The Pennsylvania colony had been founded as an idealistic experiment by the Society of Friends, or Quakers, whose pacifism and rejection of religious establishment had earned them the status of a persecuted minority in Britain. Their social connections, however—particularly those of the Penn family—had resulted in their being granted a whole colony in which to implement their religious ideals. The results were not enduring. Two of William Penn's three sons abandoned the "Friendly Persuasion" in favor of their ancestral Anglicanism, and the stresses of trying to govern a colony that was part of an empire engaged in seemingly continuous warfare soon led to an abandonment of responsibility to outsiders such as Benjamin Franklin, who had fewer scruples as to the uses of violence.[25]

By the time of the Revolution, the transformation of the Philadelphia elite's allegiance from Quakerism to Anglicanism had progressed dramatically. The crisis of conscience over the issue of the taking up of arms against perceived tyranny had become exacerbated by the revolt of the colonies, and many Quakers abandoned their ancestral principles and creed to serve the patriot cause. Although many Anglicans—particularly the clergy—in other parts of the colonies fled to Canada or the mother country after the outbreak of hostilities, their Philadelphia counterparts mainly supported the movement for freedom, and many Quakers joined them when their coreligionists refused to take sides or arms. As a result, Philadelphia's Quaker community retained a certain amount of influence and prestige in the new republic, but Christ Church and the newer St. Peter's emerged as the centers of religious and social influence in the early nineteenth century, and Episcopalians rapidly displaced Quakers as community leaders.[26] Many of Philadelphia's first families—Cadwaladers, Biddles, Morrises, Whartons, Peppers, Robertses—had begun as Quakers, but soon entered into the ranks of the Episcopalians.[27] The difference in ethos between the two communities was summed up in two words: "plain" versus "fancy."[28] Where even wealthy Quakers shunned conspicuous display, Anglicans had little compunction about emulating the lifestyles of their worldly British paragons.[29]

The heyday of Episcopal influence in Philadelphia came, as in many cities, during the late nineteenth and early twentieth centuries. It was during this period that a demographic shift among the elite took place from the core city to emergent peripheral neighborhoods. In Boston, this meant the Back Bay and Copley Square, the site of Phillips Brooks's Trinity Church. In Philadelphia, it was Rittenhouse Square, where Anglo-Catholic St. Mark's vied with the "Lower" Holy Trinity for fashionable adherents.[30] The latter's rector in the 1860s, the same Phillips Brooks who would soon distinguish himself in his native Boston, described Philadelphia's religious scene as follows:

> Philadelphia is a city where the Episcopal Church is thoroughly at home. Side by side with the gentler Puritanism of that sunnier clime, the Quakerism which quarreled and protested, but always quarreled and protested peacefully, the Church of England had lived and flourished in colonial days, and handed down a well-established life to the new Church which sprang out of her veins at the Revolution. It was the temperate zone of religious life with all its quiet richness. Free from antagonism, among a genial and social people, with just enough internal debate and difference to insure her life, enlisting the enthusiastic activity of her laity to a degree which we in Boston know nothing of, with a more demonstrative if not a deeper piety, with a confidence in herself which goes forth in a sense of responsibility for the community and a ready missionary zeal, the Church in Philadelphia was to the Church in Boston much like what a broad Pennsylvania valley is to the rough New England hillside.[31]

During the decades between 1860 and 1900 the three churches in Rittenhouse Square—St. James, which closed its doors in the 1940s, was the third—increased in membership by 338 percent, while the population of the county only grew by 130 percent. This pattern reversed itself after the turn of the century, when, as in most America cities, suburbanization took the lead, and formerly rural churches like Old St. David's in Radnor and new parishes along the Mainline and in Chestnut Hill rapidly eclipsed the growth of urban churches.[32] Wherever they were based, however, Episcopalians maintained hegemony over Philadelphia's elite institutions in a remarkable way. Quakers still maintained some influence, as did Presbyterians, whose religion was regarded by their Anglican counterparts as "not a sin . . . just a social error." Henry Coit, the founding headmaster of St. Paul's School, similarly remarked: "Never forget, my dear, that in the life to come Presbyterians will not be on the same plane as Episcopalians."[33] Even Jewish families succumbed to the temptation of assimilation. "It would be impossible," wrote Nathaniel Burt, a popular chronicler of Philadelphia's social mores, "to be more fully accepted without being eaten and digested . . . Gratzes, Ettings, and Hayes all became Episcopalians, like everybody else."[34] This is, certainly, an overstatement, since personal conviction, often in the context of interfaith marriage, played important roles in such decisions.[35] Nevertheless, the ambience radiating from the Episcopal community was difficult to elude completely among the socially eminent of any background.

In Pittsburgh, a city whose social transformation has been analyzed by social historians with more than anecdotal thoroughness, a slightly different pattern emerges. During its antebellum decades, Scotch-Irish Presbyterians established a strong base in the city and built its early fortunes. Following the Civil War, however, a metamorphosis took place parallel to that in most northeastern cities in which the old "strict no-nonsense Calvinist" stock was forced to share hegemony with their new Anglican rivals.[36] A new elite, less insular than its predecessors, began to assemble following the Civil War, making its fortunes in steel rather than the iron that had been the staple of the city's earlier economy.[37] As in other cities, the old and new elites rapidly forged alliances, abetted by new patterns of residence, sociability, and civic and religious involvement that characterized Victorian and Progressive Era Pittsburgh as much as they did other cities.[38]

Not surprisingly, the Episcopal Church played a role in this social transformation of "the dour provinciality of the iron elite," as an 1868 observer characterized the older business barons.[39] As historian Francis Couvares put it, "The Presbyterian elite was ill-suited to the role of patriciate."[40] As the East End, geographically isolated from the ethnic enclaves of factory workers, became the fashionable residence for the well-to-do, a new set of institutions rapidly developed that helped define the social identity and lifestyle of such a patriciate. These included a whole complex endowed by Andrew Carnegie featuring a music hall, library, museum, and art institute; the exclusive Duquesne and Pittsburgh Clubs; other clubs for genteel exertions such as tennis, golf, and archery; and new department stores that kept the community's women au courant with the fashions in Boston and New York. Sending one's children— sons especially—off to eastern prep schools and Ivy League colleges eroded the city's earlier provincialism, and intermarriage with auslanders further integrated the local elite with the culture of privilege that was expanding from the East Coast to form a national community.[41]

New occasions demanded new churches, and the East End soon boasted Calvary Episcopal as well as East Liberty and Shadyside Presbyterian as suitable houses of worship for this emergent suburban constituency. The first two of these were designed, in elaborate Gothic revival style, by Anglo-Catholic architect Ralph Adams Cram. East Liberty Presbyterian is something of a hybrid, a cross between a Gothic cathedral and an institutional church—much like its Chicago analogue, Cram's Fourth Presbyterian on Michigan Avenue. Except for a few details, such as the liturgical apparatus and stained glass windows commemorating Presbyterian history, it is difficult to tell that these are not Episcopal churches.[42] In addition to architecture, music came into play. As Couvares puts it, "A virtual explosion of music within a severely Low Church community served as a crucial mediator of the musical development of the city as a whole." These churches engaged professional organists, soloists, music directors, and other arts professionals from New York City, which in turn helped create a climate conducive to the organization of local musical production, both amateur and professional.[43] Although Presbyterians continued to dominate the upper class numerically, it is clear that their own churches were rapidly changing, especially in their approach to aesthetics, to come much closer to the Anglican way than their earlier austere ethos had permitted.

Calvary Episcopal also served, as did St. George's in Manhattan, as a locus of political reform in a city that, like many of its counterparts, had fallen into the thrall of machine governance.[44] During the rectorships of George Hodges (1889–94) and James McIlvaine (1900–1916) especially, Calvary provided leadership in implementing the principles of the Social Gospel—for example, by helping found Kingsley House, an urban settlement—and in implementing Progressive reform of urban government. In 1906, George Guthrie, a Calvary stalwart, was elected mayor on a reform platform; four years later, McIlvaine played a major role in producing the Pittsburgh Plan for municipal reform.[45] And, just as J. P. Morgan had steadfastly backed William Rainsford at St. George's, so did Henry Clay Frick and other "robber barons" remain (perhaps less than enthusiastic) members of Calvary in the midst of its heyday as a center of reform.[46]

Throughout the urban centers of the Northeast, the Episcopal Church seems almost universally to have played the role of social catalyst during the late nineteenth and early twentieth centuries. It became a "virtually generic upper class religion," building on its earlier strengths along the Eastern Seaboard and taking its place from early on, as an upper class began to develop in the newer cities of the Great Lakes and beyond.[47] Although the Presbyterians and other locally elite denominations by no means disappeared, they were often shaped in their aesthetics and mores by an Anglicanism that had always been at home in realm of the material world and its pleasures. Episcopalianism, in short, was the ideal church to teach a newly coalescing national elite how to conduct itself now that the imperative for rigorous self-discipline and "inner-worldly asceticism" had relaxed.[48] Although Episcopal clergy were held to high moral standards, their social and educational backgrounds and lifestyles were often similar to that of their affluent congregations. Episcopal churches and cathedrals were among the largest and certainly the most ornate among Protestants, and their architects—Richard Upjohn, H. H. Richardson, Henry Vaughan, Ralph Adams Cram—set the tone for other denominations. The Episcopal Church had become the church à la mode.

Or was it? Although Episcopal churches were not exactly in the forefront of social change in Chicago and Philadelphia, the examples of William Rainsford and George Hodges certainly indicate that they were driving forces for reform in New York and Pittsburgh, and their counterparts can be found in Boston, Cincinnati, and other cities. Even though a few Episcopal Social Gospel leaders were avowed socialists, one can argue that the major thrust of urban reform was essentially bourgeois, aimed at reinforcing the status quo rather than overturning it. This is plausible, but it complicates the argument that Episcopalians were aristocratic in their values. In fact, those values might more accurately be described as a complicated mix of aristocratic aspiration and bourgeois moralism, with an occasional dollop of social radicalism. And, although a large majority of Episcopalians during this era were most likely at least middle class in status, missions for immigrants, Native Americans, and industrial workers added a periphery of diversity.

Culture

"Culture" is an ambiguous but indispensable term for understanding yet another layer of the Episcopal experience. Culture, in the ethnological sense, refers both to the underlying templates that govern the way a coherent social group lives, as well as that group's intellectual, symbolic, aesthetic, and material production. In a more aesthetic sense, the term sometimes refers to what are in fact "taste cultures," as in "highbrow" and "lowbrow."[49] We have already touched on the issue of culture in describing how Episcopalians participated formatively in an emergent national network of social institutions—prep schools and elite colleges, urban and country clubs, boards of charitable and cultural institutions, as well as churches themselves. All these helped to define and perpetuate, if not an aristocracy, an upper class that for several decades wielded considerable influence in the broader society, a class whose tone was definitively "highbrow." But Episcopalians also participated in and helped shape a variety of discourses in Gilded Age and Progressive Era American culture—sometimes appropriating what that culture provided, sometimes taking the lead in contributing new strands, and occasionally providing distinct alternatives to what it had to offer.

Most generally, the major contribution of the Episcopal Church to American life was a religious legitimization of the material realm, not only as *not* fatally contaminated by sinfulness but as an authentic means for the experience of divine grace. This is not to say that Episcopalians, like their Unitarian counterparts, actually rejected such traditional teachings as the doctrine of original sin; they were for the most part quite orthodox in affirming the creeds of the early church. For all their theological liberalism, however, Boston's Unitarians largely clung to the old ways in carrying on worship focused on verbal proclamation and instruction in decorous meetinghouses without elaborate ritual or liturgical apparatus. Episcopalians, in contrast, reveled in architecture and accompanying liturgical arts that were as ornate as the ceremonies conducted therein and therewith. This love of material and aesthetic display not only sent out irresistible cues to the more austere Reformed denominations—Boston's Arlington Street Church (Unitarian Universalist) boasts an elegant set of Tiffany windows—but also provided an ethos in which the church's wealthier members could accumulate the treasures of European artistic culture and make them available both for their own gratification and the edification of a broader public.

This legitimation, even sanctification, of the material realm is a central emphasis in my discussion here. In addition, however, Episcopalians of this era participated in a wide variety of discourses—some mutually reinforcing, some in tension with one another—that together constituted a lively cultural and intellectual world in the broader context of the American scene. Some of these discourses were explicitly theological, and have been outlined earlier. In simple terms, Episcopalians, if they paid attention to such issues at all, tended to divide along three party lines: Evangelicals, who identified with their counterparts in the Reformed denominations; Anglo-Catholic Ritualists, who admired a great deal about Roman Catholicism; and Broad Churchmen, who shared liberal Protestant theological and social proclivities while stressing their own church's potential for bridging the denominational chasms that had traditionally divided American Christians. Active identification with any of these three options necessitated participation in theological discourse beyond the boundaries of the Episcopal Church.

One major and obvious component of American Episcopal identity was its origins in the Church of England, the break from which was only a century behind Episcopalians at the start of this era. This post–Civil War period in the United States was also a time in which a sense of Anglican identity, which would eventually acquire worldwide dimensions, was beginning to emerge. A theological and disciplinary dispute in South Africa, which was then still a part of the British Empire, resulted in the archbishop of Canterbury's convening the bishops of the entire Anglican world in 1867 for what would become the prototype of the decennial Lambeth Conferences. Although the impact of this development would only gradually impinge on American Episcopalians, it was an outward and visible sign that they were not simply an American Protestant denomination but also participants in a living tradition with firm grounding in the Church of England, the "historic episcopate," and the *Book of Common Prayer*.

That American Episcopalians were involved in and influenced by transatlantic Anglican theological discourse is apparent in our earlier discussion of the impact of the Oxford and Cambridge movements in the 1840s and the later impact of English Broad Church thinkers—Arnold, Gore, Kingsley, Maurice—and Anglo-Catholic social reformers on thought and practice on the western edge of the Atlantic. Two other English writers who had at one time considered studying for ordination in the Church of England also had a major impact, not only on Episcopalians but on Americans more broadly. These were John Ruskin and William Morris, two of the major inspirations for the Arts and Crafts movement in both Britain and the United States.

Ruskin was a critic of both art and society who saw the two realms as inextricably interlinked. He argued in *The Seven Lamps of Architecture* (1849) and other works that the value of a nation's life is manifested in the quality of its artistic production, a category that includes everyday goods such as clothing, housing, and furniture as well as painting and sculpture. Modern industrial production had seriously eroded the quality of the lives of both factory workers, who had been reduced to taking on the function of machines, and the consumers of the shoddy goods that they had mass-produced. William Morris, from his base at Kelmscott, both advocated and helped produce a wide range of objects that were intended to be at once beautiful and useful, such as wallpaper, carpets, and books. The ideas of the two men became extremely popular in turn-of-the-century American cities, where Arts and Crafts societies flourished. Prominent in these societies were Episcopalians such as Boston architect Ralph Adams Cram and Detroit publisher George G. Booth, who saw in the movement's philosophy an expression of authentically Anglican aesthetic ideals. Many of the Episcopal churches and cathedrals that blossomed during this period became veritable showcases of Arts and Crafts-inspired products designed for liturgical use.

Closely allied to the Arts and Crafts movement was the Gothic revival, already mentioned as part of the Cambridge, or Ecclesiological, movement that had commenced in the 1840s. Although Episcopalians did build in other styles—H. H. Richardson's Trinity Church in Boston, built for "prince of the pulpit" Phillips Brooks in the 1870s, is a prime example—the appeal of the specifically English strain of Gothic became the hallmark of Episcopal church design. In addition to the symbolic resonance promoted by its Ecclesiological enthusiasts, English Gothic had the merit of appealing to the Anglophilia that became a major cultural theme during an era of vast immigration and major demographic upheaval. Although many post-Revolutionary American cultural leaders had repudiated their English origins and systematically set about cultivating an authentic American identity, their postbellum successors again looked to London as the pacesetter for culture at all levels and a symbol of cultural rootedness that was lacking in their own upstart society. (The expatriations of Henry James and T. S. Eliot were extreme manifestations of this tendency, as were the marriages of myriads of socially ambitious young American women to English nobility.)

English Gothic thus became the preferred mode for church building, which accelerated with the burgeoning of America's cities during this period. In New York, as in other cities, the fashionable fortunes of neighborhoods rose and fell rapidly. Episcopal churches periodically relocated further and further north along Fifth and other fashionable avenues, creating employment and artistic opportunities for Upjohn, Cram, and other gifted architects. Their task was made easier by the abundance of money available from their clientele in the era before the graduated income tax, as well as by the availability of talented immigrant craftsworkers who were employed carving wood or stone ornaments and fixtures for these new houses of worship. In addition to this period witnessing the building of neighborhood parish churches, this was also the great age of cathedral building, culminating in such marvels as St. John the Divine in Morningside Heights and the National Cathedral atop Mount St. Alban in the nation's capital. These cathedrals were at once architectural monuments, venues for artistic and musical production, and institutions designed to project a unified and effective diocesan presence in community and social outreach.

The Arts and Crafts movement and the Gothic revival were both parts of a wider, more diffuse discourse that might be identified as "medievalism." This discourse, which began in Britain with writers such as Sir Walter Scott and Thomas Carlyle and was continued by Ruskin and Morris, looked to the Middle Ages not, as had many Protestants, as a time of ignorance and barbarism, but rather as a model organic society that contrasted favorably with the ugliness and injustice of nineteenth-century industrial cities.[50] Medievalism could be primarily aesthetic, as among the pre-Raphaelite artists such as Sir Edward Burne-Jones, whose stained glass ornamented Boston's Trinity Church, or it could have the biting social critique of Ruskin's *Traffic* (1864). The theme of an organic society, however, became an important part of Episcopal social thought and was closely connected with material expression in architecture and the arts. The architect Ralph Adams Cram gave expression to this impulse both in his voluminous writings and in the panoply of churches and cathedrals he designed beginning in the 1890s.

Although Episcopal social thought and action were deeply influenced by English sources, they also had distinctively American dimensions. George Hodges, the energetic rector of Pittsburgh's Calvary Church and later dean of the Episcopal Theological School in Cambridge, spoke very much in the language of the Progressive Era in his stress on reform for the sake of both justice and efficiency. His 1906 work, *The Administration of an Institutional Church*, set forth with a very American practicality and attention to detail a program for the implementation of this very American innovative form of ministry. The urban reform movement that had its roots in his rectorship at Calvary similarly combined elements of idealism, moralism, and practicality. The topic of the Episcopal Social Gospel is thus a complicated one, combining elements of medievalism, socialism, and "bourgeois reformism" in a variety of permutations.

Still another current of British thought that had important consequences for Episcopalians and Americans more broadly was the cult of "muscular Christianity" that emanated from the writings of Charles Kingsley and

Thomas Hughes. (The latter's *Tom Brown's School Days* of 1857 was a fictionalized tribute to the great Rugby headmaster, Thomas Arnold.) British-
educated Endicott Peabody, who became headmaster of the Groton School
at the time of its founding in 1884, was a major American spokesman for the
movement, which correlated physical fitness with Christian character. The
complex of Episcopal boarding schools—"St. Grottlesex"—that arose in the
wake of Peabody's success constituted an Episcopal attempt to popularize
this philosophy in the broader context of shaping a national elite infused
with Christian values.

A final major theme in American Episcopal life was philanthropy, a subject
intimately involved with money. Many wealthy Americans were Episcopalians who had been influenced by that lapsed Presbyterian Andrew Carnegie's
notion that the rich had an obligation to do something socially constructive
with that money, an idea he termed "the Gospel of Wealth."[51] Episcopal
philanthropy took many forms, including major contributions to the denomination for churches and cathedrals, prep schools, social services, and other
projects. In addition to specifically churchly benefactions, wealthy Episcopalians such as J. P. Morgan, who lavished funds on St. George's Church and
the new Cathedral of St. John the Divine, also spent untold sums on the arts.
Morgan himself built a fabled personal collection and supported generously
the Metropolitan Museum of Art and other cultural institutions. Just as Morgan's library became a museum after his death, so did the palazzo-like Boston
home of Isabella Stewart Gardner, whose apartments on the topmost level
included a private chapel where the Cowley Fathers still celebrate annually
a memorial service for the repose of her soul. George Booth's Cranbrook
complex near Detroit includes a variety of prep schools, a world-class art
school, and Christ Church, which combines the Gothic revival and the Arts
and Crafts impulse to remarkable effect. In the realm of historic preservation
and instruction, both the eccentrically Episcopalian Henry Ford and the
more orthodox W. A. R. Goodwin, rector of Bruton Parish Church, were the
guiding forces behind Michigan's Greenfield Village and Virginia's Colonial
Williamsburg, respectively.

Churches and Gospels

American Episcopalians were thus involved in a variety of religious, social,
cultural and intellectual activities that, diverse in their components and complex in their interactions, constituted an engaged yet distinctive sphere within

the broader society. The following chapters portray in more detail the ways that American Episcopalians attempted to fashion a church and a society in which they sought to achieve beauty and community in the midst of a tumultuous urban landscape often distressingly lacking in both. We might refer to these ways collectively as "the Episcopal project"—a program, loosely organized if at all, in which bishops, clergy, and laypeople worked to provide themselves, other Christian denominations, and the American people as a whole with a set of structures, programs, and institutions that would transform and redeem an aesthetically barren cityscape, an ethically impoverished upper class, and an unjust social order into something more closely resembling the Kingdom of Christ.

Part I of this book, "Churches," focuses on the built environment for worship that Episcopalians designed and constructed at an increasing pace as their wealth and prestige increased and American cities burgeoned. One model for these urban houses of worship was the Romanesque revival, exemplified most dramatically in Boston's Trinity Church, designed by H. H. Richardson and intended by its celebrity rector, Phillips Brooks, as a fitting place for a distinctively Protestant sort of worship. An opposing and much more prevalent vision was that of the Anglo-Catholic architect Ralph Adams Cram, who created an Americanized variety of medieval Gothic that broadly influenced not only Episcopal church design but that of a spectrum of other denominations as well. In addition to a proliferation of parish churches, a centralizing administrative vision by the church's bishops gave rise to a powerful movement toward the construction of monumental cathedrals—most dramatically in New York, San Francisco, and Washington, D.C.—designed primarily in the Gothic mode and signifying the church's hopes for leadership in a drive to Christianize the American city.

In addition to the buildings themselves, these churches and cathedrals were distinguished from most other Protestant houses of worship in their ornate interiors. Here were brought together both liturgical artifacts brought over from Europe in a vast campaign of American acquisition of Old World art, as well as the products of contemporary artists and artisans intended to create an aura appropriate for solemn worship. This artistic production, influenced strongly by the reform-minded Arts and Crafts movement, could be oriented toward the theological slants either of a liberal Protestant—"Broad Church"—ethos, such as that promoted by Brooks at Trinity, or of the "High Church" Anglo-Catholicism of Cram, as exemplified at Manhattan's Cathedral Church of St. John the Divine under the leadership of a series of bishops of alternating persuasions. Whatever the liturgical orientation, both factions converged in their advocacy of the use of material means to evoke the "beauty of holiness" in the performance of worship according to their shared *Book of Common Prayer*.

In Part II—"Gospels"—the focus shifts to a number of movements in which Episcopalians, both individually and institutionally, played leading roles, with significant consequences for the broader American social order. Although the Social Gospel was interdenominational, many of its aspects, such as settlement houses and institutional churches, had roots in British and American Anglican practice. Episcopalians in positions of social and economic leadership fostered alliances between churches, bishops, clergy, and laity and with other religious and community leaders in the advocacy of Progressive reform measures in many American cities. As with the Social Gospel, Broad Church and Anglo-Catholic Episcopalians found common cause in the emergent private boarding school—"prep school"—movement, in which clergy/headmasters aimed to steep new generations of financial and political leaders in Christian values to provide an alternative moral vision to the materialism and corruption of the Gilded Age. Finally, wealthy Episcopalians of a wide variety of theological viewpoints converged in their roles as cultural philanthropists, patronizing new urban cultural institutions, turning their homes into what would eventually become museums, and laying the foundations for the historic preservation movement. Whatever the motivations of specific individuals, these movements were united by a this-worldly focus highly compatible with an Anglican sacramental vision and an ideal of the Kingdom of Christ attainable here on earth.

The epilogue—"The Irony of American Episcopal History"—is a narrative and reflection on the aftermath of the "Episcopal project" after cataclysmic shifts in American society brought it largely to an end. The Great Depression put a severe crimp in building campaigns, while the New Deal—under the aegis of the most prominent Episcopalian of his day, Franklin Delano Roosevelt—shifted to the government much of the responsibility for social change and relief. During the middle decades of the twentieth century, much of the cultural energy emanating from Episcopalians of the Progressive Era was eclipsed by their growing identification with the stereotypes of "WASPs," "preppies," and the "East Coast Establishment." By the 1960s, a new shift was taking place. Non-WASPs such as the Kennedys were becoming assimilated into Establishment culture, while the Episcopal Church itself was transformed by an era of conflict both within itself and within the larger society.

As traditionalists fled the denomination, those who remained shifted the church's identity from that of an informal national establishment to one of prophetic witness in the causes of social justice. Much of the heritage of the earlier "Episcopal project"—that of national cultural and social leadership—remains, though often now in a pluralistic context. The notion of a church that serves the nation as an informal religious establishment, however, vanished in the vortex of civil rights, women's ordination, liturgical reform, and the challenges both of secularism and the Religious Right.

Part I
Churches

In the colonial era and the early years of the American republic, one distinctive style dominated American ideas of what a church should look like. Starting in 1721, when Boston's Anglicans built the Old North Church of Paul Revere fame, the neoclassicism introduced by Christopher Wren and James Gibbs in the "mother country" began to displace the austere meetinghouses of the Puritans and was eventually adopted across the denominational spectrum from Baptist to Roman Catholic.

Beginning in the 1840s, new modes of church design based on medieval rather than classical themes began to change the nation's religious landscape. Episcopalians, many influenced by the Oxford and Cambridge movements in England, were consistently in the forefront of adopting and popularizing both the Romanesque and Gothic revival styles for worship according to the formal dictates of their *Book of Common Prayer*. Which mode individual congregations chose often reflected the division within the Episcopal community between the Broad Church faction, which was a liberal reinterpretation of the Protestant preaching-based approach to worship, and the Anglo-Catholic, which emphasized liturgical similarities with the Roman Catholic tradition.

As the denomination expanded in both membership and wealth, it invested much of its resources in the creation of a national network of houses of worship. These ranged from the vernacular board-and-batten "carpenter Gothic" churches created by Richard Upjohn to monumental urban landmarks such as Upjohn's Trinity Church in the midst of Manhattan's financial district. Many of these great urban churches possessed not only elaborate spaces for sacramental worship but also a complex physical plant dedicated to the educational, social, and benevolent activities of the emergent "institutional church." Even grander in scale and mission were the great cathedrals, such as those in New York, San Francisco, and Washington, D.C., which served not only as architectural monuments and administrative centers but as highly visible affirmations of the denomination's role as a de facto national church.

Although these houses of worship and their staffs and parishioners differed considerably on issues ranging from emphases in worship to social outreach, they were united by at least two things: a shared, fixed, formal, sacramental liturgy; and an increasingly opulent setting in which it might be enacted. The medieval building traditions they embraced lent themselves to elaborate ornament such as stained glass, carved wood, and wrought metalwork much more readily than did their classical predecessors. Episcopal churches often became dazzling artistic ensembles in which architectural design combined with the various liturgical arts as stages for liturgical performance. These performances often combined oratory and music with the set formulas of the *Book of Common Prayer*. Such churches helped shape the landscape of the emergent American city and provided prototypes of church building that were frequently emulated by other denominations whose approaches to worship were converging with the Anglican model.

CHAPTER ONE

Phillips Brooks and Trinity Church

Symbols for an Age

If one person captured the many moods of upper class Victorian America, it was the sculptor Augustus St.-Gaudens. His *Deacon Samuel Chapin* statue in Springfield, Massachusetts—better known as "the Puritan"—expresses in that worthy's massive size and purposeful posture the pride that old New England families, a bit nervous about their status, wished to project. (Its implied subtext may very well be "No Irish Need Apply.")[1] St.-Gaudens's memorial to Robert Gould Shaw and the 54th Massachusetts Infantry on the Boston Common was a tribute to the idealism of Boston's Brahmin class as well as the heroism of the black soldiers who gave their lives for the cause of the Union. The statue commissioned by Henry Adams for the grave of his wife, "Clover," in Washington's Rock Creek Cemetery, evoked not only the husband's grief but also the failure of the era's sentimental Christianity to deal adequately with the ultimate mystery of death. And St.-Gaudens's striking design for the "double eagle"—the twenty-dollar gold piece—was a fitting expression of both the aesthetic and commercial values of "Gilded Age" America.[2]

Yet another of St.-Gaudens's works of public commemoration is the statue of Phillips Brooks that stands outside Trinity Church in Boston's Copley Square, where Brooks held forth as a "prince of the pulpit" until his elevation to Episcopal bishop of Massachusetts. During the decade of the 1870s, the coming together of Brooks, the architect Henry Hobson Richardson, the artist John La Farge, and Trinity Episcopal parish created a remarkable chapter in, at once, the history of American architecture, religion, and urbanism, as well as of the Episcopal Church. By the end of that decade, Richardson's new Trinity Church and Brooks himself had emerged as emblematic of the American Victorian city as well as of the "new" Boston itself.

The Origins of Trinity Church

The origins of Trinity Church date back to a gift of land in 1730 on Summer Street, now in the heart of Boston's central business district. Trinity was founded

Augustus St.-Gaudens, statue of Phillips Brooks, Trinity Church, Boston, 1910.
(Courtesy of Trinity Church, Boston)

to provide accommodation for the city's growing Anglican population, then served only by King's Chapel—established in 1686 by the royal governor, Sir Edmond Andros, who was sent to rein in a rampant Puritan hegemony—and Christ Church (1723), better known as "Old North," where hung the lanterns of the Paul Revere saga. (These two churches are now maintained by Unitarian-Universalist and Episcopal congregations, respectively.)[3] Although its loyalist rector fled for the duration to Nova Scotia, Trinity was the only Anglican parish to carry on worship during the Revolution. In 1829 the congregation razed its first building—a rather awkward-looking structure with a double-pitched roof and no steeple—and erected in its place an early American example of the Gothic revival, designed by a member of the parish, George Brimmer. Its High Church rector George Washington Doane departed in 1833 to become bishop of New Jersey, and was succeeded nine years later by Manton Eastburn, an outspoken Evangelical who simultaneously served both as rector and first as assistant bishop and then bishop from 1842 until 1868.[4] Eastburn and his Episcopal predecessors have been described as "not so much bishops in the traditional Anglican pattern as rectors in episcopal orders."[5]

While its rector's attention was thus divided, Trinity was beginning to experience the adverse effects of failing to respond to changing times. Prior to Brooks's rectorship, Trinity had supported itself through the common practice of pew rental, with well-to-do renters occupying the ground floor in their private pews and nonsubscribers relegated to the galleries.[6] In the words of Brooks's Episcopal successor, William Lawrence, the parish consisted of a "down-town, substantial but rather gloomy stone church; an even more gloomy chapel; a small Sunday school and a company of loyal Churchmen, most of whom were of middle age and well along in years."[7] After an earlier, unsuccessful effort, Boston's Trinity finally succeeded in 1869 in attracting Phillips Brooks, then the youthful rector of Holy Trinity in Philadelphia, to try to bail out a parish that had clearly seen better days.

Part of the context of Trinity's plight was rapid urban change. Summer Street, which had once run in the midst of a neighborhood of fashionable residences, was seeing many nearby homes succumbing to commercial development and their occupants moving elsewhere. The new Boston residential neighborhood of choice was the Back Bay. In 1856 the city had begun the process of filling in this insalubrious marshy area, not only improving public health but creating an expanse of prime real estate. Here stately new homes were being rapidly built, sold, and occupied. A home such as these played a central symbolic role in William Dean Howells's novel of new money, *The Rise of Silas*

Lapham (1885); another home was the real-life dwelling of Episcopalian art collector Isabella Stewart Gardner. Houses of worship, such as the Arlington Street Church (Unitarian) that William Ellery Channing had once served, and Frederick Dan Huntington's new Emmanuel Episcopal (1861), were quick to locate in this emergent neighborhood, where folk inclined toward these elite denominations were sure to settle or relocate. It was in the Back Bay that Trinity's future seemed to belong as well.[8]

The Young Phillips Brooks

The Phillips Brooks who would preside over the design and erection of Trinity's imposing new home at Copley Square was himself a physically imposing man. The St.-Gaudens's statue exemplifies the description of Brooks by one editor of his sermons as a "tall, majestic figure, standing six feet four inches in height, 'symmetrically massive' in build, the magnificently modeled head, the strong, exceedingly handsome face—'he was the beautiful man I have ever seen,' said Justice Harlan of the United States Supreme Court—the large, dark glowing eyes."[9] Brooks's ancestors can be traced back to the early days of the Massachusetts Bay colony, and his family connections were extensive. Among his cousins were abolitionist Wendell Phillips, orator Edward Everett, and historian Henry Adams, who were some of the most prominent New Englanders of the mid- to late nineteenth century.[10] His immediate family was prosperous but not wealthy; his mother had been raised in part, however, in the home of her maternal uncle, Peter Chardon Brooks, reputedly the richest man in New England.[11] Brooks was molded, in short, by the Brahmin elite of Boston, who dominated the city's cultural, intellectual, and religious, as well as its financial, institutions. Dedicated to a rather cautious sort of individual and collective moral uplift, the Brahmin worldview was institutionally expressed in the Unitarian Church.[12] The Boston of the Civil War era, as cousin Henry Adams acerbically noted, "had solved the universe."[13]

Brooks, not surprisingly, attended Harvard College, which was the premier educational institution of the "Hub of the Solar System," as Oliver Wendell Holmes Sr. had once memorably described Boston. Upon graduation in 1855, he took a position as "usher"—beginning teacher—at the Boston Latin School, from which he himself had graduated three years earlier. Here Brooks encountered for the first time in his young life serious failure: He was assigned a group of intractable boys who rapidly broke his spirit. The result was his resignation and a period of personal anguish finally resolved with the help of

Harvard president James Walker, a figure then available, in his role as Unitarian minister, as a counselor to the young. That consultation was apparently instrumental in helping Brooks resolve his adolescent self-doubt and enroll in the Virginia Theological Seminary in preparation for the Episcopal priesthood. In doing so, Brooks would make at least a temporary break with the family and culture that had thus far nurtured—and, perhaps, stifled—him.[14]

That Brooks should seek ordination as an Episcopalian rather than a Unitarian was indicative of a religious transition taking place not only within the Brooks family but in the culture of Boston more broadly. Brooks's mother, Mary, was descended from orthodox Congregationalist stock: Her father had founded Andover Theological Seminary in 1808 as an alternative to Harvard, which had been taken over by the Unitarian faction early in the century.[15] The Congregationalist parishes in which her mother had been raised had followed the large majority of those in the Boston area into Unitarianism, which she never accepted. In transferring their membership to St. Paul's Episcopal Church in 1836, the senior Brookses were not unusual among their social set in seeking to preserve their traditional Trinitarian Christian practice without accepting what they saw as the doctrinal excesses of Old Light Congregationalists—traditionalists opposed to the revivals of the Great Awakening—or the emotional excesses of the New Lights and Baptists. (They later transferred their membership to Trinity, just as their son was becoming a rising ecclesiastical star.)[16] The switch to Anglicanism in this context was hardly traumatic, since most of the Episcopal clergy of the period shared the modified Calvinism of their fellow Evangelicals in other denominations. One history of the diocese observes that "the Episcopalians who made up the majority of clergy and laity in the diocese until late in the nineteenth century were disgruntled Congregationalists and Baptists and Unitarians first, and Episcopalians only second."[17] These authors echo Bishop Lawrence's dictum that, in order to understand Massachusetts Episcopalians, one has to realize that they were Congregationalists at heart.[18]

The seminary in Alexandria, Virginia, at which Brooks began his theological studies in 1856, was very much in the same orthodox Protestant mode as that of Anglican Boston. Brooks, however, was bemused by its geographical isolation, put off by the manners of the southern gentry, confounded by the anti-intellectualism of his fellow seminarians, and positively repulsed by the institution of slavery that he now confronted firsthand for the first time.[19] He persevered, however, using the rigorous classical education he had previously received to good effect in reading in the original languages the texts of both Old and New Testaments as well as the Greek and Latin church fathers. Unlike other Anglicans shaped by the Reformed tradition, though, Brooks had little interest in mining these foundational documents for doctrinal formulations. He rather read them through the lenses of Romantic thought from Britain and Germany, such as that of Coleridge and Schleiermacher, who were beginning to have an impact in American literary and religious circles. This combination of Protestant biblicism and Romantic individualism would shape the distinctive message Brooks would memorably convey in his later career through both his preaching and his person.[20]

After graduating from seminary, Brooks was called in 1859 to be rector of the Church of the Advent in Philadelphia and shortly thereafter ordained. He rapidly gained attention as a preacher and received several calls to other parishes, all of which he declined. Eventually in 1861 he accepted the repeated offer of nearby Holy Trinity, which embodied the stereotype of the Episcopal Church as the province of the rich and powerful. Brooks mingled well in the upper reaches of Philadelphia society, and Holy Trinity prospered under his leadership. He was an outspoken champion of the Northern cause, becoming active in societies such as the Union League and the Sanitary Commission. His antislavery sermons, eulogy for the assassinated Lincoln, and prayer for the Civil War dead at Harvard in July of 1865 all attracted wide attention, although the Democratic candidate for governor of Pennsylvania left the parish over Brooks's public pronouncements on the issue.[21]

Brooks as Preacher

When Brooks accepted the call of Boston's Trinity Church in 1869, he had thus already acquired a substantial reputation not simply as a clergyman but more broadly as a public figure. During the remainder of his rather brief life—he died in 1893 at the age of fifty-eight—Brooks continued to shape a career that remained based at Trinity until his election as bishop of Massachusetts two years before the end of his life. Although he was preeminently known as a preacher, Brooks was also a participant in the controversies of his denomination, in the transatlantic Anglican network that connected the American Episcopal Church with the Church of England, and in the broader discourse of Victorian American culture.[22]

To read the widely published sermons of Phillips Brooks in the early twenty-first century is a very different experience from that of his auditors at Trinity or the many other venues where he preached. His preaching did undergo some shift in emphasis over the years, from a focus on biblical exegesis to the events and issues of his own day.[23] Today, however, to read one sermon is, in many ways, to read them all. Brooks generally began with a biblical text from which he derived a central theme or motif, then proceeded to weave verbal arabesques, restating the theme repeatedly with a variety of illustrations and metaphors. Unlike most Protestant preachers of the pre–Civil War era, Brooks spent little time expounding on doctrine, of which he took what one biographer has described as "an exceedingly pragmatic view."[24] His preaching was never dogmatic, but rather personal and persuasive in emphasis.[25] His message centered on one recurrent theme: the crucial role of individual personality and character, with Jesus as the ultimate exemplar. Character was exemplified primarily through right individual moral conduct, summarized in such Victorian virtues as "purity" and "service." Salvation was a matter neither of dramatic emotional conversion nor of the salvific work accomplished by Jesus's sacrificial atoning death. Rather, it was a continuing effort to overcome moral temptation and to persevere as a virtuous example for others.

The power of Brooks's message lay not so much in its originality or its profundity—his discourses seem quite banal today—but rather in his audience's experience of their delivery. Brooks was a physically imposing man, weighing in at three hundred pounds. Vested only in a black preaching robe, he read his texts from the pulpit in a rapid-fire fashion that left an enduring impression. One description evokes "the large, dark, glowing eyes . . . the low voice increasing in strength, fullness, and clarity as he proceeded, the impetuous utterance gathering momentum until he averaged over two hundred words per minute . . . giving the effect of 'an express train' rushing through the station."[26] The combination of his Victorian grandiloquence and his physical presence contributed to his impact: The medium, in short, was the message. Brooks, who was apparently celibate, was also exemplary in his seeming transparency and lack of self-consciousness, which contributed to his growing reputation as a beloved, if not saintly, figure.[27] (In this he differed conspicuously from his fellow "prince of the pulpit," Henry Ward Beecher, whose trial for adultery with the wife of a parishioner in 1875 was the media event of the day.)

When Brooks died in January of 1893—probably of diphtheria—the event occupied the entire front page of the *Boston Evening Transcript,* and the occasion was widely reported in the national press as well. Churches of a variety of denominations conducted memorial services, and the local stock exchange and many businesses closed for the day of his funeral. Thousands attended the funeral itself—conducted at Trinity by the presiding bishop, with eight Harvard crew members as pall-bearers—and thousands more were turned away. A crowd estimated at between ten and twenty thousand assembled in Copley Square, and the procession wound through Harvard Yard to the Brooks family plot in Mount Auburn Cemetery. The *Times* of London printed a lengthy account, and a memorial mosaic was laid at St. Margaret's Church, Westminster.[28] Today, Harvard students remember Brooks mainly because of the building named in his honor that serves as the central office for student volunteer work. This was a man to whom, obviously, attention had to be paid—and paid it was.

Brooks and the Broad Church Movement

Although his sermons have not stood the test of time, and his writings, specifically about theology, are practically nonexistent, Brooks nevertheless participated in and made his mark on both the short- and long-term ethos of the Episcopal Church. He vigorously disavowed any factional affiliation, but was inevitably caught up in the strife between High and Low that had plagued his denomination during the nineteenth century to the point that his election as bishop of Massachusetts was vigorously contested by the Anglo-Catholic (High) wing, who questioned—perhaps with reason—his commitment to the doctrine of the apostolic succession of bishops.[29] Brooks was in fact instrumental in the emergence of a third wing—the Broad Church movement— which distinguished itself from the two already established factions by its rejection of doctrinal dogmatism and its openness to new theological currents. Both in Philadelphia and Boston, Brooks participated in groups of clerical peers who shared his skepticism about doctrinal rigidity as well as his openness to contemporary cultural, scientific, and intellectual currents. As a generational cohort, Brooks and his allies would successfully claim the broad middle ground, as Evangelicals and Anglo-Catholics found themselves increasingly marginalized in denominational influence. (The establishment of the schismatic Reformed Episcopal Church in 1873 was both a symptom and instrument of the waning of the Evangelical, or Low, cause.)

Brooks and other Broad churchmen were strongly influenced by the writings of Hartford Congregationalist Horace Bushnell as well as a variety of British and Continental writers. Their distinction from the "liberal" Christianity that was emerging simultaneously in other denominations, however, involved a particular Anglican transatlantic connection of ideas. Brooks traveled extensively in England and developed a broad circle of acquaintance and friendship as his reputation grew. The relationship was reciprocal. Brooks was frequently invited to preach at Westminster Abbey and most of the Church of England's cathedrals, and frequently attracted standing-room-only audiences. He preached before Queen Victoria and received an honorary doctorate from Oxford.[30] His *Sermons Preached in English Churches* was published in 1883. Thanks in part to his family connections, he moved effortlessly within the upper reaches of literary as well as ecclesiastical society, and visited with "eminent Victorians" such as Matthew Arnold, Robert Browning, and Alfred, Lord Tennyson, among others.[31] On one occasion he dined with Thomas Henry Huxley at the home of James Russell Lowell, then U.S. Minister to England.[32]

Although Brooks was steeped in Anglo-American literary culture, he had also been deeply impressed since his Philadelphia days with contemporary Anglican theology.[33] He was especially impressed with the school of thought associated with Cambridge University, where the influence of Samuel Taylor Coleridge remained strong. Prominent in this lineage was Frederick Denison Maurice (pronounced as if it were "Morris"), whose notions of Christian Socialism would have a strong influence on social reform movements in both American and English versions of Anglicanism. Brooks, however, was more influenced by Maurice's aversion to dogma, his assertion that claims to exclusive truth by any Christian church were wrongheaded and obstructive, and his avowal that the distinctive teaching of Christianity is the "the headship or kingship of Christ over humanity."[34] Maurice's emphasis was on an incarnationalism without crucicentrism: The figure of Jesus was pivotal not so much because of his atoning death but rather because of his demonstration of the divine character that unites all of humanity.

Brooks had heard Maurice preach while in England but does not seem to have known the man personally; he did, however, become personal friends with younger members of the English Broad Church leadership who shared Maurice's inclusive, incarnationalist, antidogmatic vision.[35] (Maurice's son later observed that Brooks was a better exponent of Maurice's ideas than Maurice himself.)[36] Prominent among these like-minded contemporaries was Arthur Penrhyn Stanley, who became dean of Westminster in 1863. Stanley emphasized the developmental character of Christianity, the universal character of divine love manifested in Jesus, and the priority of moral and spiritual truths over dogma—themes congenial to Brooks's own thought. Brooks hosted Stanley as guest preacher at Trinity in 1878, and personally planned the American tour of another kindred spirit, Archdeacon of Canterbury F. W. Farrar, whose doubts about eternal punishment gave rise to considerable controversy in English ecclesiastical circles.[37]

For all his Anglophilia—which was part of the cultural baggage of post–Civil War Boston Brahmin society—Brooks nevertheless maintained a critical eye on the Church of England.[38] In his American-slanted view, the latter lacked vitality largely because of its established status. This status enforced an outmoded orthodoxy represented for Brooks in the rather censorious Athanasian Creed, which his English counterparts still embraced as authoritative. He also noted that "C of E" (Church of England) clergymen often seemed superficial, distracted from spiritual pursuits by more mundane tasks such as teaching school.[39]

Brooks Abroad

Brooks's travels in Britain were part of a larger agenda of sometimes rather extended excursions abroad, made possible by a rapidly improving infrastructure of transportation and communication that was creating a newly international realm of discourse during the later Victorian era.[40] His various sojourns, which he described in copious and engaging letters to friends and family, included much of Continental Europe, the Middle East, India, and, eventually, Japan.[41] In this correspondence, Brooks reveals himself as both cosmopolitan and an "innocent abroad," showing an implicit sense of the "hierarchy of civilization" model that pervaded much of Anglo-American thought of the time.[42] Outside of Britain, he was most at home in Germany: He became fluent enough in the language to immerse himself in university lectures during an extended stay, and was influenced considerably by the liberal strain of Protestant thought that had been developing there since the time of Friedrich Schleiermacher.[43]

European Roman Catholic culture, on the other hand, drew a more mixed response. Of a passion play seen in Brixlegg in Austria, for example, he remarked that "it is a good thing to have seen once, for it is a remnant of what was common in the Middle Ages." At the monastery of the Grand Chartreuse, he noted that the monks were supposed to be meditating in their cells, but "I suspect that the old gentlemen go to sleep." He compared Lourdes—"one of the strangest places in the world"—to the Ganges, and wrote an ailing niece that he would send her some Lourdes water if he thought that it would do her any good. (He apparently did not send any.) The Pope's washing the feet of twelve priests at Rome during Holy Week was "an odd and ugly sight." He was more positively impressed with the Miserere sung in the Sistine Chapel and the papal blessing on Easter Day from the balcony of St. Peter's: "Romanism certainly succeeds in being very striking in its demonstrations."[44]

If Brooks regarded the Roman version of Christianity as somewhat retrograde, he had even more skeptical views on non-Christian religions. In a burst of seasonal exuberance on his way to India, he revealed a somewhat muddled concept of the cultures he was about to encounter firsthand: "I feel almost like writing [a Christmas sermon] myself and asking some Hindoo in Bombay to lend me his mosque in which to preach it." In his description of Siva worship, he pulls no punches: "It is strange to be in the midst of pure, blank heathenism, after one has been hearing and talking about it all his life. And it is certainly as bad as it has been painted." On the other hand, his field observations had a direct bearing on his perhaps somewhat exaggerated characterization of contemporary religious enthusiasms at home. "In these days, when a large part of Boston prefers to consider itself Buddhist rather than Christian, I consider this pilgrimage to be the duty of a minister who preaches to Bostonians."[45]

Brooks also more than once visited the Holy Land, a popular destination for American Protestants—as Mark Twain satirically emphasized in his *The Innocents Abroad* of 1869—and the context of what is certainly Brooks's best-remembered work, the sentimental Christmas carol "O Little Town of Bethlehem" of 1868.[46] On his first trip abroad, in 1865–66, Brooks noted primarily the disjuncture between biblical events and contemporary appropriations of them by the guardians of their sites:

> Before dark, we rode out of town to the field where they say the shepherds saw the star. It is a fenced piece of ground with a cave in it (all the Holy Places are caves here), in which, strangely enough, they put the shepherds. The story is absurd, but somewhere in these fields we rode through the shepherds must have been, and in the same fields the story of Ruth and Boas belong. . . . We returned to the convent and waited for the service, which began about ten o'clock and lasted until three (Christmas). It was the old story of a Romish service, with all its mummery, and tired us out. They wound up with a wax baby, carried in procession, and at last laid in the traditional manger, in a grotto under the church. The most interesting part was the crowd of pilgrims, with their simple faith and eagerness to share in the ceremonial. We went to bed very tired.[47]

The following February, Brooks wrote a letter to his Sunday school students in Philadelphia that captured well his attitude toward the experience, as well as his more fundamental theological position:

The one thing I think of most is the emptiness of that tomb in Jerusalem, and the ways we have of doing honor to Jesus which are so much better than making pilgrimages to the place where he was once buried. . . . Let us, my dear children, rejoice together on Easter Day in the great Easter truth that Jesus our Saviour [*sic*] is to be found and worshiped, not in any cold tomb, but in any heart, no matter how young and humble, that is warm with his love, and bright with the constant cheerful effort to do whatever duty He desires. That is the happy temple in which He loves to live. . . . May our Lord Jesus Christ, who rose on Easter Day, rise anew on this Easter in all your hearts and be a living Saviour, a friend, a brother, a helper, and a comforter to you all, all the days of your lives.[48]

Brooks as Celebrity

Back at home, in Philadelphia and later in Boston, Brooks gained celebrity not simply among Episcopalians but more broadly as a public figure, illustrated in the remarkable turnout for his funeral, cited earlier. Part of his popularity lay in his distinctive persona, which combined physical charisma with a personality of remarkable magnetism. Another approach to understanding the phenomenon that Brooks embodied can be found through regarding him as a man of his time—a "representative man," to use a phrase of Ralph Waldo Emerson, an older contemporary whom Brooks seldom invoked but whose career he mirrored in many ways. Brooks was not such a public success because of the originality of his message but rather in the way in which that message represented for contemporary Bostonians, and Americans more broadly, a cultural ideal.

In his essay "Victorian Culture in America," Daniel Walker Howe identifies a number of cultural themes that are useful in understanding Brooks as, to paraphrase Lytton Strachey, an "eminent Victorian" American.[49] To begin with, Brooks represents an American version of Victorianism in combining attributes of a hereditary aristocracy with a democratic ethos. Boston's Brahmin class, from which Brooks had sprung, was an elite distinctively American in claiming their social position not through centuries-old bloodlines, but rather through their commercial achievements or those of their proximate ancestors. Their status was, in sociological jargon, "achieved" rather than "ascribed." The result was what Howe calls an "American gentry," analogous more to Britain's Dissenting intellectual elite than to its aristocracy.

In the United States and especially in Boston, however, these two classes were not nearly as distinct as their English counterparts, since the nouveaux riches of the early republic rapidly morphed into the upper-caste–like Brahmins of Brooks's day. The rapid growth of the Episcopal Church during this era reflected in part a desire for legitimacy on the part of an emergent mercantile elite, which was reassured by the denomination's Anglophiliac and hierarchical associations. The Brooks family was in many ways solidly bourgeois, but branches of it were also very wealthy and intimately connected through marriage with the Bostonian upper classes and their institutions, such as Harvard College. (Brooks was frequently called to preach at Harvard, served on various committees, and was awarded an honorary doctorate in 1877.)[50] Brooks may have been "to the manner born," but that manner was a distinctive mixture of cultural elitism and bourgeois republican values.[51]

Another theme of American Victorian culture that Brooks exemplified par excellence was what Howe describes as a "forensic, hortatory style of leadership" that focused on moral didacticism. This leadership was exercised both through print media as well as orally, in an age Howe characterizes as an Indian summer of American oratory. Brooks was, of course, a consummate orator, and both his sermons and his public addresses were widely circulated in book form after they had originally been delivered in person. The unvarying content of Brooks's proclamations was moral, in a way that harmonized with his own theology but that was in fact separable from it. The goal of life was the achievement of what Howe identifies as still another quintessential Victorian theme: "character." "This was not a set of rote responses but an intangible strength of purpose, combining self-reliance, self-discipline, and responsibility." For Brooks, the role of the preacher was to exemplify character, which his auditors could thereby emulate through the charismatic catalyst that effective preaching constituted.[52]

Brooks did not usually cite Ralph Waldo Emerson as a role model, and, unlike his senior counterpart, he remained explicitly Christian throughout his career. In other ways, however, Brooks's public persona was remarkably like Emerson's in his later role as "the sage of Concord." Both exemplified the power of speech in a nation that, before the heyday of electronic media, relied heavily on the spoken and printed word for inspiration as well as useful information. Both participated actively in an emergent national celebrity culture, where the persona of the celebrity began to eclipse the particular talents or message that had engendered renown initially. A celebrity is someone who is well known, it has been said, for being well known. Both appealed to a broad audience that was attracted not so much to any distinctively religious message, implicit or explicit, in both men's grandiloquence, but rather to their advocacy and personal exemplification of a value highly sought after by an emergent urban middle class: "self-culture." In the post–Civil War American city, the qualities widely perceived to be necessary for success were not so much the acquisition of traditional lore but rather active virtues such as self-discipline, what David Riesman characterized as "the inner-directed personality."[53]

After he had attained national celebrity, Emerson appealed as speaker and essayist no longer simply to the rather rarefied group of Boston literati with whom he had helped found the Transcendentalist movement, but rather to what Mary Kupiec Cayton has characterized as a "bourgeois commercial audience."[54] Brooks similarly appealed to the urban business class. When he delivered Lenten addresses at St. Paul's Church in downtown Boston and at Trinity at Broadway and Wall Street in Manhattan in the spring of 1890, businessmen in particular thronged to hear his message. (The following year he held meetings exclusively for men, since Brooks's many female Bostonian admirers, who presumably were not restricted to lunch hours, had arrived early and crowded out many of the men eager for admission.)[55]

In his "The Duty of the Christian Businessman," published in 1893 as part of his *Collected Addresses*, Brooks delivered a message that his commercially minded audience presumably found both inspiring and reassuring. Like Emerson, Brooks was inclined to ground his advice on everyday morality in soaring metaphysical principles. "Behind every specific action of man there is some one of the more elemental and primary forces of the universe that are always trying to express themselves. . . . To the merchant these are the great laws of trade, of which his works are but the merchant's expression." Merchants shared in a universal human condition in which they found themselves inevitably dissatisfied with things as they presented themselves, and were thus continually called by God to a higher life. This higher life was attainable not so much by a dramatic conversion, as evangelist Dwight L. Moody was exhorting other crowds of urbanities, but rather by embracing the implications of the Incarnation as revealed in Jesus and changing one's life. For the businessman, the particular course this change should take consisted of five parts. First, stop behaving sinfully, which, for the businessman in particular, meant eschewing "tricky business." Secondly, take up your duty, and help every struggling soul, such as "the poor boy in your shop." Then— more generically—pray, read the Bible, and seek the church. The latter is not a sectarian community withdrawn from everyday life but rather "the fulfillment of human life and society; heaven is but the New Jerusalem that constitutes all the old Jerusalems and Londons and Bostons that have been here upon our earth." Businessmen should show that they can be Christian, purify and lift business, and live so that, if everyone followed their example, the millennium would be realized here on earth, without any need of worry about an afterlife.[56]

Trinity and Boston Society

At the time of Brooks's arrival, Trinity was dominated by the prosperous classes: The building committee that oversaw the move to Copley Square consisted primarily of lawyers, bankers, and merchants. Trinity's membership grew rapidly during Brooks's rectorship, which he encouraged through his homiletical outreach to a wide variety of audiences throughout a rapidly expanding metropolitan region, his institution of open Communion, and his making space in galleries and at afternoon services available to nonmembers before the new church could accommodate a greatly expanded attendance. (Even in the new church, pews were owned or rented by proprietors, who had to pay an annual tax on them, although those not occupied by the beginning of a service were open to any latecomers. The galleries, which seated four hundred, were always free and open.)[57] Brooks boasted that Trinity and Boston's other Episcopal "churches have ceased to be mere places of worship for the little groups which had combined to build them, preserving carefully the chartered privileges of their parishioners. They have aspired to become religious homes for the community, and centres [sic] of religious work for the help of all kind of suffering and need."[58]

It is doubtful that many newcomers were drawn from the constituency that accounted for the largest component of Boston's rapid growth. In 1865, some 22 percent of Boston's residents were Irish-born.[59] These Irish were overwhelmingly Roman Catholic and remained loyal to their church; had they been tempted to stray, it would be unlikely for them to be attracted to the Episcopal Church, which was closely associated with their English oppressors. Trinity, like many other well-to-do Episcopal churches of the era, accommodated the poor primarily through the erection of mission chapels in neighborhoods where the latter were prone to reside.[60] On the other hand, about 18 percent of Boston's population in 1850 consisted of American-born migrants from rural New England or other locales.[61] It seems likely that much of the new membership came from these rising middle classes of Protestant background rather than the very rich or poor.

Brooks's attitude toward the poor—and toward the social order more broadly—was characteristic of Episcopalians, and Protestants of the comfortable classes, prior to the advent of the Social Gospel in the latter years of the nineteenth century. Brooks had from his seminary days involved himself actively in the cause of the freedmen, worked with them in Philadelphia, and continued to take an active role in their education.[62] In addition to the founding of chapels in poor neighborhoods, he established classes and societies for the poor and working classes both in Philadelphia and Boston.[63] He aligned himself with causes that were progressive by the standards of the day, such as the temperance movement—although, like most Episcopalians, he was opposed to Prohibition—women's suffrage, and prison reform, as well as supporting the New England Society for the Suppression of Vice—the "Watch and Ward" society notorious for its attempts to censor arts and literature.[64] Brooks's general attitude toward the social conflicts of urban industrial society, such as those reflected by the emergent labor movement, was that their resolution lay not in systemic reform but rather in the transformation of personal consciousness and growth in character among business and labor alike. As his rhetoric about the Christian businessman cited earlier reveals, his social vision bordered on the postmillennial, and he saw progress as being virtually inevitable as Christian principles became more and more pervasive.[65] In this he differed significantly from his English exemplar, Frederick Denison Maurice. While Brooks admired Maurice's incarnational theology, he seems to have had little interest in his theory of Christian Socialism.

H. H. Richardson and the Romanesque Revival

If Phillips Brooks was the quintessential Victorian clergyman, Henry Hobson Richardson was the quintessential Victorian architect. Although he was raised on a Louisiana plantation and in New Orleans, Richardson was a member of the Harvard Class of 1859. (Brooks was 1855.) Like Brooks and five of the eleven members of the Trinity building committee, he was a member of Porcellian, the most exclusive of Harvard's "final" clubs.*[66] Despite his (by

---

*Harvard's final clubs, which parallel but are not identical to Yale's secret societies and Princeton's eating clubs, gained their name in distinction from "waiting" clubs for underclassmen. Membership in final clubs has traditionally been a marker of high family social status, although

Harvard standards) exotic origins—Brooks described his southern heritage as "a spirit of recklessness and earnestness"—Richardson thus acquired social capital that placed him in a very advantageous position when the competition for the design of the new Trinity was announced in 1872.[67] Richardson was one of six architects invited to participate, and the only one to submit a design in a style other than the currently modish Gothic revival.[68]

Richardson's name frequently appears in conjunction with the distinctive style he created, which became a staple of the public architecture of the later Victorian era: "Richardsonian Romanesque." High-style architecture in the nineteenth-century United States had consisted largely of a series of revivals of the styles of earlier historical eras: the Roman, the Greek, the Gothic, and, to a much lesser extent, the Egyptian. These were valued for the associations they conjured: the Greek and Roman with democracy, the Gothic with religious awe, and the Egyptian with medicine and burial. The Gothic, which will be explored in considerable detail in the following two chapters, was heavily favored by Episcopalians in its English form both for its Anglophiliac associations and for its particular suitability for the ritualistic style of worship favored by the High Church—or, more properly, Anglo-Catholic—faction.

Although the Romanesque revival never attained the popularity of the Gothic, which in various forms was also adopted by Roman Catholics and a wide spectrum of Protestants, it provided a distinctive option for those concerned with the theology of worship as well as aesthetics and fashion. Its modern origins trace to the *Rundbogenstil*—"round arched style"—that became popular beginning in the late 1820s in northern Italy as well as in Germany, where its use was promoted by the Prussian government. The style soon spread to Britain, where it appealed both to urban Dissenters such as Baptists and Congregationalists as well as their Evangelically minded counterparts within the Church of England, in part because of its contrast with the Gothic revival favored by the establishmentarian-minded High Church faction.[69] In the United States it attracted a similar constituency. Among the most important early examples, which most likely influenced Richardson's designs, was Richard Upjohn's chapel at Congregationalist Bowdoin College (1844–55). Even more significant was St. George's Episcopal Church in Manhattan's fashionable Stuyvesant Square, designed by the firm of Blesch

---

in recent years they have become somewhat more inclusive and have also been forced into complete independence from the university because of their all-male character. One of Franklin Roosevelt's greatest disappointments lay in not making it into Porcellian.

Henry Hobson Richardson, Trinity Church, Boston, 1877.
(Courtesy of Trinity Church, Boston)

and Eidlitz (1846–56) and pastored by the militantly evangelical Stephen Tyng, a friend of Brooks who would participate later in the consecration of Trinity. Both churches were notable not only for their German-influenced Romanesque style but also for providing wall space for elaborate programs of murals, a project that had the same German roots as the *Rundbogenstil.*[70]

Richardson attained his early reputation as an architect with his Brattle Square Church—now First Baptist—which he designed for a Unitarian congregation in the early 1870s at the corner of Commonwealth Avenue and Clarendon Street, a Back Bay site only a few blocks from that of the new Trinity. Although Richardson had been trained at the École des Beaux-Arts in Paris in that school's eclectic monumental neoclassicism, he now turned his hand to the Romanesque in a design that anticipated many of the features of Trinity. The Brattle Square Church was made of Roxbury puddingstone laid in a random ashlar pattern in contrasting shades of light brown, with a striking red-tiled roof; it is cruciform in shape and is notable for its almost freestanding campanile. At the top is a frieze by the French sculptor Frédéric Auguste Bartholdi with trumpeting angels on the corners, earning the nickname "the church of the holy bean-blowers." (The frieze is also noted for its figural sculpture, supposedly representing the sacraments and modeled on prominent Bostonians such as Emerson, Hawthorne, and Longfellow. Bartholdi is best known for the Statue of Liberty in New York Harbor.) Although Trinity's profile would be very different, the use of Romanesque forms with the distinctive polychromy achieved by the variegated stone and tile contrast instantly identifies the two as the work of the same hand.[71]

The Making of Trinity Church

Richardson and Brooks, who already shared some institutional ties as well as both having very large physical proportions, bonded quickly once the architect had received his commission and entered into what would become a remarkable work of collaboration. Richardson, though accustomed to working from an essentially Protestant paradigm, had no theological agenda, and accommodated easily to the distinctive notions that Brooks brought to the enterprise. Although Brooks was aligned with the Broad Church movement, his liturgical style was distinctively Low. He had no use for Anglo-Catholic hierarchy and ceremonialism, and envisioned a church in which the preached Word—and, implicitly, its preacher—would be the focus of attention. Richardson's response to these requirements was a structure in a Greek cross pattern, with unobstructed sight lines from all seats, which included ample gallery space. In addition to the prominent pulpit, there was a Communion table in a large, semicircular apse, a configuration that emphasized accessibility and downplayed the distinction between clergy and laity.* As one of Brooks's early biographers put it, "The Protestant principle controls the edifice."[72]

---

*The liturgical furnishings of Trinity today bear little resemblance to the original. A monumental carved pulpit was added in 1916, and the chancel was redesigned along Anglo-Catholic lines in 1938 by Charles D. Maginnis, a prominent Roman Catholic architect. Brooks would doubtless have been appalled.

For the general design, Brooks was strongly attracted to the Romanesque style, which Richardson was already a pioneer in adapting to the modern American city. Brooks traveled to France in 1872 with Robert Treat Paine, the chair of the building committee, gathering ideas for the new Trinity.[73] Although Brooks had appreciated the Gothic style he had observed on his European sojourns, he rejected it for its Roman Catholic associations, believing—perhaps not too historically—the Romanesque to have been the dominant Christian style before papal dominance of the Western church. Richardson would later accompany Brooks on a tour of the Auvergne, where Richardson found churches that provided some of his chief inspiration for Trinity.[74] The interests as well as the personalities of Brooks and Richardson were happily converging in a memorable and authentic synergy.

Richardson was faced with the problem of how to employ the Romanesque mode to house a church that was to consist primarily of a preaching hall with a minimal sense of interior differentiation or hierarchy. Using the cathedral at Salamanca, begun in the mid-twelfth century, as his inspiration, Richardson conceived a plan in which the tower was not an adjunct to the main building, as in the case of the Brattle Square project, but rather was the church itself. This large central tower fit well into Trinity's trapezoidal site, and ensured that the church would be optimally visible from all directions. Original plans for a slender octagonal structure were fortunately scrapped in favor of the Salamanca-inspired massive square tower. This plan created an enormous engineering challenge, given the reclaimed character of the Back Bay marshland on which it stood. Its ninety million pounds of granite rest on four granite pyramids, which are in turn supported by two thousand wooden piles submerged in water, the level of which has to be continually monitored.[75]

The resulting effect is, to say the least, striking. Trinity has been described as "a volumetrically additive but nevertheless unified composition, including a sanctuary and a parish house connected by an open cloister. The building can clearly be read as a series of attached, three-dimensional spaces that together create a total composition that is more than the sum of its parts."[76] The pyramidal massing, which gives the effect of a fortress rising in the midst of the commercial and residential city, is further distinguished both by the rows of round-arched windows that break up the surfaces as well as by the play of color between the tan New England granite background; dull red Longmeadow sandstone trim arranged in horizontal bands, arches, circles, and checkerboard designs; and the semiglazed orange-red tiles of the roof.[77]

The color scheme is muted but striking, and contrasts interestingly with the more flamboyant Venetian Gothic of the New Old South Church that lies catty-corner from Trinity.[78] Together with the Italian Renaissance Boston Public Library across the street from each, these churches define a truly monumental urban public space.[79]

For Brooks, Richardson and his work were one in embodying not simply aesthetic but moral qualities that were central to his vision. The minister portrayed the architect as fundamentally intuitive: his work "was instinctive and spontaneous . . . . He was not a man of theories. His life passed into his buildings by ways too subtle even for himself to understand." A further characterization illuminates Brooks's own incarnationalism as well, perhaps, as his disinclination toward the Gothic:

> [Richardson's] is a style of breadth and simplicity that corresponds
> with his whole nature. Never somber, because the irrepressible buoyancy
> and cheerfulness of his life are in it, never attaining the highest reach of
> spirituality and exaltation, for his own being had its strong association
> with the earth, and knew no mystic raptures or transcendental
> aspirations, healthy and satisfying within its own range, and suggesting
> larger things as he himself always suggested the possession of powers
> which he had never realized and used. . . . Whoever came in contact
> with it felt the wind blew out of an elementary simplicity, out of
> the primitive life and fundamental qualities of man. And this great
> simplicity, this truthfulness with which he was himself, made him the
> real master of all that his art had ever been . . . . These are the moral
> qualities of his architecture.[80]

In this eulogy, Brooks portrays Richardson in Emersonian terms as a genius who expressed his own essence authentically and originally in his art, as well as in a more Ruskinian vein, praising his architecture for its moral qualities. There remains, however, a certain ambivalence in his depiction of the man and his work in chthonic, almost pagan terms. Brooks clearly felt a powerful affinity with the forms Richardson had created, and perhaps felt that their natural beauty was more appropriate for his particular message and performance than a more ethereal, explicitly Christian Gothic style.

There was more to Trinity, however, than its outer form and decoration and its internal liturgical arrangements. Though they did not use the term, Brooks and Richardson envisaged their joint creation as a *Gesamtkunstwerk*, Richard Wagner's Germanic coinage for a "total work of art" in which all parts organically related to one another. Richardson, for example, designed the woodwork and furnishings himself, and Brooks picked out a binding for copies of the *Book of Common Prayer* that would harmonize with Trinity's overall color scheme, which was based on a Pompeian red.[81] The interior, which is reminiscent of early Roman Christian basilicas, provided a blank slate for another major collaborator, John La Farge, who was placed in charge of the program of mural painting that would leave virtually no square inch of wall space unornamented. La Farge, of French émigré parentage and exotic appearance, was well acquainted with Boston artistic circles and would later accompany Henry Adams on a memorable voyage to Tahiti. La Farge reflected ideals of artistry promoted by John Ruskin in England and locally by Charles Eliot Norton, Harvard's first art historian, that the artists employed in a communal work such as Trinity were not there to express individual genius but rather the highest moral values of their society. His ideal was the common effort of community, artist, and patron on the medieval model, exemplified in the stained glass windows commissioned as family memorials by architect Charles Follen McKim, the designer of the adjacent Boston Public Library; building committee chair Robert Treat Paine; and Brooks himself.[82]

For the mural work—the largest scheme of wall decoration ever undertaken in the United States to that time—La Farge employed a technique that had recently been developed for the restoration of Ely cathedral: an encaustic mixture of wax, alcohol, and two kinds of turpentine. Some of the wall decorations were purely figurative, and others represented scriptural quotations chosen by Brooks. Brooks also collaborated actively in choosing themes for the paintings. In the tympana—spaces between an arch and the top of a door—are scenes of salvation by faith based on early Christian symbolism. On the sides of the central arches of the nave's opening are major scriptural figures: Moses, David, Jeremiah, Isaiah, and Saints Peter and Paul. The nave ceiling represents two Gospel stories: "Christ and the Woman of Samaria" and the "Visit of Christ to Nicodemus."[83] All these themes were soundly based, in good Protestant fashion, on biblical motifs.

La Farge also supervised Trinity's program of stained glass, in which Brooks took a very active interest. Brooks was something of an aesthete, though not as flamboyantly foppish as Oscar Wilde, and his fascination with color prompted him to buy a piece of stained glass on one of his European jaunts to carry around with him. (In this he was not nearly as self-indulgent as his fellow "Prince of the Pulpit," Henry Ward Beecher, who habitually carried precious stones in his pocket.)[84] Brooks became knowledgeable about stained glass while in Europe, visited studios while in England, and contracted with the firm of Clayton and Bell for the "life of Christ" series in the apse and other windows while on one his visits. Several windows with both Old and New Testament themes were executed by William Morris and Company, according to designs by Sir Edward Burne-Jones, a leading figure in the English Pre-Raphaelite Brotherhood that was characterized by a romantic fascination with the Middle Ages. La Farge himself designed several major windows, using his distinctive technique of opalescent glass. In later years, two local women, Sarah Wyman Whitman and Margaret Redmond, continued the windows project. Although the styles employed by artists from various countries over several decades vary considerably, their overall harmony very much fulfilled the unified vision of Brooks, La Farge, and Richardson.[85]

Trinity, the Episcopal Church, and the Arts in America

The artistry of Trinity would continue to grow over the years after Brooks, La Farge, and Richardson had left the scene, with the addition, for example, of the St.-Gaudens's statue and the Daniel Chester French portrait bust of Brooks. The result was a remarkable coming together of the arts for a goal at once religious and civic that had never before taken place in the United States, although the projects of subsequent Episcopal bishops and architects would continue the enterprise for several more decades. While most of those later projects would be in the Gothic mode, with a distinct Anglo-Catholic inclination, Trinity represented a (largely successful) attempt to create an artistic monument that was explicitly Protestant. Like its neighbor, New Old South, and Henry Van Dyke's Brick Presbyterian in Manhattan, Trinity combined a love of color, ornament, and, in some cases, figural depiction of biblical scenes and figures very different from the aniconic neoclassical meetinghouse tradition.[86]

In addition to being a religious and artistic statement, Trinity was also clearly expressing something important about the role of that congregation, and the Episcopal Church more broadly, in the emergent urban community. The building committee had stated at the outset of the project: "the conviction that our duty to the parish, to posterity, and to God has been clear, to make the new church fully worthy of the piety, the culture, and the wealth of our people."[87] Wealth was in fact an issue: Cost overruns were inevitable, and the final cost was nearly three-quarters of a million dollars (about $15,500,000 in 2010 dollars). Brooks appears to have justified the expenditure on the grounds that Trinity's opulent beauty was a powerful symbol of God's creation that would inspire its beholders toward worship and outreach. His successor, E. Winchester Donald, was quite explicit in his defense of Brooks's project on Trinity's twentieth anniversary:

> These twenty years have demonstrated a fact which I fancy will always need demonstration in the eyes of those people who immemorially have "begrudged the house of God the touch of beauty," and deplored great cost in its erection and adornment. You built a splendid temple; you meant to build a splendid temple. You spared no cost; you nobly met every demand which enlarged plan and richer beauty year by year made upon your generosity. You had to meet the plain-spoken criticism of those who insisted that the difference between slightness and solidity, between barrenness and beauty, should have been given to works of mercy, religion, and education. If the cost of this building had been funded and the interest of this fund devoted to causes universally acknowledged to be worthy the aggregate income of twenty years would not equal the munificent sum which, with the blessing of God upon it, has been offered and distributed by Trinity Church.[88]

Trinity was among the first of many such projects that in the following decades would evoke the same arguments: Why lavish money on opulent churches when the cities' poor cry out for help? Trinity did, in fact, as Robert Treat Paine directed and Donald noted, conduct extensive outreach programs for Boston's poor. Brooks himself, however, seemed focused on the building itself, as well as on his message of individual moral sanctification. Although he antedated the Arts and Crafts movement, which would mount a powerful defense of the interdependence of beauty and morality in later years, he anticipated much of its message, though focusing on the individual rather than the social implications of the beautiful, and sidestepping its critique of industrial capitalism. Trinity Church was an *haut-bourgeois* celebration of material beauty as a sacramental vehicle toward this-worldly self-realization, and Phillips Brooks was its prophet.

CHAPTER TWO

The Gothic Revival and the Arts and Crafts Movement

Boston, 1843

It was not difficult to imagine Bishop Eastburn's feelings when he made his first visit to the Church of the Advent on the evening of 23 November 1843. The rector and his assistant, Mr. Pollard, were in the robing room when the bishop arrived that evening. He was courteous and pleasant, though he was puzzled to find two priests, and had asked what role Pollard was to play. On entering the chancel, Bishop Eastburn went to the right end of the "holy table" and Mr. Croswell read evening prayer at the left. Pollard, next to the rector, knelt down during the prayers with his face toward the corner of the altar. Seventeen candidates were presented for confirmation, all of them adults. The hall was overcrowded and warm, and the atmosphere one of excitement. There was no sermon; instead the bishop, after administering confirmation, returned to the right side of the altar, and standing with his back nearly against the wall, delivered an extemporaneous address in a hurried, agitated way. After the congregation had begun to withdraw, Mr. Croswell went over to the side of the chancel, where the bishop was wiping perspiration off his face, and made some allusion to the heat.

Bishop Eastburn impatiently waved his hand toward the windows, as though to indicate that they should have been more fully let down. When the aisles were further cleared, Mr. Croswell invited him to the robing room, but the bishop preferred not to expose himself to a change of air until he was somewhat cooler. Presently he said, according to the rector,

"Mr. Pollard, what did you say St. Titus for? Why can't you say *Titus*, as everybody else does?" Pollard tried to pass this off, but the bishop wouldn't have it, challenging him further.

"And why do you kneel in that way, half a mile off from the table? I have spoken to you often enough about these mummeries, at Nantucket. These things give pious people great offence." Pollard asked the bishop how he would have him kneel.

"Turn to your chair, and kneel there," he was told.

"I do but conform to the usage of the place," he replied.

"No, you don't; Mr. Croswell did not kneel in that way" came the retort. But Croswell interceded, saying,

"Bishop, Mr. P[ollard] kneels according to our ordinary usage. When a third clergyman is present, and prefers to take one end of the altar, for symmetry's sake, I generally take the other."

This was too much for Bishop Eastburn who, up to this point, had succeeded in restraining himself. He lost his temper, rebuked Mr. Croswell for kneeling like "a Romish priest," expressed his alarm at the consequences of such innovations in England, and referred to the apostasy of John Henry Newman, whose Roman conversion had only just taken place October 9. He went on to complain of the chancel arrangements, on the substitution of a prose Psalter in place of metrical psalms, of the large cross, and of the candlesticks.

"If an Irishman were to come in here," he said, "and see that cross, he would kneel down to it at once, in the aisle. He would think he was in a Roman Catholic chapel. It looks like one."

Croswell replied that, without the "Roman," his remark was true, agreeing that it "certainly did look like a Catholic chapel."[1]

This exchange between Bishop Manton Eastburn and the staff at Boston's then recently founded Church of the Advent was one episode in an ongoing struggle between Low and High Church factions that was rending the Episcopal Church during the middle decades of the nineteenth century. The strife continued in Boston with warfare in print between the two sides. Bishop Eastburn lamented that Advent had abandoned the "masculine simplicity and dignity" that should characterize Anglican worship, and the Advent rector defended his parish's practice as conforming to the rubrics of the *Book of Common Prayer*. Eastburn refused to administer confirmation at Advent until they mended their ways, which smacked of the "idolatrous Papal communion." Advent declined to change, instead presenting their confirmands at another parish, where their numbers considerably exceeded those of the host church.[2]

A similar scene took place in 1846 in Columbus, Ohio, where Bishop Charles Petit McIlvaine, another leader of the Evangelical faction, refused to consecrate the newly founded St. Paul's Church until the altar that had been installed had been removed and replaced with a "table."[3] This was one of a number of distinctions about the material dimensions of Episcopal worship that had become hot-button issues in the battle over whether the Protestant Episcopal Church was in fact "Protestant," in the sense shared by Evangelicals both across the Atlantic and within the American denominational spectrum, or it was "Catholic," unmodified by "Roman."[4]

The Gothic Revival

Although Boston's Trinity Church was a very conspicuous exception, the overarching material context of Anglican worship that took place during the nineteenth century was the Gothic revival. Although it was eventually adopted by Episcopalians across the spectrum of "churchmanship" as well as by a wide variety of other American denominations, the use of the Gothic was for Anglo-Catholics the "only proper style" for the sacramental worship they deemed central to true Christian practice. Inspired by the Oxford and Cambridge movements in the Church of England in the 1840s, a distinctively English form of Gothic had become the norm for American Episcopalians by the later nineteenth century, with a few striking exceptions, such as Boston's Trinity. Beginning in the 1890s, its most ardent practitioner and defender was the architect Ralph Adams Cram (1863–1942), who left his mark on churches, cathedrals, and universities across the country. Cram combined a profound ability to re-create a medieval style with striking originality and an attention to decorative detail that was rooted in the Arts and Crafts movement, an Anglo-American revival of handcrafts based on a critique of contemporary industrial culture. For several decades, Cram and his partner Bertram Grosvenor Goodhue dominated the practice of American church design in a manner that combined aesthetics, liturgical theology, and cultural criticism.

The medieval Gothic tradition was carried over vestigially into colonial America in structures such as Old St. Luke's in Isle of Wight County, Virginia, but by the eighteenth century Gothic had been completely displaced by the neoclassicism of Christopher Wren, James Gibbs, and their colonial imitators. The Gothic revival in England began in a flurry of Romantic enthusiasm over all things medieval, exemplified in the architectural dilettantism of Horace Walpole and the tales of chivalric derring-do of Walter Scott. This Gothic enthusiasm also manifested itself in the Houses of Parliament, begun in 1840, and very conspicuously in the influence of the Cambridge movement in church building. The Oxford movement, which had laid the foundations for its Cantabrigian counterpart in the 1830s, began in a quarrel over state interference in church affairs. It then rapidly became a campaign for the restoration of a "Catholic" understanding of the Church of England, emphasizing historical continuity with earliest Christianity through the un- broken succession of bishops and worship in which the sacraments rather than preaching were central. The Cambridge Camden Society (later known as the Ecclesiological Society) was founded by undergraduates in 1837 to promote a deeper understanding of medieval church architecture, and rapidly became a force in its own right through its publications and lobbying. These Ecclesiologists argued that medieval Gothic was the only appropriate style for Christian churches since, according to the medieval writer Durandus, every component was laden with symbolism. They were particularly con- cerned that the chancel—the eastern end of a properly oriented church that contained the altar—be highlighted as an especially sacred place through being higher and narrower than the nave, where laypeople sat. The chancel was also to be set apart by a roodscreen, a barrier that could only be crossed by the clergy. ("Rood" is an archaic word for cross.) Their program rapidly became de rigueur for church design in the Victorian era.[5]

The Ecclesiologists soon made their mark on Episcopalians. The first American church to be designed with their approbation was St. James the Less near Philadelphia's Laurel Hill Cemetery in 1846–48. St. James was specifically modeled on plans, sent by the Cambridge enthusiasts, of the Church of St. Michael in Longstanton, Cambridgeshire, which dates back to the thirteenth century. Though now surrounded by a somewhat decrepit Philadelphia neighborhood, it was originally a small country church, enclosed by a sturdy stone wall, together with its burying ground. St. James clearly embodies Ecclesiological ideals, including a "recessed" chancel, a cruciform (cross-shaped) plan, and a tripartite interior division created by two rows of columns that symbolizes the Trinity. It rapidly became the prototype for Episcopal small parish church design in the United States.[6]

Although Richard Upjohn was viewed by the Ecclesiologists with sus- picion because his designs did not always conform exactly to the archaeo- logically precise prescriptions, he more than anyone was responsible for the realization of their ideals on the U.S. side of the Atlantic. Born in England, Upjohn emigrated with his family and began to design churches in 1835. His first major commission was the Church of the Holy Communion (1844–45) in New York City, which had been commissioned by its rector, William Augus- tus Muhlenberg. (Muhlenberg will make lengthier appearances in chapters 4 and 5.) The first asymmetrical Gothic church in the United States, Holy Communion was, like St. James the Less, an archetypal rural English parish church, though located squarely in what is now the Flatiron District of Manhattan. As the neighborhood became more and more run down, Holy Communion merged with the parishes of St. George's, discussed in chapter 4, and Calvary. Its building became, sequentially, a cultural center, a drug rehabilitation center, and a nightclub. Sic transit.

Upjohn went on to design a myriad of churches, mainly Episcopal, and virtually invented a genre of vernacular religious architecture, the "Carpenter Gothic." Churches in this mode were easily constructed by local artisans (from Upjohn's widely circulated plans) out of alternating vertical boards and "battens" (thinner wooden strips), which provided a picturesque effect.[7] His best-known work was Trinity Church at Wall Street and Broadway, royally chartered in 1697 and historically the wealthiest parish in the Episcopal Church.[8] After Trinity's second building, erected in 1790, became too dilapidated to sustain, Upjohn was given the opportunity to design a monumental urban church on Ecclesiological principles. The most conspicuous feature of the new Trinity, completed in 1846, was its soaring tower in the Perpendicular style; at 281 feet, it dominated the Manhattan skyline in an era before skyscrapers—"cathedrals of commerce"—were structurally possible. And, where earlier churches had Gothic ornament superimposed on what was essentially a rectangular box, Trinity was the first major church to be built with accurate Gothic scale and proportions, even though some structural principles had to be fudged in the interests of economy. Notable was its articulated chancel, subtly set apart from the nave, which features the first traceried stained glass window in an American church. As in medieval churches, Trinity has accrued decorative features over the decades, including an enormous reredos (altar screen)—one of the first in the country—installed in 1877.[9]

The Church of the Advent

Under the longtime rectorship of Morgan Dix (1862–1908), Trinity would become a major locus of New York Anglo-Catholicism, along with St. Mary the Virgin in Manhattan and, somewhat later, St. Thomas on Fifth Avenue. Its earliest Boston counterpart was the Church of the Advent, which we have already encountered in the vignette that opens this chapter. Founded in 1844 by a group of prominent Bostonians, including Richard Henry Dana, *père et fils*, Advent was the first Episcopal parish in the United States to be founded on Tractarian—Oxford movement—principles. Meeting at first in rented halls and former meetinghouses retrofitted with the apparatus for "Catholic" worship, the parish grew rapidly, coming under the aegis of the Society of St. John the Evangelist in 1870. These "Cowley Fathers," as the society's members were known, were the first male religious order to be established in England since the abolition of the monasteries by Henry VIII. They were joined at Advent by the Sisters of the Society of St. Margaret, an English women's order that had come to Boston to work at the newly founded Children's Hospital. Together with its elaborate worship, which became something of a tourist attraction during the later nineteenth century, the presence of these orders signified Advent's embodiment of the distinguishing features of the Anglo-Catholic movement.[10] The Cowley Fathers now reside at a monastery near Harvard's campus in Cambridge designed by Ralph Adams Cram (1924–36) on land donated by one of Advent's most celebrated members, Isabella Stewart Gardner, who is discussed at considerable length in chapter 6. The St. Margaret Sisters were based in a townhouse in Beacon Hill's Louisburg Square, which was later owned by Secretary of State John Kerry; they later moved to Roxbury and, more recently, Duxbury, Massachusetts, to be closer to their inner-city outreach. The convent chapel was designed by Henry Vaughan.[11]

The physical dimensions of Advent are significant in their detail, illustrating the intense physicality of the Anglo-Catholic enterprise. Unlike either Boston's or New York's Trinity, Advent is more discreet than monumental, fitting snugly among the elegant townhouses of Beacon Hill. Its style reflects the contemporary popularity of Venetian, or Ruskinian, Gothic, characterized by the use of polychromed (multicolored) masonry and roofing tiles. (New Old South Church [1874], which faces Trinity in Copley Square, is a more flamboyant example of the same style in contemporary Boston.) The church was designed by John H. Sturgis, the architect of homes for wealthy Bostonians such as fellow Advent parishioner Isabella Stewart Gardner, as well as the elaborately Ruskinian first home of the Museum of Fine Arts.[12] Sturgis had trained in England and was immersed in the work of the High Victorian Gothicists of the era. The church was built on hundreds of wooden piles capped with granite and constructed out of ordinary local Chelsea bricks, reflecting a Ruskinian concern with honesty in materials. In contrast with Trinity, which was intended to be an elaborately decorated preaching hall for Phillips Brooks, Advent was designed, in the words of its rector, Charles Chapman Grafton, as a "Christian temple," the object of which "is not for preaching, but worship . . . it is the privilege of grateful love to break the alabaster box, filled with the treasures of art, at His blessed feet."[13]

The interior of Advent is, in the Gothic tradition, higher than long, and the narrowing of its arches evokes a sense of receding space that creates a long vista from the west door to the high altar.[14] The central aisle accommodates the elaborate processions with which many services begin and end. Along the sides are confessionals, another feature of Anglo-Catholic sacramental practice similar to Roman Catholic usage. These booths are one of many examples of elaborately wrought woodwork by parishioner Robert Walker Turner. Another of the decorative arts that were beginning to play a major role in Episcopal church design was stained glass. Most of Advent's many windows were crafted by the English firm of Clayton and Bell, who enjoyed the patronage of the Ecclesiological Society in England. Firms and individual artisans were now arising rapidly on both sides of the Atlantic to cater to this new demand for ecclesiastical arts. Many of the windows and other crafted objects were donated by members as memorials, thus turning the church into a collective commemoration of its own past.[15]

Advent's worship space is divided into three parts, a main altar and two flanking chapels, All Saints and the Lady Chapel. The latter is dedicated to the Virgin Mary, another emphasis in Anglo-Catholic usage. The former contains the high altar from a previous building, designed by the English architect Frank Willis, and controversial in Advent's early days because of an inscription explicitly characterizing its function as a place for sacrifice. (The term "high altar" is an Anglo-Catholic usage emphasizing the sacrality of the Eucharistic service, frequently referred to in such circles as "Mass.") The reredos was designed by Ralph Adams Cram and received an award at the 1907 Boston Arts and Crafts Exhibition. Statues by the German immigrant carver Johannes Kirchmayer include images of St. Benedict of Nursia, the monastic founder, and Helena, the mother of the Emperor Constantine. (The range of saintly representation clearly transcends a more Protestant confinement to biblical figures.) The chalice-shaped pulpit was designed by Henry Vaughan, another English architect who set up practice in America and became noted for his Gothic revival work for Episcopal churches, monasteries, and boarding schools.[16]

The chancel, the focal part of the worship space that includes the high altar, is separated from the nave by a great rood suspended from the chancel arch and a tall metal rood screen, also designed by Cram. It includes choir stalls adorned with various flora and fauna and verses from the *Benedicite*, all on the theme of the entire creation blessing the Trinity. (The *Benedicite*, also known as "A Song of Creation," is a canticle taken from the apocryphal *Song of Three Children*, and is used in Roman Catholic worship and that of other

Sanctuary with rood (crucifix), Church of the Advent, Boston, Good Friday, 2015. (Courtesy of Church of the Advent)

liturgical traditions.) Other ornament is provided by copies of paintings of the Sistine Madonna and the Holy Family by the seventeenth-century artist Franceschini, as well as a polychromatic effect provided by contrasting bands of stone in the archivolts. Seven brass lamps hang above the sanctuary rail. An antique silver lamp is lit to indicate that a consecrated host is present, and a golden aumbry holds the reserved sacrament during High Mass. Other features include a late medieval French oaken-canopied bishop's throne, a row of antique chairs for the clergy, and a carved Caen stone screen donated by Isabella Stewart Gardner.[17]

The chancel is flanked on the right by the Lady Chapel, which contains liturgical apparatus and ornament donated over several decades in memory of departed parishioners. Cram designed the screen that frames the entrance. Its iconography, in addition to the Incarnation and the Virgin Mary, includes statues of James Otis Sargent Huntington (discussed at some length in chapter 4); Mother Louisa May of the Sisters of St. Margaret; Samuel Seabury, the first bishop of the Episcopal Church; William Laud, the Archbishop of Canterbury beheaded by parliamentary forces during the English Civil War; and Edward Bouverie Pusey, one of the leaders of the Oxford movement. This pantheon of Anglo-Catholic heroes also contains a bust of Charles Grafton, sometime Advent rector and later bishop of the very Anglo-Catholic diocese of Fond du Lac, Wisconsin. The baptismal font has a drain that transmits surplus water to consecrated ground. Advent also has a mortuary chapel, the first of its kind in Boston.[18]

The Nature of (Anglo-Catholic) Gothic

This copious accumulation of detail has a point—or, rather, several—all directly related to the relationship of the Anglo-Catholic version of Episcopal worship to the material realm. First, Advent's siting is significant. Though by no means obscure, it is discreet, especially when compared to its contemporary Trinity's monumentality. It is located in the midst of a residential neighborhood rather than a public center, and blends in well with its surroundings rather than calling attention to itself. It does not try to dominate public space, but rather offers an alternative to the public sphere.

Second, this alternative space is intended as a sacred space, that is, one designed to evoke an aura of the actual presence of the divine. This literally happens in Anglo-Catholic self-understanding in the presence of the Eucharist—the body and blood of Christ—during the celebration of the Mass, or afterward reserved in the aumbry. The profusion of ornament and iconography is intended to evoke a sense of the sacred. Trinity, in contrast, could be characterized as an aesthetically evocative meetinghouse, conducive to feelings of respect, but not of awe.

Third, the interior of Advent is also a performance space. What is performed is the liturgy according to the *Book of Common Prayer*, which can be treated minimally as a largely oral recitation, or, as at Advent, as a textual framework to be embellished fulsomely with vestments, chanting, incense, gestures, and music. The central aisle provides a venue for elaborate processionals and recessionals, demarcating the beginnings and ends of services with color and drama. Trinity is also a performance space, but the primary performance was that of the preacher, Phillips Brooks, upon whom the design focused attention. Though at opposite ends of the liturgical spectrum, each church provided theater enough to attract considerable numbers of visitors. (As noted in chapter 1, Trinity was retrofitted in the 1930s with a chancel more oriented toward liturgical worship.)

Fourth, the elaborate physicality of Advent has multiple levels of significance. At one level, the church is a museum, containing objets d'art from many lands and centuries. These objects serve both liturgical and aesthetic purposes. Some, such as the elaborate vestments worn by the clergy during services, are intended to enhance the solemnity of sacramental worship services. Others, such as the stained glass, wood carving, paintings, and statuary, evoke a sense of the sacred through their beauty, iconographical reference, and historical resonance. More generally, they are informed by the doctrine of the Incarnation, that is, that Christ took on human form and thereby sanctified the creation in all its materiality. This materiality informs the notion of sacramental worship, in which physical objects become the vehicles for the channeling of divine grace, and in the case of the Eucharist are actually transformed into the divine. Although Trinity also embraces materiality in its aesthetic splendor, its original purpose was primarily to showcase the preached Word, in continuity with a very Protestant, even Puritan, sense of the relationship of the divinity to humanity through that Word.

Fifth, the collection of liturgical and devotional objects that Advent embraces originated in the philanthropy of its members, and many pieces have their donors openly identified. Other objects include representations and commemorations of "saints" in an inclusive sense—Jesus, Mary, and other biblical figures; persons of importance in the history of Christianity, especially in its Anglo-Catholic lineage; and previous rectors. Their collective presence transforms the church into a sort of microcosm of the *communio sanctorum*, the corporate body of the faithful over the centuries, culminating in present-day Boston.

Sixth, although some are of European provenance, many objects were crafted specifically for Advent by contemporary craftspeople, both native-born Americans and European immigrants, who were beginning to proliferate in Boston and other American cities and who were able to support their work in part through ecclesiastical patronage. Their work was legitimized and promoted by the Arts and Crafts movement, which invoked the teachings of John Ruskin and William Morris in support of traditional handcrafts such as stained glass making.

Finally, Advent was also the product of the emergence of a cadre of architects knowledgeable in the Gothic style and in the presuppositions of Anglo-Catholic worship. Richard Upjohn had been the pioneer, and his work was continued by his son Richard M. Upjohn and his grandson Hobart. Henry Vaughan, who designed Advent's pulpit, made some important contributions during the later nineteenth century, such as Christ Church, near the Yale campus in New Haven (1898). Beginning in the 1890s and extending into the Depression era, the dominant force in this tradition was Ralph Adams Cram, whose contributions to Advent were only incidents in the sweep of a career that helped integrate the Arts and Crafts movement into architectural practice and set the benchmark for the Gothic revival across the nation during its final phase.

The Arts and Crafts Movement

Both in England and America, the Arts and Crafts movement was closely linked with the Gothic revival. An inspiration common to both was the thought of John Ruskin (1819–1900), artist, essayist, philanthropist, Oxford professor, and "public intellectual" in the grand Victorian manner. Ruskin's art criticism rooted aesthetics firmly in social and cultural morality. Part of Ruskin's achievement was to take insights already put forward by the Roman Catholic architect A. W. N. Pugin in his *Contrasts* of 1836 and recast them in a form that would be more acceptable to Protestants. (Ruskin had been raised as an Evangelical and intended by his family for a career in the Church of England, an ambition Ruskin himself rejected.) His *Seven Lamps of Architecture* of 1849 had laid out his principles of aesthetic morality, which resembled in many ways the idea of "form following function" that developed among American architects such as Louis Sullivan and Frank Lloyd Wright. For

Ruskin, however, this ideal of simplicity, functionalism, and fidelity to nature had already been realized by the artisans of the Middle Ages in Gothic architecture.

In *The Stones of Venice* (1851–53)—especially its seminal chapter, "The Nature of Gothic"—Ruskin exalted the achievement of medieval artisans who, he argued, had been free to express their inner creativity within the context of a shared faith and had been faithful to nature in their designs. The result was an organic architecture that reflected a spiritually healthy community. With the advent of Renaissance individualism, the shared moral bond that had held together an organic society became frayed, resulting in decadence in individual and communal morality as well as in artistic production. In other writings, such as *Unto This Last* (1860), Ruskin applied his principles specifically to contemporary industrial society, attacking laissez-faire capitalism, the ethos of competition, and the separation of laborers from their products as disastrous not only for the working class but for the social fabric and the national culture more broadly. In addition to his voluminous writings and public lectures, he attempted to implement his ideas through the founding of the Guild of St. George in the 1870s to promote handcrafts and traditional agriculture, and participated in F. D. Maurice's Working Men's College in London. His vision was simultaneously progressive and deeply conservative, aimed at eliminating contemporary social ills by a revival of what he and like-minded contemporaries saw as an idealized *gemeinschaftlich* society.[19]

One such like-minded English reformer was William Morris (1834–96), who had been deeply influenced by Ruskin as an Oxford undergraduate. It was there that he became associated with the Pre-Raphaelite Brotherhood of artists such as Dante Gabriel Rossetti and Edward Burne-Jones, who shared his growing affinities for a neomedieval aesthetic. Although in his earlier years he had become immersed in the Anglo-Catholic movement and had considered ordination, he abandoned his religious interests for a more secular career as an artistic polymath, beginning in architecture and painting and moving on to bookbinding—the Kelmscott Press was founded in 1891—as well as textile and wallpaper design and faux-medieval fantasy fiction. Like Ruskin's, Morris's vision of aesthetic production was rooted in a vision of contemporary society in which the ugliness of mass-produced artifacts correlated with the alienation of the laborers who had had no meaningful involvement in their production. Morris also actively espoused a version of socialism rooted in the restoration of the organic society he saw as characteristic of the Middle Ages.[20]

Although the influence of the two men was diffused widely on both sides of the Atlantic, one of the most tangible outcomes of their work was the institutionalization of the Arts and Crafts movement, which arose in the 1870s and 1880s and flourished in the two decades that followed. In 1888, the Arts and Crafts Exhibition Society mounted a show of the "useful arts" at the New Gallery in London. Nine years later, the Society of Arts and Crafts in Boston organized the first such exhibit in the United States and, in 1900, opened a salesroom for the products of local craftspeople. Charles Eliot Norton, Harvard's (and America's) first professor of art history and a friend of John Ruskin, was the president of the Boston society. Norton was the son of Andrews Norton, the so-called pope of Boston Unitarianism in the antebellum era, but represented a new generation of American literati who had largely abandoned a specifically religious faith. His reflections on medieval design and its moral implications closely paralleled those of Ruskin as well as his American post-Unitarian contemporary, Henry Adams. In his role as wielder of cultural authority Norton helped create an ethos in which Americans could become receptive to the visual and material arts on grounds compatible with a Protestant sense of morality.[21]

This Ruskinian sense of moral purpose informed the many Arts and Crafts associations and projects that began to spring up across the nation. These included art pottery firms such as Pewabic in Detroit, Rookwood in Cincinnati, and Newcomb in New Orleans, all of them employing female artists in considerable numbers, as well as Elbert Hubbard's Roycrofters collective in Buffalo and Gustav Stickley's Craftsman furniture works in New York. Although the movement was highly decentralized, its ideas were propagated widely by enthusiasts such as Hubbard and Stickley, and reflected the emphasis of Ruskin and Morris on honesty in design and a spirituality that informed the process of artistic production of objects at once beautiful and useful in the rounds of daily life.[22] This almost Benedictine sanctification of the ordinary easily lent itself to specifically religious purposes, especially for a tradition such as the Anglican, in which an emphasis on incarnational theology invested the material world with sacramental potential.

Ralph Adams Cram

The movements for the revival of both Gothic architecture and traditional arts and crafts came together most completely in the United States in the person and work of Ralph Adams Cram. Cram was born in 1863 near Hampton Falls,

New Hampshire, the son of a Unitarian minister whose family commitments had reduced him to a life of genteel rural poverty. Cram was thus deprived of a formal college education, but compensated with autodidactic zeal. At the age of seventeen he became apprenticed to the Boston architectural firm of Rotch and Tilden, where he won sufficient prize money to finance travel in Europe for a firsthand exposure to historic building. He also immersed himself in the bohemian culture of the fin-de-siècle artistic scene in Boston, where he made the acquaintance of luminaries such as Bernard Berenson, Isabella Stewart Gardner, and Charles Eliot Norton. He devoured the works of Morris and Ruskin, became infatuated with the operas of Richard Wagner, dabbled in aestheticism and the occult, and became deeply impressed with the architecture of H. H. Richardson.[23]

The most dramatic event of Cram's youth was his religious conversion from his familial Unitarianism, which took place while he was attending midnight Mass in the church of San Luigi dei Francesi in Rome on Christmas Eve in 1887. Upon his return to Boston he received instruction in the Anglo- Catholic version of the faith from Arthur C. A. Hall, later bishop of Vermont, at the Cowley Fathers' mission church of St. John the Evangelist on Bowdoin Street in Beacon Hill.[24] He also became involved for a period with W. D. P. Bliss's Church of the Carpenter, although this youthful fling with radicalism later gave way to a more conventional religiosity and political opinions of a very different sort.[25] Although his earliest architectural designs had been for private homes, his new religious orientation rapidly provided the framework for his subsequent career, which over the next several decades focused on church building.

The major exception to this was in the realm of collegiate architecture, which was also a vehicle for the Gothic style that he came to espouse vehemently. Cram contributed important buildings at West Point and Rice, served as consulting architect to Bryn Mawr and Sweet Briar colleges, and contributed designs for a number of boarding schools such as Choate and Phillips Exeter. In 1907 he was chosen by Woodrow Wilson to be Princeton's campus architect, where the Graduate College of 1913 and Chapel of 1928 stand among his finest creations.[26] Although most of his designs were for Episcopal churches and cathedrals, he also executed commissions for monumental Gothic works for other denominations, including St. Florian's Catholic Church (1928) in Detroit's Polish enclave of Hamtramck, as well as East Liberty Presbyterian in Pittsburgh (1935) and Fourth Presbyterian (1914) on Chicago's Michigan Avenue.

The premise that informed Cram's work was essentially that of the Ecclesiological movement, namely, that Gothic was the only proper style for Christian worship because of its explicit Christian symbolism and its design for the celebration of sacramental worship under priestly auspices. He departed from these early enthusiasts, however, in his interpretation of the task of the contemporary religious architect as not archaeological but rather organic. The medieval Gothic tradition, for Cram, had not ended but had simply been interrupted by the unpleasantness of the Protestant Reformation and subsequent depredations of modernity in such forms as the French and Industrial Revolutions. His own job, as he saw it, was neither to replicate old buildings, as had the Ecclesiologists, nor to apply Gothic ornament promiscuously to frames that demonstrated no knowledge of the principles of Gothic construction or design. Cram, rather, set about to create an authentically modern Gothic that began with tradition but followed it into new realms of artistic creativity that remained true to its essential structural, aesthetic, and symbolic principles. In this goal, he stood in the lineage of his hero, H. H. Richardson, who had reshaped the Romanesque tradition in a highly creative way adapted to the needs of the modern American city. He was also working in the spirit that animated other American designers such as Louis Sullivan and Frank Lloyd Wright, who had rebelled against what they saw as the inauthenticity of the work of architects such as Richard Morris Hunt, the designer of mansions for the Gilded Age elite in styles that superficially applied ornament rather than organically relating it to the underlying structure.[27]

All Saints, Ashmont

Although Cram designed dozens of churches across the nation and a few abroad, two are worth examining at some length to illustrate better his ideas and craft. Colonel Oliver White Peabody, a partner in the prominent Boston securities firm of Kidder Peabody, and his wife, the daughter of the eminent Unitarian minister Samuel Kirkland Lothrop, were converted to Anglo-Catholicism in 1879 in the wake of the death of their young daughter. The Peabodys had been attending All Saints Church in the Ashmont section of the Boston neighborhood of Dorchester. All Saints had been founded as a mission chapel for English mill workers and subsequently became the object of the Peabodys' ample benevolence. At the time of their involvement, the parish was developing a strong Anglo-Catholic identity, and now had the backing of wealthy patrons to erect a church building suitable for its

Ralph Adams Cram, All Saints Church, Ashmont (Dorchester), 1892.
(Courtesy of and © 2015, Bruce McLay, All Saints Church)

purposes. Cram had by this time become well enough connected in Boston Anglo-Catholic circles to receive the commission—his first for a church— which was completed in 1893.[28]

The prototype for All Saints was the English country parish, which was suitable for the semirural character of the Dorchester of the time—a setting similar to that in which St. James the Less had been originally built in the environs of Philadelphia a half-century earlier. Unlike the designer of St. James, however, Cram was interested not in reproducing an English church but in creating a church for New England in the English tradition. The disproportionately large, low, square tower, rendered fortress-like by its crenellations, is in the tradition of late or Perpendicular English Gothic rural churches, while the remainder of the church derives more from "hall churches" such as King's College Chapel in Cambridge. All Saints's proportions thus differ strikingly from those of its medieval forerunners. The result, however, is both coherent and powerful, lying low to the ground, and extended considerably in its horizontality by a large, articulated chancel at the rear. The use of rough-cut Quincy granite with minimal ornament accentuates the sense of rootedness in the soil of New England. The church seems almost chthonic in its adamantine character, presenting itself as a bulwark against the encroachments

Sanctuary, All Saints Church, Ashmont (Dorchester), 1892.
(Courtesy of and © 2015, Bruce McLay, All Saints Church)

of modernity. Cram himself stated that it "must show at once that it was a church of the Anglican communion, built by and for a people Anglo-Saxon by race and instinct and sympathy."[29]

The interior of All Saints has a very different feel. The church's untraditional dimensions were deliberately utilized by Cram to create a space in which the entire congregation could have unobstructed sight lines to both altar and pulpit. Two concerns underlay the interior design: that the church accommodate properly Anglican sacramental worship, and that the entirety create a unified effect, what Cram's idol Richard Wagner termed a *Gesamtkunstwerk*, a complete work of art. In articulating his vision, Cram invoked what Archbishop Laud—for Anglo-Catholics a sainted martyr—had called "the beauty of holiness," the notion that the house of God should be a place in which all the arts were invoked for His glory. Cram thus rejected the ideal of the unornamented meetinghouse of his ancestors in favor of a *domus dei*, a house in which God dwelt and which must therefore be "intrinsically beautiful."[30]

In designing the interior Cram collaborated with his partner, Bertram Grosvenor Goodhue, together with a panoply of artists and artisans stimulated by the Arts and Crafts movement, in which the two partners were locally active.[31] The center of Anglo-Catholic worship was the high altar, in this case a massive seven-ton single block of limestone. Above the altar is an elaborate reredos (altar screen) given by Mrs. Peabody in honor of her husband. It features images of Christ the King surrounded by the archangels Michael and Gabriel executed by the Spanish sculptor Domingo Mora, and a three-part painting by George Hallowell of the Virgin Mary enthroned as Queen of Heaven. (To one side of the chancel is a Lady Chapel as well.) Mrs. Peabody continued to commission further pieces, including woodcarving designed by Goodhue and executed by Bavarian-born Johannes Kirchmayer, who with Cram and Goodhue was one of the founders of the Boston Society of Arts and Crafts in 1897. Kirchmayer's work was also prominent at Advent and a number of other Anglo-Catholic churches.[32] Stained glass windows were fashioned by a number of designers, including Boston's Charles Connick, whose work in the tradition of Chartres Cathedral contrasted sharply with the palette employed by the Tiffany Studios that is featured at many Protestant churches.[33]

Perhaps the most striking feature of All Saints's interior is the crucifixion group on the rood beam that demarcates the line between the chancel and the nave. Designed by Cram himself, it consists of painted statues of Jesus flanked by the observing Saints John and Mary. The central image of Jesus has his arms outstretched upon a cross against a gold background suggesting a Byzantine icon, and forms a visual focus for those assembled in the nave. The use even of simple crosses had been controversial among American Protestants, including Episcopalians, prior to the Civil War, and had been one of the issues in the ongoing family quarrel between Evangelicals and Anglo-Catholics. By the 1870s the cross itself had become widely accepted, but the presence of a *corpus*—the body of Jesus—still smacked of Roman Catholicism. Its central presence at All Saints was a signal that corporeality in a fully literal sense was a central tenet of Anglo-Catholics.[34]

St. Thomas

While All Saints began its life as a rural church, St. Thomas, in the heart of midtown Manhattan, is a decidedly urban creation. The original church was located in Greenwich Village at the corner of Broadway and Houston Street; its founders were lawyers and businessmen, including an Astor, and its rectors were of the High persuasion in churchmanship. The building was described by contemporaries as "Gothic," but only in the sense of applied ornament related to that tradition. It was destroyed by fire in 1851—the fate of many nineteenth-century buildings—and was replaced on the same site, which soon proved to be an unwise choice, given the continuing flight of Episcopalians northward. Like many Protestant congregations, that of St. Thomas followed the flow, it was rebuilt in 1868–70 on the corner of Fifth Avenue and 53rd Street. Designed by Richard Upjohn and his son, the new church featured extensive external ornamental detail and a corner tower rising 260 feet. The interior was decorated with murals by John La Farge, who was soon to collaborate with H. H. Richardson and Phillips Brooks on Boston's Trinity Church, as well as bas-reliefs by Augustus St.-Gaudens.[35] It was here that Bishop Henry Codman Potter and a number of Episcopal and clerical colleagues presided over the notoriously reluctant marriage of Consuelo Vanderbilt to the Duke of Marlborough in 1895.[36] It was also at St. Thomas that the Easter Parade began in the 1870s, with a procession by the church's choir to nearby St. Luke's Hospital, where they carried flowers from the sanctuary and provided patients with a concert. The parish has a lengthy tradition of choral music.[37]

When Upjohn's iteration of St. Thomas burned in 1905, the parish turned to the by then well-known Cram, Ferguson, and Goodhue for a replacement on the same site. Cram, who was primarily responsible for the exterior, provided a striking contrast with the ornate *Kölner Dom*-inspired St. Patrick's Cathedral that stands catty-corner across Fifth Avenue. A blend of English and French Gothic forms, St. Thomas anchors its corner lot with a single tower at the southeast. Where St. Patrick's dominates its site, even in the shadow of the later Rockefeller Center that has stood opposite since the 1930s, St. Thomas fits in discreetly, a stately but unobtrusive presence on bustling Fifth Avenue. Its exterior belies its considerable size: it seats 1,700, compared with St. Patrick's 2,500.*

---

*St. Patrick's, designed by Episcopalian architect James Renwick Jr., was inspired by the Cologne Cathedral (*Kölner Dom*) that had been recently completed in Germany after centuries of arrested development, stimulated by the historical studies of French architectural restorationist Viollet-le-Duc. Dedicated in 1879, St. Patrick's was, unlike its Baltimore and Cincinnati predecessors, less a bid for full Catholic participation in the democratic republic than an act of public defiance of a culture in which Catholics were perceived as unwelcome and potentially dangerous aliens. Financed in part with countless small contributions from impoverished immigrants, it stood as an urban fortress against all enemies. Renwick was also the architect for Grace Church (Manhattan) and the Smithsonian Institution's "Castle."

Bertram Grosvenor Goodhue and Lee Lawrie, altar and reredos, St. Thomas Church, New York City. (Courtesy of Saint Thomas Church Fifth Avenue)

Leaving "the crowded ways of life" of midtown Manhattan and entering into the silence of St. Thomas when no services are in progress is a liminal experience. The church's interior is, simply, luminous. Some of the light comes through the stained glass windows from London's Whitefriars Studio, which consist collectively of some nine million panes.[38] But the visual focus of the church is the overwhelming great reredos, designed by Goodhue and executed by the sculptor Lee Lawrie, which measures eighty by forty-three feet. The reredos, for which Goodhue was awarded a gold medal by the American Institute of Architects in 1925, is carved of Dunville stone and emits an ivory glow when illuminated. It consists of representations of some sixty figures from the history of Christianity, ranging from St. Stephen to Samuel Seabury to Phillips Brooks, and twice including the church's patron, St. Thomas.[39] The interior also features playful iconographic touches such as carvings of moneybags with the initials "J.P.M."—J. P. Morgan—as part of a series representing the professions.[40]

The inclusion of Lee Lawrie in the design team was another step in the achievement of the *Gesamtkunstwerk* ideal first attempted at Ashmont. The German-born Lawrie worked closely with Goodhue both in collaboration with Cram and after the breakup of the architectural partnership in 1924; their later works included both religious buildings such as Rockefeller Chapel (1923) at the University of Chicago and ostensibly secular structures such as the Nebraska State Capitol and the Los Angeles Public Library (both 1924). Lawrie and Goodhue together were drawn to projects involving complex iconographical schemes, which Lawrie executed in the stylized character of the Art Deco that was emerging as the distinctive fashion for the age of the skyscraper.[41] It also complemented Cram's exteriors, which shaped Gothic "truth" according to a minimalist aesthetic, emphasizing composition and massing rather than ornamental detail.[42] An instructive contrast with Lawrie's work at St. Thomas is his great statue of Atlas at Rockefeller Center, just a block to the south. Cram, whose vision accommodated an admiration for the secular art of the skyscraper as manifested in the Gothic-ornamented Empire State Building, roundly denounced this newer creation as the spawn of a decadent civilization whose preoccupation with commerce now manifested itself aesthetically in tawdriness.[43]

Together with the Cathedral Church of St. John the Divine, which is discussed at considerable length in chapter 3, All Saints Ashmont and St. Thomas illustrate many of the major themes that inform Cram's extensive career of ecclesiastical design. Cram was, however, a medievalist in theory as well as architectural practice. Over several decades he published a lengthy series of books, many of them compilations of articles and speeches, in which he expounded his apotheosis of Gothic style, complemented with an ongoing jeremiad against contemporary civilization.[44] For Cram, the medieval culture that had produced the great Gothic cathedrals illustrated the necessity of a religious core to society that would harness individual talent and effort to a transcendent goal. He shared to a considerable extent the nostalgia of post-Unitarian contemporaries such as Charles Eliot Norton and Henry Adams for what seemed a culturally vital "age of faith." Unlike them, he believed that it was still possible for the United States to achieve such a culture. First, however, it had to overcome the social and ideological detritus of centuries of revolutionary upheavals—religious, industrial, and political.[45]

Cram's later social views were shaped by his early experience. His essay "The Last of the Squires," published originally in the *Atlantic* in 1930, was a celebration of his maternal grandfather, Ira Blake, who presided over his domain in Kensington, New Hampshire, and represented for his grandson the finest flourishing of "the last phase . . . of feudalism."[46] This evocation of a benign but vanished organic, agrarian society has strong affinities with *I'll Take My Stand*, a collection of essays defending the Southern heritage that Cram admired, published in the same year.[47] Cram held this evocation of the austere tradition of New England republicanism in a tenuous balance with the royalism he had playfully espoused during his Boston "bohemian" days as a member of the Order of the White Rose, a whimsical celebration of the English House of Stuart. (He argued that the society should espouse a Hamiltonian political philosophy, since a monarchy, however romantically desirable, was not practical in the United States.) Underlying this seemingly eclectic flirtation with incompatible ideologies—which continued in later years in admiration for aspects of both Mussolini's Fascism and Roosevelt's New Deal—was a yearning for a society that was both hierarchical and organic, in which all members had a place of repose from which they could contribute according to their particular talents to a greater, commonly acknowledged good.[48]

For Cram, however, the ultimate paradigm for the good society was the later Middle Ages, during which a deeply held communal belief underlay the production of an authentically beautiful artistic tradition, that is, the Gothic. Although fixated on an era in which Aristotelian philosophy enjoyed a renewed primacy in Thomas Aquinas's synthetic thought, Cram was at heart a Platonist and believed that the Gothic was more the visualization of a spiritual impulse than a method of construction or the material expression of an intellectual concept.[49] Cram expatiated on the superiority of medieval over modern life on numerous occasions throughout his career, but perhaps the most succinct and radical expression of this idea came in his brief book, *Walled Towns*, published in 1919. Cram explicitly conflated his neomedieval vision with his nostalgia for preindustrial New England. The latter, however, had its drawbacks: it was a place where "there was a hard and unlovely religion, the arts had wholly disappeared, and the exquisite environment man had always made for himself had vanished from life. The stimulus and the vital communal sense of the old guilds, the games, the merrymaking, the living religious practices, had faded into a colder and more austere neighbourliness [sic]."[50]

Chapter 4 of this curious work describes a visit to such a town, named "Beaulieu"—"beautiful place." Cram's community of the past/future is a closed-off, self-sufficient, deindustrialized realm of small-scale agriculture. Modern inventions are limited to emergency use and owned communally: automobiles must halt at the Bar Gate at the town's edge. Local crafts are protected, handcrafts have largely replaced machine-made goods, and "useless luxuries" are banned. A single parish church (presumably Anglo-Catholic) serves the entire community, and religious orders have prominent houses nearby. The franchise is limited to landholders, and civic affairs are conducted with considerable pageantry. "Taxation is almost wholly in the form of rent of land." There is no division between capital and labor, since production is for use rather than profit. Education is aimed primarily at basic literacy and character development; beyond the primary level it is entrusted mainly to trade guilds and religious orders.

Cram goes on in considerably more detail in his evocation of a postindustrial utopia that evokes the medieval town, the Puritan village, Edward Bellamy's enormously popular *Looking Backward*, and a variety of other attempts to provide imaginative alternatives to the bleak urban-industrial society that still exists at the margins of Cram's walled towns. His vision was, to be sure, fanciful, but arguably no more so than Bellamy's, which had inspired a widespread movement of "Nationalist Clubs" after his best-known work's publication in 1888. The popular reaction to *Walled Towns* was considerably more muted, to the point of invisibility. Cram's ideas can be read more positively as, in Jackson Lears's words, "a thoroughgoing corporatist critique of centrifugal liberalism."[51] His works can also be read as an idiosyncratic late chapter in the Episcopal version of the Social Gospel—described in detail in chapter 4—in their embrace of a distinctively Anglican sense of churchly responsibility for shaping and informing an organic community. His architecture has proven considerably more enduring than his thought.

Coda: Bertram Grosvenor Goodhue and St. Bartholomew's

St. Bartholomew's is only a short walk from St. Thomas—two blocks east and another two south. The histories of the two parishes were in many ways parallel, although St. Bartholomew's from early on had a distinctly Evangelical identity. "St. Bart's," as it is familiarly known, was founded in 1836 at Lafayette Park, and its congregation followed the northward path taken by many Episcopal congregations. With a Roosevelt and a Vanderbilt on the building committee, a new "Lombardic" church designed by James Renwick Jr. was completed at Madison Avenue and 44th Street in 1876, featuring a monumental three-door portal by Stanford White. (White, a principal in the prestigious firm McKim, Mead, and White, of Boston Public Library fame and a celebrated bon vivant, was shot and killed by a jealous husband in a 1906 cause célèbre.) Its theological orientation shifted with the coming of David Hummel Greer as rector in 1888. Greer, who would later serve as bishop of New York, was one of the most articulate spokesmen of the Broad Church movement. At his death in 1919, the *New York Times* eulogized him as having "built up at St. Bartholomew's a great educational, patriotic, labor, race-amalgamated, and generally useful system of Christian charity and helpfulness."[52]

By the time of its final move uptown in 1923, St. Bartholomew's had developed a considerable reputation in two areas: music and social outreach. Under the direction of Richard Henry Warren, an adult choir replaced the quartet, which had been a staple of nineteenth-century church music. Upon his retirement in 1905, Warren was succeeded by Leopold Stokowski until the latter's departure for the Cincinnati Symphony four years later. In 1915, Amy Beach, perhaps the most prominent female American composer of her day, settled in New York and soon became a virtual composer-in-residence for the church, which commissioned and performed a lengthy series of her works.[53] In addition to serving as a venue for "high" artistic performance, the church had also sponsored a "Chorus of Homeless Men" as part of the extensive programming of its parish house. During the 1890s, the parish house flourished as one of New York's premiere "institutional churches," a phenomenon described in considerably more detail in chapter 4. The parish's outreach activities included a temperance society, the Rescue Worker's Practical Training School, a night dispensary, a hospital for gastrointestinal diseases, and services conducted in Armenian, Chinese, German, Persian, Swedish, and Syriac.[54] The new Park Avenue venue also included a substantial parish house that would become the subject of considerable controversy in later years.*[55]

The present-day iteration of St. Bartholomew's was the result of the collaboration of two apparently disparate men whose visions united to produce a remarkable structure. Leighton Parks was the rector who oversaw the church's design and construction. Continuing in the direction of his predecessor, Bishop Greer, Parks was clearly in the camp of theological modernism: he openly denied the Virgin Birth, a touchstone of Christian orthodoxy, and from his pulpit he dared Bishop Manning to try him for heresy. (The bishop tacitly declined the challenge.) Parks at the same time openly criticized those in the congregation who took a more traditional position; one Vanderbilt took umbrage as well as membership in St. Thomas.[56]

Parks's theology had clear implications for the design of the new church. In many ways he stood in a direct line with one of his heroes, Phillips Brooks, who had supervised Richardson's creation of a church that was both a Protestant preaching hall and aesthetically conducive to the contemplation of the sublime. One of the key teachings of Parks's version of Broad Churchmanship was the notion of divine immanence, that is, the idea that God exists and can be experienced in the here-and-now rather than only in some transcendent realm. This idea correlated with Parks's faith in democracy and in the need for community outreach, which continued to inform the parish's commitment to the Social Gospel.[57]

In a manner reminiscent of John Ruskin in his *Seven Lamps of Architecture*, Parks argued that the primary goal of religious building was moral uplift, for the entire community as well as the congregation. The church was to be "an instrument for the ministry of beauty."[58] Like Brooks, he favored the Romanesque as more appropriate for his day, arguing not simply in terms of proximity in time to the early Christian community but also for the specific

---

*St. Bartholomew's was designated an historic landmark in 1967 as part of the reaction to the 1963 destruction of Penn Station, a status opposed by the rector and vestry. This became a serious point of contention in 1981, when the vestry wanted to replace the parish house and adjoining terrace with a fifty-nine-story office building to raise funds for community outreach activities. After the New York City Landmarks Preservation Commission rejected these plans, the case was appealed as far as the U.S. Supreme Court, which declined to hear it.

associations of the style's components. The round arch, for example, stood for human brotherhood, the dome for divine immanence, and the campanile for progress. It also fostered democracy, allowing the minister and congregation to gather together around the altar like family, as opposed to the more hierarchical scheme of the Gothic, exemplified in St. Thomas. Parks also wanted a church with good acoustics for musical performance and a pulpit visible from all parts of the nave.[59]

To implement these desiderata, the vestry of St. Bartholomew's in 1914 selected Cram's sometime partner, Bertram Grosvenor Goodhue, just as the two were parting company. Like Cram, Goodhue came from a venerable but financially shaky New England family, never received a formal higher education, and began his career as part of Boston's bohemian arts scene. Unlike Cram, he never experienced a religious conversion; in later times, his attitude toward such matters might be described as "spiritual, not religious," and he was fascinated with elaborate iconographical schemes that informed not only his churches but also the previously mentioned public buildings on which he worked with Lee Lawrie. Although he collaborated with Cram on a number of Gothic revival churches, including St. Thomas, he had no commitment to the style on either aesthetic or theological grounds. He was inclined toward a rather romantic but not too clearly defined sense of the numinous that evoked the exotic and remote while simultaneously expressing his own era's zeitgeist.[60]

The result of the collaboration between the modernist rector and the romantic architect was St. Bartholomew's, which Goodhue in retrospect described as looking less like a Christian church than something from the *Arabian Nights* or the final act of Wagner's opera *Parsifal*, in which the Holy Grail is unveiled.[61] Its first impressive feature is the entry portal. This was not new at all, but rather had been transferred in its entirety from the Madison Avenue venue, where it had been designed by Stanford White as a memorial to Cornelius Vanderbilt II. Modeled loosely on the Romanesque church of St. Gilles-du-Gard in Provence, the entry consists of three doorways, each by a prominent sculptor, and is held together visually by a screen of marble columns and a sculptural frieze of biblical scenes. The west window of the façade, which delineates the beginning of Goodhue's church, contains statues of four prominent preachers, including the now literally iconic Phillips Brooks.[62]

The main body of St. Bartholomew's is based on a variety of historical sources, most notably the Cathedral of San Marco in Venice. San Marco and

Bertram Grosvenor Goodhue, St. Bartholomew's Church, New York City, 1916–17. (Photograph by Christopher Little. Courtesy of St. Bartholomew's Church)

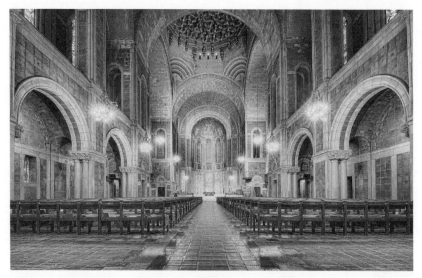

St. Bartholomew's Church, Byzantine-influenced interior. (Photograph by
Virgelio Carpio. Courtesy of St. Bartholomew's Church)

other Byzantine-influenced prototype churches differed from their Gothic
counterparts in their centralized, cruciform plans.[63] Unlike Cram, who
preferred traditional masonry construction unless absolutely necessary—
as when St. Thomas was threatened by underground urban vibrations—
Goodhue had no qualms about concrete and structural steel, justifying this
as well as stylistic innovation and eclecticism as a fortunate blending of old
and new. The dominant space is the central domed crossing, from which
emanate the nave, an apsidal choir, and two transepts. The overall drama of
the interior, experienced as a single unified space, is evoked by the play of
large, enclosed volumes composed of flat and curved planes in which the
ornament is structurally embedded. The ornament consists of shimmering
mosaic tiles designed by Hildreth Meière, one of Goodhue's and Lawrie's
regular collaborators.[64] Although the mosaic ensemble was commissioned
after Goodhue's death and is more elaborate than his original vision required,
it has become an integral part of the luminous aura that the combination of
volume and ornament evokes in the beholder.[65]

Christine Smith, the church's foremost interpreter, provides an evocative
interpretation of St. Bartholomew's overall effect: "The exterior—razor-sharp,
aggressively self-confident—projects an image of leadership and of no-
nonsense efficiency. But the voluptuous sensuality of the interior—with its

great, vaporous spatial volumes, in which the air trembles with a more-than-human living force—invites the spectator to experience an inner mystery."[66]

Together, St. Thomas and St. Bartholomew's represent two contrasting yet ultimately similar evocations of a new kind of Episcopal church in the age of the city. Cram's St. Thomas is Anglo-Catholic and Gothic, and its interior is a hierarchically arranged processional space. Goodhue's St. Bartholomew's is centralized and intended to minimize the distinctions between clergy and laity. They stand, respectively, in the traditions of Advent and Trinity in Boston, and are based on very distinctive visions of the place of the Episcopal Church in the Christian tradition.

But the two have much in common. Each is a large urban church that stands prominently on a major avenue in midtown Manhattan, and each attracts a predominantly well-to-do clientele. Each includes an assemblage of the liturgical arts, representing the heyday of the Arts and Crafts movement and its contemporary practitioners, their individual work shaped into a harmonious whole through the vision of the supervising architect. Each is a performance venue, providing space for musicians and composers to participate in corporate worship. Finally, each is designed to evoke an aura of sacrality, an air of the numinous produced through the combination of space, light, materials, and art, "the complete consort dancing together."[67]

They, and other churches like them, are also cultural institutions of a distinct period in American urban history. In the decades that lay between the Civil War and World War I, the United States experienced not only the dizzying growth of its cities but also a corresponding drive to create cultural institutions that would place those cities and their elites on a par with the long-established cultural centers of Europe. The cultural philanthropy of many prominent Episcopalians, such as J. P. Morgan and Isabella Stewart Gardner, is discussed at considerable length in chapter 6. But it is worth noting at this point that the great urban churches of this age were also cultural institutions—architectural displays, art collections, and performance venues for music and oratory. Conversely, explicitly cultural institutions such as museums, libraries, symphony halls, and theaters were intentionally designed to evoke an aura of the sacred—to be "temples of the arts."[68] And, although other denominations played some role in this process of cultural hybridization, it was the Episcopal Church that indubitably took the lead.

CHAPTER THREE

The Great American Cathedrals

The word "cathedral" suggests a very large church, such as the late Robert Schuller's famed "Crystal Cathedral" in Anaheim, California. Schuller's erstwhile domain, however, was not originally a cathedral in any but a metaphorical sense, since it did not belong to a denomination with bishops as part of its governance. (This changed in 2010 when Schuller's heirs were forced into bankruptcy and sold the plant to the Roman Catholic Diocese of Orange.) An authentic cathedral is not necessarily a very big church; many Episcopal cathedrals in the United States are no larger than an average parish church, which is what many of them originally were. A bona fide cathedral is a bishop's church, one where that dignitary's emblem of office, the chair (Greek καθέδρα, Latin *cathedra*), permanently stands as a symbol of episcopal authority. Cathedrals are located in cities designated as sees (from the Latin *sedes*, "seat"), in which the bishop resides and which are usually the most prominent in their respective dioceses. (Dioceses in the United States are areas—usually a state or section of a state—in which a bishop exercises ecclesiastical authority.)

In Europe, cathedrals had for centuries symbolized the power of the institutional church—Roman, Anglican, or Lutheran—in a given region, which enjoyed establishment status and exercised authority in conjunction, or sometimes in competition, with the secular government. The Gothic cathedrals erected over periods of decades or even centuries in late medieval England, France, and other countries represented vast investments of wealth and artistic talent and stood as the premier symbols of the social, cultural, and religious orders of their day. Henry Adams's *Mont-St.-Michel and Chartres*, first published in 1904, portrayed Chartres Cathedral, built near Paris in the twelfth and thirteenth centuries, as a sublime incarnation of the power exerted by the Virgin Mary over the France of its time. It stood for Adams in stark contrast with the impersonal force of the "dynamo," which he saw as the most fitting embodiment of the culture of the twentieth-century United States.

Although cathedrals have continued as a feature of the Church of England from medieval times through the Reformation era to the present day, the establishment of the Protestant Episcopal Church as an independent Anglican body in the newly formed United States in 1789 by no means automatically implied the simultaneous appearance of this venerable institution. The first suggestion that a cathedral in the American church might be desirable appears to have arisen from John Henry Hobart, the first bishop of New York. Hobart mentioned the possibility of such a structure, perhaps in Washington Square, to former New York mayor Philip Hone in 1828 after an inspiring trip to Britain.[1] Although the cathedral idea meshed well with Hobart's High Church ecclesiology, the idea was shelved until the era of the Civil War. James Lloyd Breck, missionary to the upper Midwest and cofounder of Wisconsin's Nashotah House, a seminary for the training of priests in the Anglo-Catholic tradition, revived the idea in Minnesota during the 1850s on the grounds that a cathedral would "ennoble society."[2] Working with Breck, Henry Whipple, the bishop of Minnesota, dedicated the Cathedral of Our Merciful Savior in Faribault in 1869. Although there have been several other claimants to the title, Minnesota's seems to have been the first proper Episcopal cathedral in the United States—appropriately in the heart of the "Biretta Belt," that enclave of Anglo-Catholicism in the upper Midwest.

The establishment of Episcopal cathedrals began gradually to take shape in the decades following the Civil War, bolstered both by the rise of Anglo-Catholicism and by a growing denominational impetus toward administrative centralization and a corresponding increase in the importance of the office of bishop. Although there was no national mandate for cathedral churches—in the early twenty-first century there are still some dioceses that lack them— many dioceses proceeded to create them, although not in any uniform fashion. One common pattern was the designation of an already-extant parish church in the premier city of the diocese as having cathedral status. This usually came about through Episcopal vision and initiative.

Boston

In Boston, the cathedral was the result of an unexpected opportunity. The successor to Phillips Brooks as bishop of Massachusetts was William Lawrence, the descendant of two of Boston's wealthiest families, the Appletons and the Lawrences. In his autobiography, Lawrence recalls his concern at the end of the nineteenth century that "each parish and mission was a unit in itself; and while the people recognized the Bishop as the head, they were, to a large degree, Congregationalists."[3] He did not find adequate precedent for a cathedral as a means of symbolizing diocesan unity in either England, where most cathedrals had been built on monastic foundations, or in those that already existed in the United States, which were either bases for missionary bishops or parish churches where bishops had been invited to store their miters (assuming they wore them—Low Church bishops trended to shun such manifestations of what they regarded as "popish" affectation).[4]

While in 1898 Lawrence was pondering the question he had posed for himself—"Would it be possible to found in this country a real American cathedral?"—he was informed that a wealthy donor had an interest in making a substantial bequest to the diocese for just that purpose. Four years later, that donor—Miss Mary Sophia Walker, with her sister Harriet Sarah Walker—left a bequest of over a million dollars to the diocese for a cathedral. The Misses Walker—"very modest and retiring women of pure New England blood and type," according to Lawrence—had been raised as Congregationalists, but had been led to the Episcopal Church by their pastor in Waltham as well as by Lawrence's charismatic predecessor, Phillips Brooks. The bulk of their wealth was in the form of the Governor Gore estate in Waltham, an inheritance from their uncle. "Had I been a follower of Anglican Episcopal tradition of pre-Trollope days," Lawrence mused, "I might have driven in coach and four from the door of the Bishop's palace in Waltham to the Cathedral of St. Botolph, whose tower standing upon the Cambridge bank of the Charles was reflected from the calm surface of the water."[5] ("Boston" is a contraction of "St. Botolph's Town.")

Lawrence readily dismissed the aristocratic pretensions that he saw implicit in the commissioning of a grand new structure, and instead opted— as many of his counterparts had done or would do—for the retrofitting of an already extant parish church. The choice was presumably not difficult. His Appleton grandfather had been among the founders of St. Paul's Church, which in Lawrence's day was conveniently situated at the population center of the diocese in downtown Boston. (It sits near "Brimstone Corner," named after nearby revivalist-oriented Park Street Church, a short walk from the hub of the city's public transportation system at Park Street.) St. Paul's had been built in 1819 in the Greek revival mode, and has always been the only Episcopal cathedral of that style. It had originally been conceived as the first truly American Episcopal church in Boston, since Christ (Old North) and Trinity had been founded in colonial times. Even at this early date, however, St. Paul's followed a practice of historical memory that would be continued in many subsequent cathedrals by incorporating stones from three resonant sites: its namesake, St. Paul's Cathedral in London; its city's namesake, St. Botolph's church in Boston, England; and Valley Forge, Pennsylvania, which richly evoked the founding of the American nation. St. Paul's was thus something of a microcosm, incorporating itself physically as well as associating itself symbolically with significant elements of the political and religious cosmos in which it was situated.[6]

Like many bishops who were drawn into the business of cathedral building, Lawrence felt the need to articulate the reasons that justified such a potentially costly undertaking, even though in this case all that was involved was the modification of an already extant structure. Though from an enormously wealthy family, he played the role of the frugal Yankee, reluctant to deprive parish churches of resources.[7] In explaining the cathedral's purpose, he employed a biblical phrase, "a house of prayer for all people" (Isaiah 56:7), that would be similarly invoked by many other Episcopal cathedral builders. Most urban dwellers of his age, Lawrence argued, were unchurched, and a downtown cathedral would serve as a mission center for them:

> The millions of dollars that go into the structure of cathedrals lay upon the Church heavy responsibility so to use them as to give back returns in character, public spirit, and glad sacrifice. While we are constructing great fanes in our city—the tens of thousands of poor and helpless, the anarchists, the Bolshevists, and radicals—have before them fruits which they have a right to expect from great churches in the pure and unselfish character of clergy and worshipers.[8]

Although it is not recorded what reception was given the cathedral by Boston's anarchists and Bolshevists, Lawrence did implement some reforms to remove the deterrents to lower-class attendance that still existed at many Episcopal churches. He was quite emphatic in declaring that his was "now a free and open cathedral," and proceeded to have the doors removed from the building's pews, thus signaling that the purchase or rental of pews that had barred the poor from attending Episcopal services in many places was a thing of the past. This appears to have been effective, as Lawrence speaks of the cathedral holding four or five services daily to accommodate popular demand, as well as staging hymn-sings, led by the choir from the steps, in which crowds, which flooded onto the street and across onto the common on Sunday and holiday evenings, enthusiastically participated.[9]

Philadelphia

In the case of Philadelphia, ambitious plans for a cathedral were in the air early in the twentieth century. Bishop Philip Mercer Rhinelander espoused a vision similar to that of Boston's Lawrence in which the functional independence of individual parishes—the de facto Congregationalism that Lawrence had identified—might be subordinated to a more unified diocesan identity symbolized by a cathedral, one in keeping with the broader theme of administrative centralization in the American society of the day. In 1918, Rhinelander launched his cathedral project and received an enthusiastic response from his elite constituency, who viewed the enterprise as a matter of civic as much as religious import. Women from families with major holdings in Curtis Publishing, the Drexel Bank, and the Pennsylvania Railroad were active in the Cathedral League, and Senator George Wharton Pepper composed a pamphlet boosting the enterprise. A vast Gothic structure that would be part of a complex including a bishop's house, deanery, and other facilities was to be built on a tract in Upper Roxborough and would constitute "a permanent center of diocesan life" near the geographic center of the diocese. Construction did not begin until 1932, after economic circumstances had changed dramatically, and the project was abandoned in the 1960s, with only the deanery and Lady Chapel completed. The diocese of Pennsylvania never did get its cathedral.[10]

The cathedrals in Boston and other cities such as Detroit were sizeable structures that served prosperous and well-populated dioceses at a time when wealthy parishioners were at hand to foot the hefty bills. In a few key cities, however, even grander plans were being launched to erect cathedrals on an even more monumental scale. These would be accompanied by a panoply of outlying structures that would emulate the functions that cathedrals had provided under the Church of England, a paradigm that was increasingly becoming the model for Anglophiliac Americans.[11] Such cathedrals would simultaneously take on the roles of centers of diocesan programming, administration, and outreach; symbols of both episcopal and Episcopal presence; museums of liturgical arts; microcosms celebrating the story of God's church, the history of the nation and region, and the glories of human achievement; and various other things besides. Three such cathedrals launched during this age of ecclesiastical magnificence were Manhattan's St. John the Divine; the National Cathedral in Washington, D.C.; and San Francisco's Grace.

New York

The Cathedral Church of St. John the Divine in Manhattan's Morningside Heights was the first of these cathedrals to be launched and remains to this day, as its nickname indicates, "St. John the Unfinished." As noted earlier, Bishop John Henry Hobart was the first of New York's bishops to propose a cathedral in 1828, but anti-English sentiment lingering from the War of 1812 stood in the way of its gaining significant support.[12] After the Civil War, prosperity, civic pride, growing Anglophilia, and the implicit challenge presented by St. Patrick's Roman Catholic cathedral worked in favor of both the Episcopal Church and a cathedral project. Bishop Horatio Potter revived the notion, only to be thwarted by the Panic of 1873 and the financial hard times that ensued.[13]

The beginnings of St. John the Divine as an actual project rather than simply an idea were the work of Potter's nephew and successor, Henry Codman Potter. In 1887, the younger Potter issued a call addressed "To the Citizens of New York," appealing to the moral instincts and civic pride of all of that city's inhabitants to join in a campaign to build a cathedral "worthy of a great city."[14] This was the era in which New York and other American cities were engaged in a burst of civic boosterism and vied with one another to acquire the institutional amenities—public libraries, art and natural history museums, symphony halls, monumental government buildings, railroad stations—that would demonstrate to the world that the United States could hold its own with the great cities of Europe as centers not only of commerce but of culture. New York's newspaper editorials enthusiastically supported Potter's call. One of the first major contributions to the campaign—one hundred thousand dollars—came from Presbyterian business magnate D. Willis James, who saw the cathedral as potentially "a permanent power for good to the nation through its entire history."[15] Less enthusiastic was the local Roman Catholic press, which perhaps not surprisingly felt that the project was an elitist venture that slighted their own community's cathedral as a civic monument.[16]

A suitable three-square-block site was found for the new cathedral on land that had belonged to an orphanage on the edges of a plateau near the north end of Central Park, an area in which residential neighborhood development was rapidly taking place. In 1889 a design competition was declared that drew sixty-eight submissions, but immediately aroused controversy over the secrecy that surrounded it. (Henry Yates Satterlee, then rector of Calvary Church

and later the chief promoter of the National Cathedral after he became bishop
of Washington, was one of the protesters.) Two years later the plans of the
four finalists were revealed, none of which drew more than a tepid response
from architectural critics. Eventually the firm of Heins and LaFarge, both of
the principals of which were Roman Catholics, was selected as the winner
for their hybrid Byzantine-Romanesque-Gothic design, over the protests of
Bishop Potter himself.[17] The plan, characterized by the *New York Times* as
"a compromise cathedral," was inspired in part by the Hagia Sophia mosque
in Istanbul. Their design was characterized by a central plan in which most
of the congregational seating would be not in the nave but rather under an
enormous central dome, similar to Boston's Trinity Church. At the insistence
of the trustees, it was modified to include more elements of what for Episcopalians was becoming the normative English Gothic, and the alignment
shifted from north-south to east-west, in keeping with ecclesiastical tradition but interfering with the goal of having the cathedral's façade and towers
help to shape the Manhattan skyline. Not, perhaps, the most auspicious of
beginnings.[18]

The building of St. John's lurched on, with architects and trustees quarrel-
ing over such issues as the use of newly available poured concrete (rejected)
and George Heins's death in 1907. The first building campaign was for the
completion of the choir and crossing, which would serve as worship space
while other parts of the cathedral were being erected. One innovation intended as temporary, but which became a permanent feature after its significance was fully realized, was the construction of a roof over the crossing by
Spanish architect Rafael Guastavino, who had invented a low-cost system of
tile vaulting that was at once elegant, durable, and acoustically resonant.[19] In
1911, the apse, choir, crossing, and two of the apsidal chapels were completed.
At this point, the trustees fired Christopher LaFarge and instead engaged
Ralph Adams Cram. Cram's hiring, before LaFarge had been notified of his
dismissal, was another in a string of public relations blunders that characterized the early years of St. John's.[20]

Cram had actually admired the Heins and LaFarge scheme and wanted
to collaborate with LaFarge after the death of Heins, although the trustees
vetoed this notion.[21] He saw the already realized portion as both a challenge and opportunity to break free of the English Gothic tradition with
which Anglophiliac American Episcopalians were enamored, and to turn
to French and Spanish precedents as well.[22] His first task, however, was not
the cathedral itself, but rather the outbuildings that were planned for the

Ralph Adams Cram et al., The Cathedral Church of St. John the Divine, New York City, 1892–. (Courtesy of the Cathedral Church of St. John the Divine Archives)

ample grounds on its outskirts. These included St. Faith's House, a school for deaconesses established in 1890 by William Reed Huntington and already executed by LaFarge; Synod House, Cram's first project on the grounds, rendered in French Gothic, which had been donated by J. P. Morgan and railroad magnate William Bayard Cutting as a meeting hall for the Episcopal Church's General Convention in 1913; a choir school designed by the firm of Cook and Welch in English Collegiate Gothic; and Cathedral House, which contained the bishop's residence and deanery, and which Cram modeled on a French chateau. Cram also drew up a plan for the whole complex, which he conceived of as a medieval "walled town," "enclosed and set apart from the secular city without."[23] For better or worse, this scheme was never realized.

After the completion of these projects in 1913, construction largely halted until work began in 1924 on the octagonal baptistery, the gift of August Van Horn Stuyvesant and his sisters—the last lineal descendants of Dutch governor Peter Stuyvesant—in memory of their parents. The structure included in its iconographical scheme coats of arms of the Stuyvesants and other Dutch families, as well as statues of major figures in the history of the Netherlands, New Amsterdam, and New York. (Synod House had similarly included a statue of George Washington between its two main doors, as well as thirty-six smaller figures representing the work of men and women in the arts, sciences, and industry.)[24]

The cathedral, however, could not be financed entirely through such targeted gifts of munificent patrons.[25] In 1925, Bishop William Manning launched a major fund-raising campaign, kicked off by Franklin Delano Roosevelt at Madison Square Garden. Though this campaign was not as successful as hoped, it permitted construction to resume on the nave and west front.[26] Two years later construction began on the north, or "Women's" transept, so named because its funding came entirely from donations from women. A donation of a half-million dollars from Baptist philanthropist John D. Rockefeller Jr. was cheerfully accepted by Manning, but the episode led to misunderstanding and resentment after Manning refused to implement his benefactor's request for representation of non-Episcopalians on the cathedral's board of trustees. Rockefeller, seeing that his aim at a truly interdenominational church for the city was not to be realized in St. John's (despite Manning's characterization of it as "a shrine of prayer and worship for all people"), instead launched his own project, Riverside Church, very close to the cathedral in Morningside Heights.[27]

In addition to its financial and architectural dimensions, St. John the Divine should be understood in terms of the rhetoric it generated as its episcopal sponsors attempted to explain its rationale and justify its existence, not only to Episcopalians but to the urban public at large, to whom they repeatedly appealed for financial support. Not surprisingly, Henry Codman Potter was particularly diligent in this regard. Potter developed two rhetorical strategies, one for fellow churchmen and the other for a broader audience that included non-Episcopalians. The first strategy was presented fully in a sermon, "The Cathedral and Its Uses," preached in 1888 at the dedication of All Saints' Cathedral in Albany.[28] In this discourse, Potter contrasted the situation of cathedrals in England, where the great monuments of medieval building had come under fire by critics arguing that they had become irrelevant to contemporary challenges such as social welfare and evangelization, with that of those in the United States, where they stood at the forefront of efforts of the Episcopal Church to establish a presence in thinly populated areas.[29]

After quoting at length from other bishops on the need for cathedrals to support evangelization, Potter went on to list and expound systematically four contributions that the cathedral could make to the contemporary life of the Episcopal Church. First, it could serve "as an elevated type and example of the Church's worship." He maintained that worship in the Church of England is conducted to a far greater degree with "that noble combination of dignity and simplicity" than in the American church. A major barrier to American liturgical excellence was the decentralization of religious culture that prevailed in dioceses without a strong Episcopal presence, without the example of which "it is still in many places pretentious, obtrusive, and bad." Cathedrals, on the other hand, promoted a style of worship and music that was free from the eccentricity and individualism that prevailed in parishes lacking compelling examples of contemporary best practices.[30]

Second, the cathedral could serve as "a distributing centre [*sic*] of diocesan work." Potter here cites two problems facing the Episcopal Church in his day. First, parish clergy were too preoccupied by their parochial responsibilities to be available for the task of evangelization. Secondly, charitable work was seriously hampered by the duplication of effort and waste of resources that resulted from a multiplicity of pet agencies with local sponsorship. Centralization of welfare efforts at a cathedral could thus result in economies of scale that would make charitable contributions far more effective.[31]

Third, the cathedral could serve as "a school and home for the prophets." Potter contrasted the importance, even the primacy, of the prophetic office not only in the Hebrew Bible but in the early Christian Church as well, with its subordination to and confusion with the priestly domain that prevailed in the church of his own day. Exactly what distinguished the prophetic office from that of others is left a bit vague, although he did state that the church needs to be "a voice of warning, of authority, of instruction to a perverse and evil generation"—presumably an adumbration of the values of the Social Gospel that he frequently championed.[32]

Finally, the cathedral was also "the home and center of the work of the bishop." Potter at once echoed the lament of his Massachusetts counterpart, William Lawrence, that the contemporary Episcopal Church was de facto more congregational than episcopal in polity, and also assuaged any American fears that a strong bishop is necessarily despotic. Diocesan and national canons placed strict limitations on episcopal power, and contemporary bishops actively sought out advice and cooperation from a variety of clergy in their dioceses. Once a bishop had the appropriate resources—symbolized by and centralized in a cathedral—he could draw on the cathedral chapter as the cabinet of the bishop, to be made up of preachers, missionaries, rectors, canons, and scholars, each one of whom shall have a double tie, first to the Cathedral, and then to some mission field, to some outlying cure, to some organized parish, to some college, or school, or seminary. . . . This I maintain is the lost ideal of the Episcopate, whereby his office and his seat become of paramount importance to the whole diocese, as expressing and impressing his influence, as binding together the active life of the diocese not only in one polity but in one policy, as the centre of institutions which surround the Cathedral and grow out of it."[33]

Potter was, in this discourse, articulating in detail the emergent rationale in the Episcopal Church, based on appeal to historical precedents, for a church that was at once American in its stress on efficient centralized administration and a polity based on checks and balances, but also Anglican in its setting off an empowered and effectual hierarchy against a laity whose influence had from colonial days frequently approached that of their Congregationalist counterparts. Such arguments, however, would presumably be of little interest to the broader public on whom he and his successors were to rely for extensive financial support. To the end of reaching this broader public, Potter published a number of articles in general-interest periodicals aimed at an educated readership in which he tried to make the case for the cathedral as a significant player in the life of the broader community.

In "An American Cathedral," which appeared in the May 1898 edition of *Munsey's Magazine*, Potter first made a cultural argument, namely, that religious design in America had never progressed beyond what he regarded as a rather primitive state. Part of the problem lay in the nation's Reformed heritage. Puritans, Huguenots, Quakers, and others "were weary and impatient of a conception of religion which made it to consist largely in costly and splendid ceremonial, and in a pampered and indolent hierarchy." The result was "a certain stern impatience of the decorative in architecture."[34] Another problem lay with collective cultural priorities. Domestic architecture had made aesthetic strides, in part due to increasing wealth, while commercial buildings, which originally had been simply ugly, were now both ugly and huge. Apartment houses and hotels were particular offenders, the opulence of which seduced their residents "to extravagance, and to wanton and reckless living."[35] Here Potter was mounting a critique of the aesthetic of conspicuous consumption that characterized the "Gilded Age," a lifestyle notably embraced by many of his wealthy constituents.

While Americans lavished money, if not taste, on their residences and emporia, Potter maintained that they were simply too busy to care for the appearance of their churches, which they were not entirely sure really needed to be beautiful. "The popular conception [of a church] consists mainly of a huge auditorium, with a platform and a more or less dramatic performer, and a congregational parlor, and a parish kitchen."[36] Here again Potter was identifying the ethos of Congregationalism, to which he attributed many of the nation's cultural and religious shortcomings, as a model to which Anglicanism offered a necessary counterweight. Puritan austerity had, in his view, generated a "debonair indifferentism" in the culture at large, which he saw as corrosive of the basic human instinct of worship and, ultimately, of the survival of religion itself in an increasingly secularized culture. The antidote, of course, was a cathedral on the Anglican model:

> The cathedral, instead of being an anachronism, is a long neglected
> witness we may sorely need. . . . The greatest ages of the world, the
> greatest nations of the world, have not been those that built only for
> their own comfort and amusement; and it is simply inevitable that
> a great idea meanly housed, and meanly expressed in those forms in
> which we express reverence for our heroes and love for our dead, and
> loyalty to our country—in which, in a word, we express toward our
> best and greatest among our fellow men, or toward human institutions,
> veneration and affection and patriotism—it is inevitable, I say, that
> a great idea meanly treated will come to be meanly esteemed.[37]

Americans, who in Potter's view did not collectively possess five churches worthy of respect among them, needed "visible institutions . . . representing honesty and integrity and faith" as much as they needed electric railways and protective tariffs. The solution, not surprisingly, was at hand. Potter began to describe the progress that had already been made on St. John's, located on a "site of preeminent dignity and ample proportions overlooking the whole city," while proximate to the sector of Manhattan into which population was most likely to expand. Potter here shifted his argument from the cultural to the social, justifying the cathedral with many of the arguments that had earlier been used to promote Central Park. Its spacious grounds would provide breathing and resting space for "all sorts and conditions of men" (to invoke the language of the *Book of Common Prayer*), including mothers and children and workingmen and their wives. A pro-cathedral already stood on the site, which included much of the apparatus of the institutional church movement:

Tomb of Bishop Henry Codman Potter. (Courtesy of the
Cathedral Church of St. John the Divine Archives)

schools, a gymnasium, a community house, and other instrumentalities of
social outreach beyond the worshipping community. The Cathedral Church
of St. John the Divine, in short, would simultaneously uplift the city's culture
while also extending much-needed relief to its working people.[38]

One aspect of St. John's that reflected Potter's social vision was one of the
first to be erected, namely, a series of seven apsidal chapels representing what
Potter conceived to be the major ethnic groupings that made up the urban
population that the cathedral would serve. These "Chapels of the Tongues"
were dedicated respectively to St. James the Apostle, representative of Spain;
St. Ambrose, for Italy; St. Martin of Tours, for France; St. Saviour, for Greek
and Slavic peoples; St. Columba, for Celts; St. Boniface, for Germans; and
St. Ansgar, for Scandinavians. Architects and architectural styles differed, and
were chosen in part for their historical resonance with these different regions
of Europe.[39] Missing were the English—presumably because the entire cathedral was a monument to their heritage—as well as those of non-European
origin.[40]

Henry Codman Potter died in 1908 and is interred in an above-ground
tomb in the Chapel of St. James in the manner of a medieval bishop.[41] He
was succeeded by his coadjutor, David Hummell Greer, who while rector of

St. Bartholomew's in midtown Manhattan had shown little interest in the cathedral project. After his accession to the *cathedra*, however, he worked to utilize St. John's as a forum for the promotion of the democratic ideology that undergirded the rationale for American participation in the Great War. Greer invited clergy of other denominations, laymen, and visiting English clergy to share the cathedral's pulpit. British foreign secretary Arthur Balfour spoke at the cathedral's dedication service on the theme of Anglo-American friendship in 1918, and Elihu Root gave the major address at a service of thanksgiving following the Armistice the next year.[42]

Greer and his staff continued the themes of Potter's rhetoric, which they adapted to the ideological climate of the war era. The cathedral's Dean Howard Chandler Robbins proclaimed that "the Cathedral is the home of Christian democracy" as well as "the House of Prayer for all people." "Working people of the artisan class could come," he declared, "because the Cathedral is great, democratic, free."[43] Special services were held for particular groups such as letter carriers, actors, patriotic societies, and Freemasons and other fraternal orders, as well as union confirmation services for the twenty African American churches and missions of the diocese.[44] In 1917, Bishop Greer issued "A Cathedral Vision," a pamphlet in which he articulated his own interpretation of the work of St. John's. The ultimate aim of social service work, for which the cathedral provided an administrative base, was not simply the improvement of the material conditions of the working classes, but also their spiritual transformation. It was further an instrument for church unity, providing a center around which the various factions of the Christian community could rally, and helping to liberate the church to participate in civic and political affairs without hindering its own growth.[45]

Most centrally, perhaps, the cathedral was a rebuke to contemporary American materialism. This was not to deny the reality or goodness of materiality as such: Anglicanism was, after all, an incarnational faith that believed that "spiritual realities are mediated to us through the mediating means of material signs and symbols." The cathedral, though firmly rooted in the reality of this world, was potentially an institution that could serve as a counterweight to the commercial and practical emphases of contemporary American education. Both the church and the world, Greer argued, were "training schools of God." Greer's was "A CATHEDRAL VISION for men of vision in the Church to work for and towards. A vision to work with until it has been at last accomplished and fulfilled, and all those false and cruel and self-exalting aims which are working now in human life and crushing the people down, shall be driven out, shall be driven out, and the Kingdom of God shall come, and He Whose right it is to reign in righteousness shall reign."[46] Greer here combined the ecumenical vision of William Reed Huntington with contemporary Anglican incarnational theology and, above all, the rhetoric of the Social Gospel, with its stress on ushering in the Kingdom of God through the application of the Gospel to the social conditions of the day.

Greer was succeeded in 1921 by British-born William Thomas Manning, the Anglo-Catholic rector of Trinity Church at Broadway and Wall Street, who has been evocatively described as "a symbol of progressive aristocracy."[47] Manning's vision of the role of the cathedral was conditioned by a number of factors: his catholic vision of the Anglican tradition as a source of religious and social unity; his embrace of the popular notion of his era that the Anglo-Saxon or English-speaking peoples shared a special providential role in human affairs; his belief that the church should enter into an alliance with education and commerce for social progress; and his conviction that unity was needed in a nation that had been torn apart by controversies over immigration, radical ideology, and participation in the Great War, with results that disappointed those who had bought into the Wilsonian rhetoric that had justified American involvement.[48] Manning was also a creature of the 1920s and utilized his rhetorical and organizational talents to organize large-scale fund-raising drives that included celebrity appeal and mass rallies—the sort of "ballyhoo" that characterized the campaigns of revivalists such as Aimee Semple McPherson and Billy Sunday, although much more genteel in tone.[49]

Work on St. John's continued into the 1930s—Manning defended the expenditure as providing jobs for the unemployed—and was suspended during World War II. After the peace, Manning tried to raise another ten million dollars, but abandoned the effort in favor of a drive for half that sum to replace Episcopal missions abroad that had been destroyed during the war. Manning's successor, Bishop Charles Gilbert, regarded further work on the cathedral as incompatible with the need for funds to help alleviate the plight of the Harlem neighborhood against which the cathedral abutted, and construction was suspended for three decades. Work on the west front was resumed in 1978 in a program through which local youth were to serve as apprentice stone cutters, but the project was abandoned after a few years, with little new work completed. One architectural historian comments: "Today, the partially completed church stands both as a monument to the faith of many New Yorkers, but also as a monument to the overreaching of those who planned such an enormous and inevitably impractical building project." St. John the Divine thus seems perpetually destined to remain "St. John the Unfinished."[50]

Washington

The germ of the idea for a national cathedral in Washington, D.C., can be traced back to the original city plan by the French engineer Pierre L'Enfant, who developed that city's unique system of radiating and intersecting avenues named after individual states, so that the city constituted a virtual microcosm of the nation as a whole.[51] L'Enfant envisioned "a Great Church for National Purposes," a sort of cathedral of a civil religion that would be used "for national purposes, such as public prayer, thanksgiving, funeral orations, and be assigned to the use of no particular denomination or sect, but be equally open to all."[52] Nothing came of this project until 1890, when Miss Mary Elizabeth Mann donated property valued at seventy thousand dollars to the diocese of Maryland, which then included the District of Columbia. Bishop William Paret convened a committee to consider the best uses for this gift, and they recommended a cathedral. In 1893 the U.S. Congress granted a charter for such a cathedral, which was signed by President Benjamin Harrison in what, in retrospect, seems a rather odd blurring of church-state boundaries. (Congress became involved apparently through a technicality about the actual ownership of the land, but the federal government's role gave the enterprise a certain cachet of quasi-establishment that was presumably not unwelcome.)[53]

The erection of a cathedral in the nation's capital was complicated by the fact that the city of Washington was not yet the seat of a bishop. The General Convention of 1895 proceeded to constitute the new diocese of Washington, and Henry Yates Satterlee, the rector of Manhattan's Calvary Church, was shortly thereafter elected the first bishop and consecrated the following year.[54] Satterlee was the scion of a well-to-do New York family who was educated at Columbia and, following his conversion by Arthur Cleveland Coxe, the rector of Calvary Church, attended General Theological Seminary. He was then assigned by Bishop Alonzo Potter in 1866 as the assistant at Zion Episcopal Church in the upstate town of Wappingers Falls.[55]

Satterlee was not unusual in this era for combining a concern for proper High liturgy with a strong sense of social justice. He took a High Church view of his parochial responsibilities in that he saw himself and his congregation as

Henry Vaughan et al., Washington National Cathedral, 1907–90.
(Courtesy of the National Cathedral Archives)

carrying a responsibility for the entire community, not simply for its Episcopalians. In his roles as assistant and, after 1875, rector, he worked to remodel
the church to make it more appropriate for liturgical worship and also to
establish a wide range of activities and institutions for the benefit of those
in need, such as a home for factory girls, a sewing school for women, and a
town library.[56] In 1882, Satterlee, who had enjoyed a cordial relationship with
both of the bishops Potter, accepted a call to the same Calvary Church he
had attended as a college student and proceeded with a similar program of
liturgical and social outreach, transforming Calvary along the "institutional
church" model pioneered at St. George's.[57]

Although some Maryland clergy had already taken some initiative in promoting the Washington cathedral project, it was Satterlee who, once installed as bishop, made it his own. After some negotiation, a site on Mount St. Alban's, where a parish of similar name had already been established, was selected, in part for its commanding view of the capital city.[58] In 1905, an advisory committee was selected to decide on a style and engage an architect.[59] The committee was indeed select. It consisted of two of the nation's most prominent "signature" architects: Daniel Burnham, the chief overseer of the design and construction of the "White City" at the 1892 World's Columbian Exposition in Chicago, and Charles Follen McKim, the principal architect of the Boston Public Library.[60] Both were associated with the École des Beaux-Arts style, a sort of eclectic neoclassicism on a grand scale, which informed the wave of public building and city planning that dramatically changed the appearance of the nation's cities during this "American Renaissance."[61] Both Burnham and McKim were also members of the McMillan Commission, which devised the plan that transformed the National Mall into a monumental public space. Perhaps not surprisingly, both Burnham and McKim favored a Renaissance plan for the cathedral. They were, however, balanced out by two of the committee's other three members, Harvard medievalist Charles F. Moore and Casper Purdon Clarke, the director of the Metropolitan Museum of Art in Manhattan. Moore and Clarke favored Gothic, a judgment upheld by the cathedral trustees. This pleased Satterlee, who wrote Burnham that, appropriate as Beaux-Arts classicism might be for governmental buildings, "in the building of a Cathedral there is another Consideration surpassing even that of Monumental Unity. First, last, and always, the Cathedral is 'House of Prayer for All People' that was Our Lord's own description of the Church. . . . And experience has plainly shown that the Gothic is the distinctively Religious and Christian Style of Architecture which exceeds all others in inspiring prayer and devotional feeling among all sorts and conditions of men."[62] (The last phrase is a conscious echo of the *Book of Common Prayer*.)

After the issue of style had been settled, the choice of an architect came to the forefront. In 1906, without the sort of public competition that had become so controversial in the planning of St. John's in New York, the committee selected two prominent Gothicists, George Bodley and Henry Vaughan. Bodley, who had learned his trade with Sir George Gilbert Scott and had collaborated with Arts and Crafts leader William Morris, was arguably Britain's premier church architect of the later Victorian period and a proponent of fourteenth-century English Gothic. Vaughan, the "American" half of the duo, was actually born in England and immigrated in 1881 to Boston, from which base he designed a number of the most significant Episcopal churches and chapels of the era. (These included Christ Church in New Haven, Connecticut, a bastion of Anglo-Catholic worship; the chapels of Groton and St. Paul's schools; and portions of St. John the Divine Cathedral.) Bodley died in 1907, and was succeeded by Vaughan, who survived him by ten years. Vaughan in turn was succeeded in 1921 by Philip Frohman, the designer of the chapels at Trinity College and the Kent School, both in Connecticut, and who remained the cathedral's primary architect until the time of his death in 1972. Although a Roman Catholic, he was interred in the cathedral's Chapel of St. Joseph of Arimathea through a special dispensation from the Washington archdiocese.[63]

The rhetorics that came into play in the formation of the National Cathedral—more formally known as the Cathedral Church of St. Peter and St. Paul—reflect the convergence of the structure's intersecting rationales.[64] On the one hand, it was an Episcopal cathedral that was shaped by both a bishop and a succession of architects immersed in the Anglo-Catholic movement of the era. Like Cram, both Satterlee and Frohman were enamored of the Gothic style as expressive of the sacramental symbolism of the Catholic—though not necessarily *Roman* Catholic—tradition of worship. Satterlee was also deeply imbued with the thought of England's *Lux Mundi* movement, in which theologians such as Charles Gore expounded a theology where the doctrine of the Incarnation was regarded as central to a distinctively Anglican understanding of the relationship between God and creation, including humanity.[65] Such a theological approach reconciled a penchant for liturgical worship in richly symbolic churches with a concern for the amelioration of human suffering in the social and economic realms.[66] The fusion of these two themes was unique to the emergence of a distinctive Episcopal identity during this era and manifested itself with particular clarity in the cathedral project.

Another context in which the building of American Episcopal cathedrals, and particularly the National Cathedral, took place was the deep-seated notion that the Episcopal Church was destined to be in some sense an established national church, on the model of its prototype, the Church of England.[67] Since literal establishment was prohibited by the First Amendment, Episcopalians had to seek other strategies, much as had the Evangelical denominations in their creation of the "Benevolent Empire" of evangelistic and reform voluntary agencies in the 1820s. By the late nineteenth century, this establishmentarian quest had taken on a number of aspects. One was the notion, promoted especially by William Reed Huntington, that the Episcopal Church, as the "bridge" between Catholic and Protestant traditions, was the ideal candidate to serve as the nucleus for a national church in which all ecumenically minded denominations could join.[68] The Chicago-Lambeth Quadrilateral, adopted by the Episcopal Church in 1884 and two years later by the Church of England as a basic affirmation of the foundations of Anglican Christianity, was originally formulated by Huntington as the basis for ecumenical conversations that never, at least in the short run, bore a great deal of fruit.[69] (Henry Yates Satterlee's tomb at the National Cathedral is surrounded by four pillars representing the four points of the Quadrilateral.)

Another way in which the cathedral was entwined with the establishment idea lay in the relationship of the Episcopal Church with the national government. Although the newly independent American branch of Anglicanism suffered in its initial existence from the taint of Loyalism, it had by the early nineteenth century rapidly attained a prestige rivaled only by the Presbyterians among Protestant denominations. In the civic realm, this prestige expressed itself in the disproportionate number of Episcopalians among holders of high public office, including the presidency.* St. John's Episcopal Church, for example, located close to the White House, has been dubbed "the Church of Presidents"; it is rich in presidential iconography and boasts that every president to date has worshiped there, even though the majority have not been actual members.

By the late nineteenth century, other denominations were beginning to establish monumental presences in the capital city. In 1869, the Metropolitan Memorial Methodist Episcopal Church was erected near the Capitol, with memorials to historic figures in the Methodist tradition and pews reserved for governmental officials.[70] Others included Catholic University and its nearby Basilica Shrine of the Immaculate Conception, the Methodist-sponsored American University, and churches of a variety of denominations.[71] Part of

---

*American presidents of Episcopal provenance, if not always active affiliation, in the eighteenth and nineteenth centuries included Washington, Jefferson, Madison, Monroe, W. H. Harrison, Tyler, Taylor, Pierce, and Arthur. Theodore Roosevelt, although Dutch Reformed, attended Episcopal services at Oyster Bay with his second wife, and his funeral was held in Christ Church in that town. His cousin, Franklin Delano Roosevelt, served as senior warden of St. James Episcopal Church in Hyde Park. More recently, Gerald Ford and George H. W. Bush have been active members of the Episcopal Church.

this flurry of activity antedated the cathedral; more came as a reaction to the nascent cathedral's implicit claims to be *the* national church, as when President Wilson was persuaded to participate in a service of thanksgiving after the Armistice in which only Episcopal clergy took part.[72] In any case, the Episcopal Church could not take for granted the preeminent status to which it aspired, and the National Cathedral project from its inception played a role in this campaign and in Satterlee's vision in particular.

One of the Satterlee's first major promotional projects was the erection of the Peace Cross to coincide with the meeting of the General Convention in Washington in 1898. The cross, which was hurriedly quarried and carved in time for the event, was ostensibly a commemoration of the ending of the Spanish-American War and an implicit tribute to Admiral George Dewey, the hero of Manila Bay, whom Satterlee particularly admired and who was a trustee of the cathedral. President McKinley was induced to speak at the site, with the Marine Band providing the music. Satterlee also arranged for the transfer of the remains of Thomas Claggett, the first Episcopal bishop to be consecrated in the United States, together with those of his wife, for reburial at the cathedral, thus adding further ecclesiastical legitimacy to the project. He also secured the services of Thomas Nelson Page, a writer of popular fiction who had romanticized the antebellum South in such works as *In Ole Virginia* (1887) and later served as ambassador to Italy, to write *The Peace Cross Book* as a piece of publicity. All of this display proved successful in persuading the General Convention to recognize the cathedral project formally.[73]

Another promotional coup for Satterlee occurred in October of 1903, when the All American Conference of Bishops—including those from Canada and the West Indies—convened in Washington. Satterlee arranged for them to converge on the cathedral site on a Sunday afternoon for an outdoor service. A total of sixteen thousand attended the service, where the Marine Band again played, and President Theodore Roosevelt provided some hortatory words about the moral responsibilities of religious leaders.[74] The cathedral was rapidly gaining an identity as an icon both for the Episcopal Church and for the nation.

Satterlee was an accomplished promoter of a project that in his mind and rhetoric brought together a complex of themes and objectives. He saw the cathedral as playing three roles: "A House of Prayer for All People"; "Chief Mission Church of the Diocese"; and "A General Church for National Purposes."[75] Although the ecumenical and national roles he envisioned for the cathedral were never completely fulfilled—in part because he always insisted on the centrality of the Episcopal Church in any attempt at religious unity—he accomplished a remarkable amount in planning the project, generating publicity, and obtaining widespread support and funding. However much involvement in worldly activities such a project necessitated, it remained firmly anchored in Satterlee's distinctively Anglican vision of the cathedral as a sacramental presence that could help sanctify the life of the city and the nation as well as that of the church.

Satterlee's successor once removed, James E. Freeman, who became bishop of Washington in 1923, was cut from a very different piece of cloth. Prior to his ordination, Freeman had been a businessman who had attended neither college nor seminary, and his approach to the project has been characterized as "a businessman's ecumenism."[76] Although their theologies may have differed, Freeman had a great deal in common with his New York counterpart, William Manning, in their common embrace of the techniques of advertising and promotion that characterized the "Jazz Age." Freeman saw the cathedral as an icon of Christian presence for the nation as a whole and pitched his campaign for support in that direction. To this end, he did his best to obtain for the cathedral literal remnants of prominent Americans, so that the public would associate the structure with civic patriotism. Although his attempt to have Warren Harding buried there was unsuccessful, he had better luck with Woodrow Wilson, convincing the twenty-eighth president's widow of the propriety of the concept. That Wilson, the son of a Southern Presbyterian minister, should lie here may seem odd, but his second wife, Edith Bolling Galt Wilson, was an Episcopalian who conducted much of the business of the presidency after her husband had become incapacitated.[77] Mrs. Wilson later took offense when she came to believe that the presence of her husband's body was being exploited by Freeman for fund-raising, and the latter reluctantly but rapidly backed away from such efforts.[78]

San Francisco

The story of San Francisco's Grace Cathedral is similar in many ways to that of its grand counterparts in New York and Washington, but with some regional distinctiveness. William Ingraham Kip, the first bishop of California, had promoted the idea, even to the point of having "Grace Cathedral" stamped on the prayer books of the church he had served as rector, but little came of the plan. William F. Nichols, his successor, was inspired by the example of St. John the Divine to revive the notion, but found little support until nature intervened in the form of the 1906 earthquake. Grace Church was destroyed, as were the Nob Hill mansions of one of its wealthy parishioners, the Crocker family. When banker William H. Crocker, the spokesman for the second generation of the family, indicated to Nichols that a major gift was in the offing, Nichols traveled to New York to negotiate the matter with the Crockers on board the *Elsa II*, the private yacht of William's brother-in-law. The result was the gift of the Nob Hill properties to the diocese as the site of the new Grace Cathedral.[79]

The Grace Cathedral Corporation was organized in November of 1906 and included equal numbers of clergy and prominent local businessmen, including William H. Crocker. George Bodley, one of the two original designers of the National Cathedral, was appointed architect, but died shortly thereafter and was succeeded by his assistant, Cecil Hare. Although the cornerstone was laid in 1910, construction did not begin until 1927 under Lewis Hobart, a local architect who had come to be in charge of the project (and was also Crocker's cousin by marriage). The ubiquitous Ralph Adams Cram served as consultant. The cathedral functioned out of the Founders' Crypt from 1914 until 1941. Grace itself, which combines features from a variety of medieval French Gothic cathedrals, was not consecrated until 1964 under controversial Bishop James A. Pike. Its use of steel-reinforced concrete is a concession to the vicissitudes of California geology.[80]

Bishop Nichols had been laying the conceptual and rhetorical foundations for what would become Grace Cathedral as early as his address to the 1896 diocesan convention, which he expanded upon in 1913 after the project was already well under way. Nichols's primary rationale for a diocesan cathedral was its utility in domestic missionary work, and he quoted William Reed Huntington to the effect that "in all our large cities there is a steadily increasing population of unattached Christians . . . [who] live for the most part concealed in flats and are exceedingly inaccessible to the shepherds of souls." He invoked the twin ideals of *leitourgia* (worship) and *diakonia* (service) as two intertwined fundamentals of Christian practice that cathedrals symbolized and facilitated. Nichols touched other notes, including an invocation of Congregationalist theologian Horace Bushnell on the sublimity of European cathedrals and of the magnificent San Francesco Church standing against the skyline of Assisi. Given all this, Nichols asserted, "we need not stop to discuss whether Cathedrals are not superfluous in this practical utilitarian age, or whether they are not in danger of becoming an Episcopal fetich [*sic*]."[81]

The Significance of the American Cathedral

The various rhetorics used to promote the cathedral enterprise among Americans in general and Episcopalians in particular reflected the ambiguities involved in reviving the architectural expression of an era remote in time and culture as an expression of the values of Americans in the Progressive Era. To be sure, American architecture from the time of Independence at least had been characterized by a series of stylistic revivals, but a reasonably plausible case had been made for the affinities of the Greek and Roman modes with modern democratic ideology. Bishops and architects alike stressed not only the appropriateness of Gothic as the "only proper style" for Christian worship—an argument that worked more comfortably for parish churches than for the more public cathedrals—but also as a modern style, just as the cathedral was framed as a modern institution. The results were expressed in the great American cathedrals of the era not simply in verbal rationales aimed at gaining legitimacy and, especially, financial support, but in the fabric of the buildings themselves. ("Fabric" in this context refers to the entire physical makeup of a structure.)

One way of understanding the distinctiveness of these cathedrals is by constructing a typology, reflected in the list below, that highlights both their novelty and their continuity with the past. I place particular emphasis on the cathedrals in New York, Washington, and San Francisco that have just been discussed.

1. *Scale.* Although cathedrals need not be large—or any size in particular—the three under consideration here are enormous. Since there are no universally agreed-upon criteria for determining "largeness," there is an irresolvable rivalry among cathedrals as to which is the largest in the nation or world. Many lists put St. John the Divine at the top—certainly for the United States, arguably for the world—and the National Cathedral also makes some worldwide "top ten" lists.[82]

2. *Siting.* All three are located on elevated sites: St. John's in Morningside Heights, Grace on Nob Hill, and, most spectacularly, the National Cathedral on Mount St. Alban's, the highest elevation in Washington. As with size, the effect here is one of majesty and dominance.

3. *Plant.* In addition to the cathedral building itself, the plant—that is, the totality of physical components—of larger cathedrals typically

includes a substantial plat of grounds on which reside the *close*, that is, a compound of buildings that adjoin the main building, often in the shape of a quadrangle. Such buildings may include diocesan offices, the bishop's house, meeting spaces, and educational facilities. The National Cathedral has a particularly elaborate close, with spacious landscaped grounds, a "Cathedral College" for continuing education, and shops for the sale of books, gifts, and herbs. Grace Cathedral is distinguished by labyrinths, which serve as meditative aids, on the model of Chartres.[83]

4. *Style.* Although the original plan for St. John's was an amalgam of earlier medieval styles, and there were prominent advocates for the Renaissance in the early stages of the planning of the National Cathedral, Gothic emerged as the winner in each case. English Gothic predominated in the National Cathedral, as it did in Anglican church and cathedral design more broadly during this era. (Cram's final design for St. John's included French elements, and these predominated at Grace.) The prestige of Gothic in general and English Gothic in particular seems unsurprising in retrospect, given the English antecedents and continuing connections of the Episcopal Church. The predominance of the Gothic style also stemmed from the fact that this was an era in which Anglophilia exerted a strong pull on American taste more generally; from the influence exerted by architects Upjohn, Vaughan, and Cram in ecclesiastical circles; from the success of John Ruskin in legitimizing Gothic for contemporary use; from the continuing influence of the Oxford movement in emphasizing the continuity of the Christian church over the centuries; and from the influence of the Cambridge movement in pushing Anglicans (other than dyed-in-the-wool Low Churchmen) in the direction of traditional liturgical worship.

5. *Worship Center.* These American cathedrals, like their medieval prototypes, were designed for a particular kind of worship that was quite distinct from the main run of Protestantism, at least until the 1920s, and that had more in common with Roman Catholicism than with the Methodists or Presbyterians of the day. The internal arrangements of the structure were hierarchical, beginning with a *narthex* that provides a transition from the secular realm into that of the sacred; a *nave* in which the congregation is seated, in the midst of which is located a broad aisle for liturgical processions; and a *sanctu-*

ary area, elevated above the nave, in which the altar resides. (The choir may be situated in various arrangements.) The cumulative effect is one of increasing degrees of sacrality as one advances from the west entry to the east-oriented altar. This liturgical arrangement is closest in affinity to the Anglo-Catholic tradition, reflected in the churchmanship of bishops such as Satterlee and Manning. Form here follows function in a very explicitly theological manner.

6. *Administrative Center.* A principal rationale for American cathedrals offered by Henry Codman Potter and other early advocates was that they could serve as a central administrative center for the diocese, thereby promoting efficiency while simultaneously providing a symbol of diocesan unity. Cathedral closes thus provide office space for bishops, deans, and members of the cathedral chapter, who function as a sort of cabinet for the bishop, each having a particular administrative responsibility. Cathedrals also provide meeting rooms, educational programs, and other facilities and activities that draw together laity and clergy from throughout the diocese.

7. *Educational Center.* In addition to providing a place of worship and diocesan administration, the closes of many cathedrals include educational facilities. In the very earliest stages of the National Cathedral project, Phoebe A. Hearst, the widow of California businessman and Senator George Hearst, donated $175,000 for what would become the National Cathedral School for girls. This was the first part of the close, designed in the Renaissance mode by Ernest Flagg.[84] St. Albans School for boys was established shortly thereafter, and an elementary school, Beauvoir, was added to the complex in 1933.[85] Today's Cathedral School of St. John the Divine was founded by Bishop Potter in 1901, originally for the training of choirboys (as was St. Albans).[86] The St. John's complex also included a school for deaconesses, which was abandoned, as that office became obsolete. Grace Cathedral later opened a boys' school. Cathedrals in recent years maintain a variety of educational outreach programs for the broader community.

8. *Arts.* Like many of the grand parish churches of the era, the great cathedrals were from early on collections of and repositories for the liturgical arts, including mural painting, stone sculpture, wood carving, metalwork, embroidery, and stained glass. The era of great immigration had brought with it a variety of artists and skilled

craftspersons on a remarkable scale, such as the Italian stonemasons who were major players in the National Cathedral's extensive sculptural programs.[87] Polish émigrés Samuel Yellin, the premier metalworker of his day, who wrought the National Cathedral's intricate gates, and Jan Henryk de Rosen, who painted Grace Cathedral's rather fanciful historical murals, were among others whose talents were available to the ecclesiastical patrons of this age. Glass artists abounded, among them Boston's Connick Studios, which worked carefully with Cram in re-creating the techniques of Chartres Cathedral. In addition to the many pieces commissioned especially for the cathedral projects, others ranging over a broad span of the history of Christian art were acquired over the years. Cathedrals also often host musical activities, as exemplified in the choir schools that several of them sponsor.[88]

9. *Iconography.* Much of cathedral art is representational and, not surprisingly, much of what is represented are themes from the Bible and the subsequent history of Christianity. Since Episcopalians had, by this time, overcome the traditional Protestant antipathy to the depiction of human figures, cathedral art—sculpture, painting, glass—abounds with motifs taken from both Hebrew and Christian scripture, especially those having to do with the life and work of Jesus. In addition, the Virgin Mary, the Apostles, and the entire *communio sanctorum* find their place in the art of the cathedrals. Another aspect of medieval iconography carried over into modern cathedral decoration is the gargoyle, a small, fanciful grotesque sculpture used as a waterspout. (Water runs out through the figure's mouth.) An updated version can be found in the National Cathedral in the shape of Darth Vader, the archvillain of the *Star Wars* film series.

   In addition to this narration of sacred history in a catholic manner, American cathedrals introduce other narratives into their iconographical programs. The National Cathedral, not surprisingly, abounds in imagery from the history of the United States, ranging from statues of Washington and Lincoln to the actual body of Woodrow Wilson. The de Rosen murals at Grace interweave elements of the introduction of Christianity into England, the founding of the Franciscan Order by its city's namesake, the coming of the English and their church to California, and the founding of the Episcopal

Church.[89] Grace's windows extend the story of the continuing work of the Spirit, through Christianity, but also through images of human achievement such as the figures of astronaut John Glenn and physicist Albert Einstein. Similarly, the "bays"—divisions of the nave—of St. John's pay tribute, on the model of the medieval guilds that sponsored various cathedral segments, to a wide variety of human activities, from sports to motherhood. The main window of the Sports Bay, also known as St. Hubert's Chapel, has medallions commemorating twenty-eight sports, including baseball, auto racing, fencing, and bowling. Its clerestory (upper-level) window features the Old Testament Nimrod, "the mighty hunter," and St. Hubert of Tongres, an early medieval bishop who was also particularly fond of hunting.[90]

10. *Funerary Monument.* Following the precedent of European churches, cathedrals, and, most notably, London's Westminster Abbey, American cathedrals memorialize the eminent dead with wall plaques or, on occasion, through the actual interment of their remains. Frequently these are churchmen associated with the cathedral. Bishops Horatio Potter, Henry Codman Potter, and William Manning lie in repose in tombs reminiscent of those of medieval bishops in St. John's, and Henry Yates Satterlee's sarcophagus is located behind the altar of the National Cathedral's Bethlehem Chapel, "above the Foundation Stone and below the Jerusalem Altar, surrounded by the four pillars representing the Chicago-Lambeth Quadrilateral."[91] The bodies or ashes of a variety of other notables interred in the National Cathedral include cathedral architect Philip Frohman; Helen Keller and Annie Sullivan; Admiral George Dewey, who had played a role in the cathedral's inception; Secretary of State Cordell Hull; and Missouri Senator Stuart Symington.[92] The National Cathedral's most notable interment is that of Woodrow Wilson, whose sarcophagus lies in the south aisle. The presence of a presidential tomb also may render the cathedral a pilgrimage site in the national "civil religion."[93]

11. *Microcosm.* Historian of religion scholar Mircea Eliade has noted that sacred buildings often have the character of a microcosm, that is, a recapitulation of the cosmos in miniature symbolic form. Medieval cathedrals such as Chartres can be read in this way not

The Space Window in the Washington National Cathedral contains a piece of rock from the moon. It was designed by St. Louis artist Rodney Winfield and dedicated in 1974. (Courtesy of the National Cathedral Archives)

only in such features as orientation—the altar stands at the east end, associating it with both the rising sun and the risen Christ—but also in artistic schemata that recapitulate the entirety of Christian *Heilsgeschichte*—the "history of salvation" from the creation through the Incarnation to the final consummation. Thus the stories and figures of both biblical testaments and the subsequent history of the Christian church are illustrated in painting, sculpture, and stained glass. (Eastern Orthodox churches carry out the same tasks on a smaller scale in their iconographical layouts.) The translation of this motif to the American scene is well illustrated in our earlier discussion of the iconography of Grace Cathedral.

American cathedrals carry out a similar task in the depiction of sacred scenes and in the literal incorporation of objects from other sacred sites that have particular relevance to their identity and mission. One good example is the great bronze doors of Grace Cathedral, which were cast from the molds of Lorenzo Ghiberti's "Doors of Paradise" at the baptistery of the *duomo* (cathedral) in Florence, Italy, and which consist of a series of frames depicting biblical scenes from both testaments.[94] Among the earliest activities in the construction of the National Cathedral was the acquisition of a series of iconic objects: twelve marble blocks from King Solomon's quarry near Jerusalem for the high (Jerusalem) altar; twenty carved stones from the ruined abbey of Glastonbury in England for the Glastonbury Cathedra; and other stones from the "mother ship" of Anglicanism, Canterbury Cathedral, out of which the Canterbury Pulpit was fashioned.[95] Incorporated into the fabric of the building itself is a stone from Mount Sinai. These structures deliberately echo earlier monuments of Jewish and Christian art and history, and they recapitulate that history by selectively incorporating small pieces of earlier structures with iconic resonance. Perhaps the ultimate act of literal incorporation is the piece of moon rock contained in the National Cathedral's Space Window.*

---

*It is also worth noting that secular structures of the era indulged in this practice. The Chicago Tribune Tower, the great Gothic skyscraper completed in 1925, incorporated, at the request of publisher Robert McCormick, stones from a wide range of historic world structures, including the Great Pyramid, St. Peter's Basilica, Angkor Wat, Notre Dame and Trondheim cathedrals, Hagia Sophia, and the Great Wall of China. Another, less literal, display of recapitulation is Yale's Gothic revival Sterling Memorial Library (James Gamble Rogers, 1931), which bears more

12. *Tourism and Pilgrimage Site.* The combination of many of the above-mentioned features—scale, siting, art, funereal monument—with their somewhat exotic appearance in highly urban, commercial settings, as well as active efforts at promotion by bishops and their staffs, turned the great national cathedrals into attractive sites for religious pilgrims, secular sightseers, or, in many cases, people who combined both motives in differing degrees. The burial of Woodrow Wilson at the National Cathedral, as noted above, seems to have been the result of Bishop Freeman's desire to have an attraction that would appeal to historically and patriotically minded tourists. (By 1925, shortly after Wilson's interment, the cathedral had attracted as many visitors as Arlington Cemetery and Mount Vernon, and the number reached a quarter of a million the following year.)[96] All of these cathedrals now have gift shops and groups of "friends" who are encouraged to become generous donors for the cathedrals' upkeep and programming. (The National Cathedral as well as Boston's Trinity Church now charge admission to visitors arriving when worship is not being conducted.)

13. *Public Ritual Site ("Civil Religion").* From early on, the great cathedrals provided appropriate sites for public rituals, particularly sermons or other addresses, memorial services, and funerals of public dignitaries. The appearances of British statesman Arthur Balfour and his American counterpart Elihu Root at St. John's in the final phases of the Great War are a good example of the civic purposes to which the cathedrals could be put, and for which, in fact, they had been partially intended. Although in the early decades of the cathedrals only Episcopal clergy were permitted in most cases to officiate at services, in more recent years the cathedrals have taken on a deliberate ecumenical role, and have opened their pulpits to prominent religious figures of a variety of backgrounds, such as Martin Luther King Jr. and the Dalai Lama.[97] The National Ca-

---

than a passing resemblance to a cathedral and incorporates carved sequences illustrative of the history of the book and of the university and its setting, The Nebraska State Capitol (1922–32), designed by Cram's sometime partner Bertram Grosvenor Goodhue, has also been likened to a cathedral and is something of a "cosmogram"—that is, a map of the universe—that incorporates extensive Native American symbolism into its iconographic scheme. Lee Lawrie, the German-born sculptor who collaborated with Goodhue on the interior of Cram's St. Thomas Episcopal Church in Manhattan, was notably involved in the two latter of these projects.

thedral especially has served as the site for state funerals both for Episcopalians, such as Gerald Ford, and non-Episcopalians, such as Dwight Eisenhower and Ronald Reagan, and provided a venue for the second President Bush's addressing the nation after national disasters such as the 2001 "9/11" attacks and hurricane Katrina.[98] (A notable fictional appropriation of the National Cathedral took place in a 2001 episode of the popular television series *The West Wing*, in which President Josiah Bartlet argues with God in Latin and grinds out a cigarette butt on the cathedral's floor after a memorial service for his secretary, who had been killed in an auto accident.) Although the term "civil religion" is elusively vague, it is evocative when applied to these cathedrals' playing a significant role in framing the collective life of the American nation as a locus of religious meaning.

14. *Sacred Space.* Like "civil religion," "sacred space" is a term that is protean and much contested, but nevertheless indispensable. A plausible argument has been made that the capital city itself—or at least the monumental structures on and in the vicinity of the Mall— are a collection of sacred spaces, or *tout ensemble* constitute one such unified space.[99] Although the National Cathedral has a special role to play in the collective iconography and ritual space of the nation's capital, it shares with the other great American cathedrals the attributes cataloged above, most of which can be seen as constituent components of sacrality in a religious building: elevated siting; setting for sacramental worship; memorial to and site of repose for the dead; cosmic iconography; symbolic and physical linkage with other sacred sites; pilgrimage destination. Although Anglican theology—unlike that of the Reformed tradition—is somewhat ambiguous about the sacred character of worship settings, its Anglo-Catholic wing is quite emphatically positive on this point, and it is difficult to read these particular cathedrals as other than quite intentional attempts to create such an effect.

The significance of the "great American cathedrals" is complex and should be pursued in a multiplicity of contexts. First, the cathedrals were begun in a distinctive moment in the history of the American city. This was an era in which monumental buildings of all sorts—commercial, cultural, governmental, even residential—were converging to create a cityscape on a far grander scale than any that had existed prior to the Civil War. This expansive new program of design and construction had many sources: vast new wealth, the explosion of urban populations, the desire of urban elites for cultural legitimacy in the eyes of Europe in general and England in particular, improved building technology, and the aesthetic of the "City Beautiful" movement that envisioned cities not simply as commercial sprawls but as expressions of neoclassical beauty and repose. These same cities were arenas of religious competition, with Roman Catholics and Jews aggressively making their presence known as actors in the public sphere, and Protestants trying both to hold their ground and also to reach out to new urbanites through theatrical worship and programs of social amelioration. The three great cathedrals considered at some length here raised the ante in this competition by building on such a scale, on such prominent sites, with such elaboration of detail, and at so great an expense as to assert definitively, if not defiantly, the preeminence in cultural, social, and religious leadership that many Episcopalians believed to be rightfully theirs.

These campaigns of cathedral building also reveal something of the dynamics of the self-understanding of the Episcopal community of the day. Many of the rationales expressed by the cathedrals' advocates reflected a desire to present these projects not as retrograde exercises in archaism but rather as thoroughly modern, democratic, reformist, and American in spirit. (Ralph Adams Cram was arguably an exception.) The Social Gospel was at least implicit in the mission proclaimed for these new entities, namely, the spiritual and material enhancement of the urban masses, who were falling through the cracks of the new social order. Cathedrals could not only provide outreach to "all sorts and conditions," they could do it efficiently through centralized oversight and economies of scale.

This message of rationalized social outreach, however, was frequently given a distinctively Anglican twist in the establishmentarian assumption of the responsibility of the Episcopal Church not only for its own flock but for the entire social order—the city or the nation as corporate entities in need of a spiritual center. An undercurrent of Anglo-Saxon, or Anglo-American, providential mission was also implicit in this notion. The Gothic form that these institutions inevitably assumed was an implicit reference to the kind of corporate social order once, allegedly, manifested in medieval society, but dispersed in the wake of industrial age individualism. The simultaneously modern and archaic cathedral could stand in judgment against a secularized culture in which materialism and acquisitiveness reigned. The cathedral might thus be seen as an ecclesiastical counterweight to the "cathedrals of commerce," such as Manhattan's Woolworth Building, that were claiming material primacy in many of the nation's central business districts.[100]

In creative tension with the social mission of the cathedral was its sacramental character. Cathedrals were, after all, places of worship as well as of administration, and the kind of worship that was to take place there was far different in kind from that which might be found in the Methodist or Presbyterian preaching theaters that were a distinctive feature of contemporary urban Protestant life.[101] Unlike these churches, which took as their model the secular theater of their day, the cathedrals were material settings for sacramental worship, and all their features converged to evoke a sense of sacrality, of mediation between everyday life and the supernatural realm. This notion of sacramental worship was in part a result of the Anglo-Catholic proclivities of bishops such as Manning and Satterlee, but was also consistent with the incarnationalism of the *Lux Mundi* movement that influenced Broad Churchmen as well as High.

Another context for understanding the cathedral movement was the impulse toward administrative centralization manifest during this age in both secular and ecclesiastical culture. Both "Robber Barons" and Roman Catholic bishops gained success in their respective spheres through the consolidation of wealth and power in hierarchical organizations. Although Episcopal bishops were institutionally constrained from the sort of absolute authority that their Roman counterparts enjoyed, they nevertheless sought to enhance their influence in their diocesan domains, with the cathedral as an "outward and visible" sign of their power as well as an actual center for administrative work. One perhaps unintended consequence of the cathedral movement was that these bishops were compelled, willingly or otherwise, to take on the roles of financiers and promoters that were necessary to raise the vast funds that building the cathedrals entailed.

The cumulative effect of these contexts was that the American cathedral could be seen as exhibiting a tension, if not a contradiction, between the affirmation and rejection of the dominant culture. Episcopalians were a self-admittedly worldly lot, and in self-definition the opposite of sectarian in their embrace of life within and responsibility for the secular world. Though frequently elitist and Anglo-Saxonist, they spoke a language of democracy and inclusiveness. The cathedral was promoted as a place within that world from which prophetic judgments could be made upon that world's ways. It was also, physically, a place quite remote from that world, in which the worshipper could withdraw into a realm of sacrality from which the secular was excluded. But it was also a massive physical plant, the construction and maintenance of which required a constant strenuous campaign of promotion and fundraising, with bishops and deans cultivating the wealthy and powerful as potential donors. The cathedral was, in short, as complex and ambiguous an entity as the Episcopal Church itself.

Part II
Gospels

Between the Civil War and the Great Depression many Episcopalians participated in a number of discourses—or "gospels"—intended to improve, morally and materially, the quality of American life. These included social and educational reform as well as cultural philanthropy. As social reformers, a number of prominent Episcopal bishops, clergy, and laity provided leadership for the "Social Gospel" not so much in terms of theology but rather in the praxis of reform on the ground. They were instrumental in developing the "institutional church," a response to the social crises of the city based on the traditional Anglican notion that each parish was responsible for the welfare of all who lived within its bounds, and that welfare had a material as well as a spiritual component. Many laity, especially women, also participated in the settlement house movement that aimed at Americanizing immigrants while also teaching them to value their own cultural heritages. Both of these movements were predicated on the creation of community, a phenomenon their advocates perceived as singularly lacking in the unforgiving, competitive, and faceless jungles of the new American city.

Educational reform manifested itself in the private boarding, or "prep," school. Although many parents may have conceived of this novel institution as an elite alternative to the more plebian public school, the founders and leaders of the movement saw it as a vehicle for the fashioning of a national class of leaders imbued with the values of Christian gentlemen (or, in some cases, ladies). The prep school was also conceived of as a community in which students learned the values of group life in addition to pursuing individual success. Like the Social Gospel, the movement was informed with the spirit of noblesse oblige in which an emergent national elite had to take a responsibility for a common good that could not be trusted to secular private enterprise.

Cultural philanthropy among Episcopalians, whose wealth enabled them to serve as exemplars, had complex motivations, including sensual gratification and conspicuous consumption. But collectors and patrons of the arts were also influenced by religious and moral currents in the Anglican and broader cultures of the day. These included the Anglo-Catholic theme of the "beauty of holiness" as expressed in elaborately designed physical settings for worship; the "Gospel of Wealth," formulated by Scottish industrialist Andrew Carnegie, that called on the wealthy to invest in the enhancement of the general welfare, including education and culture; and the Ruskinian denunciation of both the moral and aesthetic ugliness of the products of the machine age as well as the negative impact of modern industry upon its employees.

American Episcopalians were not prominent among theoreticians of these discourses, but they were hardly oblivious to these ideas. Some influences were American thinkers such as Horace Bushnell or Continental European educators and economists. The most influential source of theory, theology, and practical example, however, was the Church of England. Just as the Oxford and Cambridge movements had provided much of the inspiration for the great age of church and cathedral building, so American Episcopal programs for cultural and social reform were informed by English voices such as those of Frederick Denison Maurice, Charles Kingsley, Arnold Toynbee, Thomas Arnold, Edward Thring, John Ruskin, and William Morris, all of whom had been nurtured in the Anglican matrix. More broadly, Episcopalians were informed by a distinctively Anglican sense of collective responsibility for a church-centered community in which the material and cultural as well as the specifically religions dimensions of existence were nurtured.

CHAPTER FOUR

The Social Gospel

When in New York, usually on settlement business, I would often stay in
the home of my uncle, E. P. Dutton, the publisher, a stately house where the
foot sank deep into rugs, where good pictures graced the walls, where all was
ordered softly to suit the two dear elderly people who lived a curiously quiet
life. . . . From there I would go down to the pushcarts, the crowds, the grim
excitement of Rivington Street. I found the contrast excruciating. Always I have
remembered a response of my devout uncle, one of the most sincerely religious
men I ever knew. I had reproached him gently for his pew at aristocratic Saint
Thomas's and had persuaded him to go with me one Sunday to Saint George's,
where Dr. Rainsford was then in his prime. My uncle did not enjoy the service.
He complained that a stout and, to speak frankly, smelly man was shown into
the same seat. "I was not comfortable," said he.

"Christ was not always comfortable," returned his impatient and slightly
irreverent niece.

"No," said the dear uncle slowly, thinking the matter out. "No-o. But he became
uncomfortable in order that we might be comfortable."

—Vida Dutton Scudder, *On Journey*

Vida Scudder was a member of a prominent New England family who broke
with their traditionalist ethos to become an outspoken advocate of new and
critical views of the American social and economic system in her role as a
"public intellectual."[1] More specifically, she became an advocate of what by
the turn of the twentieth century would become known as the "Social Gospel."
The Social Gospel was an interdenominational movement that broke with
an earlier Protestant emphasis on personal conversion as the essence of the
Christian Gospel, and personal moral reform, such as temperance, as the
solution to social problems. Instead, its advocates interpreted the message of
Jesus as applying to the transformation of the entire social order. These new
Social Christians addressed the issues of a nation that was being dramatically
transformed by the simultaneous and complementary processes of industrialization, urbanization, and immigration, especially from southern and eastern
Europe, on a vast scale. These issues included the growing separation and

estrangement of capital and labor, whether financial, physical, or psychological; the rights of workers to organize; protection for women and children, in the workforce and elsewhere; housing and sanitation; medical care for the poor; and a host of other concerns. These problems had, in earlier times, been seen to by families and local communities or simply did not yet exist in rural America. Perhaps surprisingly for a church associated with the well-to-do, the Episcopal Church often took the lead among American denominations in addressing rapid social change and its ensuing problems.[2]

Within the Episcopal Church—unlike some other denominations—there was considerable room for argument on matters of social and economic issues as well as those of "churchmanship."[3] During this era, many Episcopalians, both clergy and laity, remained attached to the laissez-faire economics that had dominated American thought during much of the nineteenth century. Others, however, grew highly critical of this economic system in the American social and political context. Some were Progressives, seeking a variety of reforms affecting the situation of labor in particular. Others were more radical, advocating varieties of socialism with a Christian twist. A few found in the Middle Ages a paradigm of an organic society and longed for a return to its social structures. Sometimes the lines blurred, and strands of various arguments were combined. Institutionally, some notable Episcopalians became involved in the settlement house movement, living and working among immigrants. Many Episcopal parishes became pioneers in the "institutional church" movement, devising a whole new mixture of physical plant and programming that could provide a wide variety of services to poorer parishioners. Some of these parishes were served by deaconesses, women who were dedicated to a religious life of skilled good works, at a time when only men could be ordained as clergy. Although many of their ideas and practices were shared with other denominations and secular agencies, Episcopalian "Social Gospellers" often differed from their counterparts in their association with the thought and experience of the Church of England, with which American Anglicans maintained a lively relationship during this era.

English Origins

England first experienced the Industrial Revolution and all the social dislocation that ensued in its wake. England also had an Established Church, which provided a matrix very different from the denominational competition of the United States, in which responses to social upheaval were—gradually—

formulated. Evangelicals took the first steps to bring the Gospel to urban workers who had left the church behind when they exchanged England's "green and pleasant land" for the "dark satanic mills" of the industrializing cities, but did little to address the systemic issues underlying urban poverty. By the 1840s, Tractarians—the High Church Oxford movement that would morph into later Victorian Anglo-Catholicism—did revive the notion of an organic society in contrast with Evangelical individualism. In their early years, however, they too failed to address social issues squarely. Instead of advocating reforms that would improve the earthly lot of the poor, the Tractarians exalted the poor as a means of grace: They existed to be a blessing to the rich.[4]

Particularly influential on both sides of the Atlantic in supplying a theological foundation for a critique of urban-industrial society was Frederick Denison Maurice (1805–1872), a Church of England clergyman and scholar. Maurice had been dismissed from his post at King's College, London, for his questioning of the doctrine of eternal punishment for sin, but was later awarded a chair at Cambridge. Although Maurice eschewed party labels, he is generally credited with helping lay the foundations for the Broad Church movement in both England and America. The insight that made him particularly influential on the Social Gospel was the notion that the Kingdom of Christ was social and universal in character and that the entire body of Christians, past and present, were witnesses and participants. Christ was the divine Λόγος (Logos, Word) that was present in all humans. National churches such as the Church of England were particular embodiments of this universal Kingdom; their duty was to purify and elevate the national mind. The state was also divinely ordained to serve as a moral educator when there was no central religious authority to do so. Maurice's Christianity was thus simultaneously ecumenical, immanentist, incarnational, evolutionary, optimistic, and social in its character.[5]

For Maurice, Jesus had come to establish a Kingdom in which all humans were inextricably involved with him and with one another. He had come to redeem the whole of humanity, and that redemption was social in character. For Maurice, there was no distinction between the realms of the sacred and the secular; all of human life came under the scope of Christian belief and action. The condition of the poor was due neither to divine decree nor to their own lack of industry; rather, it arose from the improper ordering of social relations and institutions, which could be remedied through human action. Maurice was also active in promoting the implications of his thought in the social realm. He joined with Charles Kingsley, John Ludlow, and other kindred spirits in the early 1850s to promote what they called "Christian Socialism," which was based on the premise that reform must be grounded in morality, which in turn had to be grounded in the Christian faith. In various combinations they published a journal, promoted worker's cooperatives, and established the Working Men's College in London, an endeavor in which the pre-Raphaelite artist Dante Gabriel Rossetti and critic John Ruskin collaborated. None of these ventures lasted very long, but collectively they helped disseminate the notion that Christianity and social reform should not be separate, not to say incompatible, spheres of action. Much the same idea would inform the American Social Gospel in subsequent decades.[6]

The Conventional Wisdom

During the middle decades of the nineteenth century, the dominant paradigm in American social and economic thought—including that of the Protestant churches—was also of British derivation. Seniors at most American colleges were required to take what might now be called a "capstone" course in "moral philosophy," a concept that would later be displaced by social ethics on the one hand—a creation of the Social Gospel movement—and the various social and behavioral sciences, based on secular scientific paradigms, on the other. The moral philosophy expounded in popular texts such Francis Wayland's *The Elements of Political Economy* (1837) was derived in part from the "classical" laissez-faire teachings of the Scot Adam Smith and his followers, who held that there was an "iron law of wages" dictated by the free market that could be violated only at the cost of economic catastrophe. This doctrine received religious legitimation through the Scottish "common sense" school of philosophy, which informed the thought of American Protestants in the early nineteenth-century and resulted in the "clerical laissez-faire" expounded across the denominational spectrum from the Baptist Wayland to theologically progressive Unitarians.[7]

What in some ways was the ultimate conclusion drawn from the premises of laissez-faire was expounded by William Graham Sumner (1840–1910), whose career bridged the transition from moral philosophy to modern social science. Sumner, the American-born son of an English artisan, studied for the ministry at Geneva, Göttingen, and Oxford and was ordained an Episcopal priest in 1869. After a brief career as a parish minister in New Jersey and editor of *The Living Church* (still an Episcopal periodical), Sumner returned in 1872 to his alma mater, Yale, as professor of political economy. As such he offered some of the first courses in sociology in the United States, incurring the displeasure of the Congregationalist president Noah Porter for his use in the classroom of Herbert Spencer's 1873 *Study of Sociology*. Spencer, whose work was enormously popular both in the United States and his native England, embraced the Darwinian concept of evolution—he, rather than Darwin, coined the phrase "survival of the fittest"—and combined it with Comtean positivism in his exposition of a universal natural law that applied to all aspects of human existence. Sumner embraced Spencer's secular evolutionary scheme, as well as his laissez-faire approach to political economy, in such works as *What Social Classes Owe to Each Other* (1883), which gained for his thought the label of "Social Darwinism." Whatever the accuracy of this philosophy, Sumner had clearly left the realm of Anglicanism, and Christianity more broadly, behind him in his quest for a "scientific" sociology. Like most early practitioners of sociology, however, he held firm, morally grounded views on the application of social theory to public policy.[8]

Other prominent Episcopal clergy shared Sumner's position that governmental interference in the economic realm is disruptive both of fundamental economic laws and of the social order, without following Sumner into the realm of secularism. These included the rectors of what were arguably the two most prestigious Episcopal churches in America. As we have already seen in some length in chapter 1, Phillips Brooks at Boston's Trinity Church was focused on the redemption of the individual through character transformation and had little conceptual sense of the significance of broader forces in the shaping of character and fortune. For Brooks, social inequality was not only inevitable but desirable. Education, wealth, and social position were gifts of God to those upon whom He saw fit to bestow them. Poverty had its own virtues and sources of happiness. Workers could improve their lot through patience and self-improvement, aided, presumably, by the message preached by Brooks. Although Trinity did sponsor programming for the poor, Brooks had little sense of the systemic causes of poverty. Although he had found inspiration in the teachings of Maurice about the Kingdom of Christ, it stopped far short of Maurice's "Christian Socialism."[9]

Brooks's career illustrates, among other things, that a Broad Church theological position did not necessarily correlate with sympathy for an emergent Social Gospel that involved a serious critique of the contemporary social order. Anglo-Catholics were similarly at various places along the spectrum of social critique. Morgan Dix, for example, was the longtime (1862–1908) rector of Trinity Church, Wall Street, which to this day continues to be the wealthiest Episcopal parish in the United States. (Its vast real estate holdings derive from a 1705 bequest from Queen Anne.)[10] Trinity had been the target of social critics since the 1840s as a slumlord and owner of land occupied by saloons and brothels; in 1910 Ray Stannard Baker, a leading muckraking journalist, indicted it as a paradigm of unaccountable and soulless capitalist greed.[11] Dix, who for many years presided over the House of Deputies at the General Convention, was not unsympathetic to the poor: He utilized some of Trinity's vast resources to sponsor a series of chapels and a Mission House that was home to a variety of outreach programs typical of the institutional church movement exemplified at St. George's. These Trinity programs were funded in considerable measure through Astor family money—just as St. George's benefitted from the largesse of J. P. Morgan.[12] (Baker and other critics dismissed this programming as ineffectual window-dressing.)

Dix's attitude toward the poor is visible in his collaboration with a group of the parish's laity in the founding of the Trinity Church Association in 1880. The association focused on educational work aimed at civilizing the poor and inculcating in them a spirit of self-respect. Its Relief Bureau embodied the emerging philosophy of "scientific charity" characteristic of the emergent social work profession, distinguishing between the "worthy" and "unworthy" poor through an investigation into the character and circumstances of applicants for its services. Dix was generally progressive in his politics, supporting St. George's vestryman Seth Low in his campaigns for mayor. He was, however, appalled by strikes and demonstrations, and opposed the labor movement as demagogic and anarchistic. On the other hand, he shared the attitude of many contemporaries in denouncing the Gilded Age *nouveaux riches* as contributors to social unrest:

> What shall we say of the aristocracy of mere wealth, whose implements are sharpness, shrewdness, and unscrupulous conduct, and whose badge is pretentious and extravagant display. . . . Purse pride is the lowest form of all. We see it full blown where fortunes are rapidly made, and where men who do not know the right use of money find themselves suddenly in its possession. This is the sin which is accountable for modern discontent, and the alienation and hostility of classes.[13]

Dix's attitude toward contemporary social issues might be characterized as patrician: critical of the excesses at both ends of the social spectrum, but more frightened by the prospect of working-class anarchy than upper-class vulgarity.

The Institutional Church

Dix's posture was characteristic of many contemporary Episcopalians, lay and clerical. Trinity's ventures into social service, however, indicated the ambiguity of the role of their church in responding to the crisis of the American city. The provision of such "secular" services was a major hallmark of the institutional church movement of the late nineteenth century, a movement in which Episcopal churches set the pace. The forerunner of the institutional church was William Augustus Muhlenberg's Church of the Holy Communion at Sixth Avenue and West 20th Street in Manhattan, designed by the prominent Gothic revivalist architect Richard Upjohn in 1844. One significant step that Muhlenberg took as rector of Holy Communion was to abolish pew rents, a pervasive practice among Episcopalians dating from colonial times, in which individuals or families bought or leased rights to a particular pew annually or in perpetuity. More desirable pews, usually those toward the front, fetched higher prices, and nonpew holders were seated in the rear or a balcony, if anywhere. The movement to abolish pew rentals as undemocratic and unwelcoming became a major issue in Episcopal churches, in particular in the later decades of the nineteenth century. Many followed Holy Communion's example, while others retained the practice well into the twentieth century. (In some churches today many regular attendees still maintain a proprietary attitude toward their accustomed seats, and ushers try to steer the unwary clear of them.)[14]

Muhlenberg also sponsored other progressive measures at Holy Communion, which was unique among the New York Episcopal churches of the day in embracing persons from across the entire social spectrum in its membership. The parish sponsored a dispensary that provided the poor with free medicine and medical advice; an infirmary that would evolve into Saint Luke's Hospital; a fresh-air fund to provide summer vacations away from the crowded and insalubrious city; an employment service for poor women; and a parish school for boys and girls. To staff these enterprises, Muhlenberg sponsored the Sisterhood of the Holy Communion, founded in 1845 as the first religious order for women in the United States outside the Roman Catholic Church. Anne Ayres, who would later serve as his biographer, was received by Muhlenberg as its first and, for several years, its only member, in 1845.[15]

The term "institutional church" would not come into usage for several more decades, but Muhlenberg's Holy Communion exhibited many characteristics of a mode of church design and operation that would become extremely popular among Episcopalians and other Protestants as a practical response to the challenges of living in a city crowded with poor immigrants at a time before the wealthy had fled to the safety of the suburbs.[16] Churches were seldom founded with this model in mind; rather, individual churches, whether missions or regular parishes, responded pragmatically and experimentally to the local needs they confronted. Both the idea and paradigm of the institutional church evolved together as a response to changing environments.

One example of this evolution was Boston's South End, in which, during the 1870s, the private homes of middle-class Protestants were rapidly being converted into rooming houses for immigrants.[17] (In *The Late George Apley*, John P. Marquand's gently satiric 1947 novel of Boston Brahmin life, the protagonist's grandfather quickly sells his South End home when he sees a man in shirtsleeves on the street.) St. Stephen's Church had been established in 1845 by the Episcopal City Mission as a chapel for the poor in the West End. (Mission chapels differed from parish churches in being subsidized by the diocese and having less autonomy than self-supporting parishes.) Following a disastrous fire in 1872 and a long period of indecision as to its future course, the church was reestablished in the South End two decades later by then bishop Phillips Brooks under the direction of Brooks's former assistant, Frederick B. Allen, who was then the superintendent of the City Mission.[18] The church, which was unencumbered by tradition, wealth, or vestry, was seen by Brooks and Allen as an opportunity for practical work among the poor. It was originally staffed by two former members of the Cowley Fathers religious order, Henry Torbert and Charles Brent.[19] Although Brooks had seen mission work as an opportunity for personal service and evangelism, Allen, Torbert, and Brent, who were all experienced in slum ministries, began to move toward more practical aid to their constituents. In order to help the poor achieve character change, they first had to get the attention of potential converts through material relief. By providing such relief, the enterprise shifted its goals unobtrusively from those of a mission church aimed solely at religious conversion to a ministry in which social service and spirituality were inextricably linked.[20]

St. Stephen's thus began rapidly to take on the character of an institutional church. Its programming included a children's laundry in which, under the supervision of a deaconess, girls would learn to wash, iron, and mend clothes for a living. It also provided a safe haven for prostitutes in a rented house supervised by the deaconess, and another rental building, which formerly housed a billiards parlor, served as a meeting room for various boys' and men's clubs. As these modes of outreach proved popular, other activities and staff, including a young men's boarding house, a rescue mission for the "utterly lost," a lecture series, a kindergarten, a nurse, and a five-story parish house were added. Although the clerical staff, as their previous monastic affiliation might indicate, were Anglo-Catholic by inclination, they were skeptical as to whether the formal liturgy of the *Book of Common Prayer* would appeal to their constituency. Instead, they held daily sessions of intercessory prayer according to the Cowley ritual, which became a hallmark of the institution.[21]

Both Allen and Brent reflected publicly on the theological implications of the innovations in worship and programming that St. Stephen's was developing in response to its environment. Allen reflected that "the distinction between the religious and the secular is not so rigidly observed as once in missionary work. This happens not by making sacred things more secular, but by recognizing the sacredness of much that once was thought to have no religious character." Brent framed their enterprise similarly. For him, the performance of the corporal works of mercy—the relief of physical suffering— was to minister to Christ himself. Social service thus took on an explicitly sacramental character, grounded in a distinctively Anglican understanding of the Incarnation as bringing the entire realm of creation within the purview of the sacred. By implication, the "machinery" of the parish house had become as integral a part of the church's mission as preaching and sacramental worship.[22]

Perhaps the most influential institutional church in the Episcopal fold was St. George's in New York City. The parish, which dates back to a 1752 chapel in lower Manhattan, had, like many Episcopal churches, migrated northward with the flow of their constituents—"the spoor of the rich," as the parish's historian evocatively phrased it.[23] In 1846 it relocated in then fashionable Stuyvesant Square and employed Leopold Eidlitz to design a building in the *Rundbogenstil* (Romanesque revival) style. The parish prospered under the midcentury rectorship of Stephen Tyng (1800–85), an Evangelical whose oratory drew over a thousand auditors each Sunday. St. George's also sponsored mission chapels in the lower reaches of the borough for the growing number of immigrants, especially Germans, who were settling there.[24]

As the wealthy continued to move uptown, St. George's fell onto hard times. By 1883, five years after Tyng's resignation, the parish consisted of only twenty families and had sold off most of its property holdings. It was in that year that it called William S. Rainsford, who would serve as rector for the next

St. George's Church, corner of Sixteenth Street and Rutherford Place.

Charles Otto Blesch and Leopold Eidlitz, St. George's Church, Stuyvesant Square, New York, 1846–56. (Courtesy of St. George's Church)

twenty-two years and transform St. George's into a national phenomenon. Rainsford had been born into an old Anglo-Irish family of many clergy. His father, whom Rainsford described as "an unworldly, simple-minded man," scraped out a living as a vicar in a poor Irish village until his call to a fashionable London parish in 1865, where he became a leader in the Evangelical faction of the Church of England. It was through the connections made in this parish that the younger Rainsford both obtained the resources for extensive

The Reverend William S. Rainsford (second from right) with J. P. Morgan Jr. (center), Rocky Mountains, 1884. (From Rainsford, *The Story of a Varied Life* [1923])

European travel and a Cambridge education, as well as a glimpse of the social stratification that the church embodied rather than attempted to rectify.[25]

As a young man he exemplified "muscular Christianity" during a lengthy, harrowing trip through the Indian country of western Canada to the Pacific Coast in 1869, a journey that began as a project to help poor English relocate in the New World. (Rainsford would later become a close friend and fellow wilderness enthusiast of Theodore Roosevelt.) Despite persisting doubts about matters of doctrine, he obtained a position as a curate near Norwich, Connecticut, and soon became a powerful revivalist after beginning to preach in the city's streets to attract the poor. In 1876 he began a career as an itinerant mission preacher in the United States, where he rapidly gained a reputation that led to an invitation by Phillips Brooks to preach at Trinity in Boston. This period culminated with Rainsford's appointment to the staff of the Cathedral Church of St. James in Toronto, where he remained for four years.[26]

After the bishop refused to confirm Rainsford's election as rector of the Toronto cathedral, Rainsford accepted the call to St. George's. He did so on the conditions that pew rents be abolished, that all committees be dissolved and replaced with appointments of the rector's choice, and that he be given a fund of ten thousand dollars a year for outreach work. To these demands, J. P. Morgan, the longtime senior warden, simply said: "Done." Rainsford thus received carte blanche to transform the church, with virtually complete control and no financial worries.[27]

"Well Backed," a 1903 cartoon depicting William S. Rainsford and his accomplishments at St. George's resting on the backs of his wardens—including J. P. Morgan, far left—and vestry. (From Elizabeth Moulton, *St. George's Church, New York* [1964]. Courtesy of St. George's Church)

St. George's was in a peculiar situation. Its membership base, though seriously diminished, included some of the wealthiest and most influential men in the United States, who provided Rainsford entrée into New York's best clubs and social circles. Although a few of the old guard resisted—one sat on the hat of a newcomer in what were now free pews—the vestry now took turns standing at the front door before Sunday services, welcoming in "all sorts and conditions." Rainsford spruced up the church and successfully manipulated the Tammany Hall machine into cleaning up a badly neglected Stuyvesant Square.[28] He also beefed up the church's music program, substituting congregational singing for paid quartets and adding surpliced choirs of boys and parishioners. One controversy that Rainsford successfully weathered was his invitation to Harry Burleigh to be a soloist. Burleigh was an African American baritone who had studied at the National Conservatory of Music, where he had assisted Antonin Dvořák and introduced the Czech composer to black religious music. Burleigh overcame initial hostility and continued to perform at St. George's for several decades, while also acquiring a lasting national reputation for his arrangement of art songs and spirituals.[29]

Rainsford's concern was not primarily with African Americans, who generally participated in Episcopal life only in mission congregations or an occasional parish of their own, such as St. Philip's up in Harlem.[30] It was rather with lower New York's poor, many of whom were fellow immigrants. One of Rainsford's early attempts at evangelism was to open a mission in the back of a saloon, at which he once knocked down a drunken intruder. His major outreach project, however, was the erection of an elaborate parish house that would provide the facilities that an institutional church needed to carry out the kind of recreational and educational programming that would attract and serve the poor. One parishioner offered to fund the enterprise, on the condition that Rainsford turn over the church's music program to his control. Rainsford refused, and the parishioner departed St. George's. After a lengthy lobbying campaign by Rainsford, carried out over their weekly breakfasts, Senior Warden J. P. Morgan eventually agreed to fund what became known as "The Memorial House of St. George's."[31]

Although Rainsford disliked the term "institutional church," St. George's rapidly became a paradigm of that emergent genre, and even the subject of a book entitled *The Administration of an Institutional Church: A Detailed Account of the Operation of St. George's Parish in the City of New York.*[32] This tome was written in part by John Reichert, a down-and-out German sailor whom Rainsford befriended and who became a fixture of the parish staff, especially

Harry Burleigh, arranger of Negro spirituals and longtime soloist at St. George's.
(From Moulton, *St. George's Church*. Courtesy St. George's Church)

Gymnasium, Christ Church, Cincinnati, Ohio. A typical piece of
institutional church apparatus. (Courtesy of Don Prout)

in its outreach to the many German immigrants in the neighborhood. Much
of the parish programming focused on the young: Rainsford had written off
many adults as beyond help. St. George's offerings included recreational
facilities, which began with a bowling alley in the church basement and
expanded into a gymnasium that occupied an entire floor of the parish house;
a kindergarten, only the second of its kind in the city; an industrial school;
a Sunday school, which enrolled two thousand students in its heyday; and
a panoply of other facilities and activities described in minute detail in the
Hodges and Reichert volume. In addition to numerous lay volunteers, which
included luminaries such as New York mayor Seth Low, staffing was provided
not by seminarians, whom Rainsford considered useless, but by a succession
of young priests who lived with their rector in a clergy house and for whom
Rainsford served as mentor. Among them was Frank Howard Nelson, who
would later turn Christ Church in Cincinnati into yet another exemplar of
the institutional church.*[33]

---

*Rainsford resigned his rectorship in 1906 in the face of deteriorating health and the prospect
of charges of heresy for his increasingly humanistic interpretation of basic Christian teachings. He later participated in twenty-two African safaris, including a 1912–13 expedition for the
American Museum of Natural History in pursuit of the black rhino.

Progressive Episcopalians

In addition to building up this vast empire of outreach, Rainsford openly aligned himself with reformist politics. Like his bishop, Henry Codman Potter, he grew increasingly sympathetic with the labor movement. In 1896 he denounced the calling out of the militia to break up a trolley strike in Brooklyn, even though the trolley company was controlled by Senior Warden J. P. Morgan. (Morgan, typically, defended his rector's right to speak out on public issues.) Rainsford testified at slum clearance hearings, and accused a vestryman at another Episcopal church of receiving bribes.[34] St. George's was further linked with the Progressive movement by the active presence of Seth Low (1850–1916), elected mayor of New York in 1901 by an anti-Tammany Hall coalition. Low had inherited a considerable fortune and had previously been president of Columbia University, where he greatly expanded programs, moved the campus uptown, and personally endowed the Low Memorial Library in honor of his father. In his single term as mayor he reformed the police department, expanded the public school system as well as public health facilities, and vigorously enforced housing laws. "Short, stocky, humorless, and very wealthy," he was defeated in his 1903 bid for reelection. Low spent the remainder of his career as a labor mediator and advocate, as well as a trustee of the Tuskegee Institute.[35]

A particularly clear example of the intersection of the Episcopal Church and Progressivism can be seen in Calvary Church in Pittsburgh. Its rector, George Hodges, had been deeply influenced by the English reformers Maurice and Kingsley. Taking the entire community as their charge for mission, Hodges and Calvary helped introduce a previously dour Presbyterian-dominated local elite to a richer aesthetic life, and employed professional organists, choir directors, and soloists for a congregation aspiring to participation in a national elite culture.[36] Hodges saw this programming in Mauricean social terms: "We want to have the Kingdom of Heaven come in Pittsburgh, and we are beginning to see that praying is not enough: we have got to set to work ushering it in. And the first thing to do is to cultivate this sense of social inclusion, of social fraternity and responsibility, and to share our good music with our neighbors, who have not so much good music as we have, is a small beginning."[37]

Another of Hodges's English-inspired enthusiasms was the social settlement. In 1890 he visited London to study Toynbee Hall, the prototype of that movement, and corresponded with Jane Addams and other leaders in the United States. The result was Kingsley House, which Hodges recruited a multidenominational committee to organize. This committee included the wife of steel magnate Henry Clay Frick, and engaged Kate C. Everest, a protégé of Addams and student of labor economist Richard T. Ely, as its head. In addition to hosting the sorts of educational and recreational activities associated with such foundations, Kingsley House became a center for the systematic study of the roots of poverty, with a charge from Hodges to produce "a moral map of the Twelfth Ward," a project later realized as the "Pittsburgh Survey."[38]

Hodges departed Calvary in 1894 to become dean of the Episcopal Theological School in Cambridge, where he continued to be involved in settlement house work as well as prolific speaking and publication.[39] In 1900 James McIlvane assumed the Calvary rectorship and continued Hodges's work. During the next few years Calvary became the nexus of the reform movement in Pittsburgh, as McIlvane and a group of influential laity used it as a base for what became known as the "Pittsburgh Plan." Whereas earlier Presbyterian-led reform efforts had focused on the elimination of the enablers of personal vice, such as liquor and Sabbath breaking, this new breed of Progressives used the findings of the Pittsburgh Survey as an empirical basis to address the city's social ills more systemically. Prominent in this mobilization of the laity to implement Social Gospel principles were Calvary members H. D. W. English, the president of the Civic Commission, and George W. Guthrie, the "reform mayor" elected in 1906. (Another Calvary layman, Henry Clay Frick, who had ordered the violent suppression of the 1892 Homestead Strike, was unsurprisingly not supportive of these efforts.)[40]

If Hodges and "the D_____ Calvary Crowd," as his cohort of civic reformers were dubbed by their antagonists, represented the alliance of clergy and laypeople in the active reform of urban politics under the banner of Christian morality, Richard T. Ely (pronounced EE-lee) contributed an academic and theological foundation to the movement, which also had a profoundly practical dimension.[41] Ely (1854–1943) was born to an economically challenged, strict Presbyterian family of old New England stock in upstate New York. Having converted to the Episcopal Church while an undergraduate at Columbia, he remained an active member for the rest of his life.[42] While studying at Heidelberg for his doctorate—American universities were only beginning to offer serious graduate study—Ely became exposed to the German civil service system firsthand, as well as to economists such as his mentor Karl Knies. While British economists of the laissez-faire persuasion—*Manchesterthum*, as they were known collectively in Germany—took a dim view of the role of government in economic affairs on deductive, theoretical grounds, Knies and his collaborators took a more empirical, historically based view of the matter, arguing that economic laws were not abstract and timeless but rather that different specific situations called for different, pragmatically grounded approaches. In Germany, this resulted in an activist role for the state, which seemed to the young Ely to have resulted in a marvelously efficient and humane civic realm.[43]

Upon his return to the United States, Ely participated in the beginnings of the new era of the American research university, holding positions first at Johns Hopkins, which had been founded for the purpose of advanced scholarship, and later at the University of Wisconsin and Northwestern. Ely lived at a time when what are now known as the social sciences, including economics, were emerging as distinctive empirical disciplines rather than as part of the realm of "moral philosophy," the catchall rubric under which they had traditionally been included in the undergraduate curriculum of colleges under a Protestant aegis. These new "sciences," however, were in their early days by no means either "pure" (as opposed to applied) or "secular" (divorced from religious and ethical content). The American Economic Association (AEA), which Ely first convened in 1885, and which he served as secretary for seven years, presented itself as dedicated to scientific investigation rather than propaganda, but was clearly opposed to laissez-faire and saw itself as having an active ethical mission of reform. (The AEA was founded during a meeting of the American Historical Association, indicative of the porosity of disciplinary boundaries in these early years of the professionalization of academe.)[44]

Although Ely's thought on political economy had been shaped by his German educational experience, he was also influenced by the theology of F. D. Maurice, on whom, among many other topics, he lectured at Chautauqua.[45] His Chautauqua lectures became the basis for his *Outlines of Economics* (1893), which sold over a million copies and was at one time the most widely used economics textbooks in the United States. In this and many other books, such as his *Social Aspects of Christianity*, a collection of essays published in 1889, Ely aimed his teachings at a broad audience. Robert T. Handy has described this teaching as a "mild evolutionary socialism," interpreted as an application of Jesus's commandment to love thy neighbor. To accomplish this, Ely invoked a Mauricean notion of human solidarity with a positive role for both church and state in the implementation of Christian social ethics. His vision of the state was expansive: In its ideal form it would virtually absorb the church.

The state would thus become a sort of public church, similar to the Church of England in concept, but acknowledging the de facto diversity of religious opinion that characterized American society.[46]

At the University of Wisconsin, where he taught from 1892 to 1925, he became an active figure in promoting the "Wisconsin Idea," an alliance of university social scientists with the state government promoted by Progressive governor Robert Lafollette. The programs that Ely promoted were not particularly radical or distinctive—he supported civil service reform, publicly owned utilities, and moderate government regulation of industry; favored labor unions; and opposed child labor. What distinguished him from more secular-minded reformers was the Christian framework he employed for justifying the positive role of the government in the economic order.[47]

While at Wisconsin, Ely inadvertently found himself at the center of a drama that would have long-lasting repercussions for the right of American academics to advocate controversial ideas such as the Social Gospel. In 1894, Oliver E. Wells, the state superintendent of schools, in a letter to the *Nation*, accused Ely of teaching socialism. Wells, curiously, had come to his post by accident. He had been nominated by Wisconsin Democrats in a moment of inattention: when they were thinking that they had no chance of victory and were about to adjourn their convention, it was pointed out that they had neglected to provide a nominee for this office, and Wells was selected after someone in the group shouted out his name. The Democrats, benefitting from an unpopular Republican law that had placed religiously operated schools under state supervision, found themselves dumbfounded when their ticket, including the previously unknown Wells, carried the day. Ely was in fact a leading advocate of economic reform, but hardly a socialist. The university regents not only rejected Wells's charges but took the occasion to issue what became a fundamental statement of the principle of academic freedom—*Lehrfreiheit*—in American higher education.[48]

While Hodges had been a clergyman and Ely a layman, another leading Episcopal advocate of Progressive causes was a bishop. Also the son and nephew of bishops, Henry Codman Potter (1835–1908) was, as it were, "born to the purple." After stints as an assistant at Trinity in Boston and then rector of Manhattan's fashionable Grace Church, Potter was elected bishop of New York in 1887, in effect taking over the family business from his uncle Horatio.[49] While at Grace, Potter continued the work begun by his predecessor, Thomas House Taylor, turning the parish into an institutional church before the term had come into being. During Potter's rectorship, Grace added an employment program for poor women, an industrial school for their children, and free medical aid for the needy, as well as establishing Grace House as a center for these and a myriad of other outreach activities. Potter unsuccessfully lobbied his vestry to abolish pew rentals, but did promote the mingling of social classes among his parishioners for their mutual benefit.[50]

As bishop, Potter continued to straddle the proverbial railroad tracks, mingling with rich and poor alike. (George Hodges once observed that "Bishop Wilberforce, after a good deal of experience, came to the conclusion that society could not be saved by dining with it. Bishop Potter was not so sure.")[51] Potter, for example, presided over the marriage of Consuelo Vanderbilt to the Duke of Marlborough in 1895, the archetype of the American heiress matched against her will to a British nobleman.[52] His ability to mix easily with the cream of New York society enabled him both to raise funds on a vast scale—recall his role in the building of St. John the Divine—as well as to serve as an effective advocate of labor.

It is in this latter capacity that Potter made a mark on his times. Potter was no radical. Wealth, for him, was a blessing if used for the public good. The problem, however, was the moral corruption of the wealthy as well as the alienation between social classes that was resulting from the selfish use of wealth. By the 1890s, Potter's rhetoric began to emphasize not only proper stewardship by the moneyed classes but also the need for justice for the poor and unemployed. He was now beginning to endorse the fundamental premises of the emergent Social Gospel, namely, that Christianity was best expressed not simply in prayer and worship but in a ministry to all aspects of human nature, including the material.[53]

In addition to promoting the New York cathedral as a center for social service, Potter became personally involved in a variety of projects that illustrated his call for mutuality rather than a detached paternalism. These ventures also illustrated a distinctively Anglican "middle way" approach to social issues. One of the "hot button" issues of the Progressive era was the alcohol question, which had begun in the earlier nineteenth century as a campaign by Evangelicals for Protestants to "take the pledge" to refrain voluntarily from the use of alcohol. By Potter's time, this campaign had morphed into a drive first for local and state and then eventually for national prohibition by the government of the manufacture and sale of intoxicants. Prohibition was no longer a drive for self-control, but had now taken on an aspect of social control in the context of a vast influx of southern and eastern Europeans and their folkways involving beer, wine, and whiskey.

Potter recognized that the saloon was not simply a place for individual imbibing, but a venue for socializing as well. Like many Episcopalians (who had their own folkways involving Scotch and sherry), he was opposed to coercive prohibition, although he was a founder of the Church Temperance Society. Rather, he favored constructive alternatives to the saloon and its associations with crime, political corruption, and overindulgence that harmed the workingman and his family. He supported experiments such as the Temperance Society's Squirrel Inn, which he praised as a "poor man's club" that provided an alcohol-free gathering place for workingmen. In 1904, more controversially, he presided at the dedication of the Subway Tavern. Based on a prototype by the English reformer Earl Grey, the tavern, which had come about in part through Rainsford's efforts, was intended to be "an ethical stimulant-selling establishment," that is, a saloon free of vice (regarded by most temperance advocates as an oxymoron). Perhaps not surprisingly, neither of these experiments was very successful.[54]

Prohibition has faded from the American scene, but immigration has not. Potter's service as bishop coincided with the floodtide of European immigration into the United States, with New York as the focal point of entry and settlement. Many Protestant clergy—notoriously, Congregationalist Josiah Strong in his *Our Country* of 1885—looked upon immigration with alarm, as contributing to the degradation of urban life.[55] Potter, along with many Episcopal clergy, began by sharing Strong's Anglo-Saxonism, arguing that American culture and values had been molded by its English heritage. In 1878, his "Plea for the American Sunday" defended the Evangelical tradition of Sabbatarianism—Sunday as a day in which commerce and secular amusements were severely restricted—against the "continental Sabbath," where leisure activities such as patronage of the *Biergarten* were culturally endorsed. In following years, however, Potter changed his emphasis, blaming Sabbath disrespect less on immigrants and more on the commercialization and material spirit of American life, a theme that became increasingly central to his rhetoric. While maintaining his commitment to the Anglo-Saxon heritage, Potter refused to endorse the movement for immigration restriction that was gaining headway, favoring instead a policy of assimilation. As rector and bishop he promoted mission chapels for Germans, Italians, and Chinese, as well as the celebration of a multiplicity of ethnicities at St. John the Divine. Here, too, Potter followed a very Anglican "middle way."[56]

The issue most associated with Bishop Potter, however, was that of labor. By the late 1870s Potter was beginning to denounce economic individualism and Social Darwinism in his sermons and other public addresses, invoking instead the theme of social solidarity. In the wake of the 1886 Haymarket riots in Chicago, Potter issued a pastoral letter renouncing repressive measures against strikers, and called instead on the laity to acknowledge the origins of labor unrest in the inequitable distribution of wealth. In later public statements he acknowledged the legitimacy of the labor movement and the need for governmental intervention for the protection of labor and consumers. He invoked the teaching of Jesus as the basis of the principles that needed to be applied to the realm of business and labor, and employed the rhetoric of a this-worldly Kingdom of God and the brotherhood of humanity that was becoming the common currency of both British and American Christian social teachings. Potter gained the trust of many labor leaders and worked behind the scenes with J. P. Morgan to try to settle the 1901 steel strike and the anthracite coal strike of 1902–3. As an active member and honorary vice president of CAIL (Church Association for the Advancement of the Interests of Labor), he served—together with Seth Low, among others—as a mediator of several labor disputes. In 1901, the General Convention appointed Potter chair of the Joint Commission of the Relations of Capital and Labor, a group that included George Hodges, Seth Low, and William Lawrence. In this and other capacities he helped bring the national Episcopal Church to acknowledgment and institutionalization of its role as arbiter in the industrial economy.[57]

Henry Codman Potter was, throughout his career, modeling a new role for the Episcopal bishop as a player in the broader social and political arena of the American city. Potter's self-fashioned persona was that of the benevolent patrician who served as an honest broker between social classes. He called on the elite, who were his more natural constituency, to observe high ethical standards in business, government, and the professions, and denounced their tendency to succumb to self-indulgence. "Political righteousness" was one of his continuing themes, and he publicly denounced police and political corruption, supporting, for example, Seth Low's successful campaign to become mayor of New York in 1901.[58] Although critical of the excesses of capitalism, his positions were never radical, acknowledging the essential soundness of the American system while continually calling its leadership to public responsibility rather than private gain. Although at home in high society and perhaps at times overly accommodating of its foibles, he won the confidence of many in the labor movement through his reputation for fair-mindedness: A biography by Harriette Keyser, longtime secretary of CAIL, hailed him as *Bishop Potter: The People's Friend*.[59]

Women and Society

Although only a few women, such as Harriette Keyser, occupied visible positions of leadership in the Episcopal version of the Social Gospel movement, much of the actual work of social outreach was carried out by women. Since many female Episcopalians were ladies of leisure, they were able to serve as unpaid volunteers for a variety of parish-based social services, such as sewing classes for poor women and girls. Before the Civil War, such outreach was rare; by 1900, however, there were sixty-two such community institutions in New York City alone.[60]

Although the priesthood would not be open to women until 1976, the Episcopal Church did begin to provide institutional opportunities for formal female service during the later nineteenth century. William Augustus Muhlenberg, who had established forerunners both of the institutional church and the private boarding school, was also instrumental in sponsoring the first Episcopal religious order for women in the United States. Anne Ayres, who became the first (and for several years the only) member of the Sisterhood of the Holy Cross, became Muhlenberg's "domestic administrator" for his programs of social outreach at Holy Communion. Among these was St. Luke's Hospital, where Ayres and her eventual colleagues helped structure nursing education, and the profession more generally on the English model, in which early Anglican sisters worked with Florence Nightingale to the same end.[61]

Although some of these orders came to resemble those of the Roman Catholic Church, their original model was not Catholic sisterhoods, which required perpetual vows and were generally shocking to Episcopal sensibilities. Rather, they were based on a German prototype, that of Lutheran Pastor Theodor Fliedner in Kaiserswerth-am-Rhein in the 1830s, the same model that had inspired Nightingale and that Henry Codman Potter viewed first-hand. These women in service to the church were called neither nuns nor sisters, which sounded too Roman to many, but rather deaconesses, an office adopted by several American Protestant denominations. Deaconesses, which were first recognized by the national Episcopal Church in 1874, were not the same as deacons: the latter (διάκονοι) were one of the early Christian orders of clergy (together with priests and bishops), and were restricted to males until the 1970s. Unlike nuns or sisters, deaconesses did not take long-term vows, but were required to be unmarried and undergo a two-year training program such as that offered at St. John the Divine, which equipped them to be missionaries, social workers, administrators of schools or orphanages, or religious teachers. They took short-term vows, wore distinctive uniforms, and received salaries. They were not ordained, but rather "set apart." Never numerous, deaconesses began to decline in number in the 1930s and disappeared among Episcopalians when women became eligible to be ordained as deacons and priests.[62]

Deaconesses became a mainstay of the institutional church movement, and provided much of the staffing in many parishes. Another institution of the era in which Episcopal women participated enthusiastically was the settlement house, a creation of Victorian Anglicanism. Its prototype was Toynbee Hall, founded in Whitechapel in London's East End in 1884, named in honor of Arnold Toynbee (1852–83), the Oxford economic historian who popularized the term "Industrial Revolution" in English-speaking countries and died at an early age after exhausting himself in slum work. (Toynbee was the uncle of his better-known namesake, Arnold J. Toynbee, the author of the multivolume *A Study of History*.) Toynbee Hall, which is still in operation, provided an opportunity for students from Oxford and Cambridge to serve as resident volunteers among the urban poor. Its founders, Church of England vicar Samuel Augustus Barnett and his wife Henrietta, were deeply influenced by the teachings of Maurice and Kingsley as well as those of John Ruskin. Their goal was not so much systemic reform but rather the spiritual renewal of the poor through education, together with the better mutual understanding of social classes who had been separated as the result of industrialization.[63]

American versions of Toynbee Hall began to arise in the late 1880s almost simultaneously in a variety of cities. The idea resonated strongly among Social Gospel advocates, and most of the young people who helped implement it were church members, primarily Episcopal, Presbyterian, and Unitarian. American settlement houses founded under Episcopal or other church auspices usually found it more expedient to operate without overt denominational affiliation.[64] Among the numerous Episcopalians who became involved with the movement, two women deserve particular attention: Ellen Starr Gates and Vida Dutton Scudder.

Gates (1859–1940), the cofounder of Chicago's Hull House in 1889, has largely been overshadowed by her collaborator and longtime companion, Jane Addams. Gates and Addams had met while students at what was at the time known as Rockford Female Seminary in Illinois, an offshoot of Mount Holyoke College that focused on the preparation of young women as foreign missionaries. Gates was not inclined in this direction, and instead became immersed in the work of Carlyle, Dickens, and Ruskin. While the two were on a study tour in Europe in 1887, Addams visited Toynbee Hall, and she and Gates soon became involved in planning a similar venture in Chicago. The result was the founding of Hull House on Chicago's Near West Side, a "community of university women" who undertook an ambitious program of work with the Italians and other immigrants who were settling in the neighborhood. This work included medical and childcare services as well as educational and cultural programming. Hull House sponsored concerts, lectures, and classes in the liberal arts as well as more practical subjects such as sewing. Its residents also became political activists, successfully promoting public services such as a playgrounds and gymnasiums for the neighborhood and juvenile courts and child labor laws for the broader community. Hull House— which Jill Ker Conway has called "a salon in a slum"—also provided a context in which young women in particular could pursue "vocational goals [that] were innately tied to friendship circles," combining professional, political, and personal pursuits within a close, supportive community of social service.[65]

Like many Hull House and other settlement residents, Gates performed various sorts of social outreach work and also became a political activist. In 1896 she joined the picket lines of Chicago's garment workers to seek higher wages, and was arrested in a 1914 restaurant strike and again in another garment workers' demonstration the following year. In 1911 she became an active member of Chicago's Socialist Party, advocating a Christian vision of a unified, cooperative society. "I became a Socialist because I was a Christian," she declared, citing the Hebrew prophets as well as Jesus on the need for social reform. At one point she became a candidate for alderman of the 19th Ward as an opportunity to promote her agenda.[66]

In addition to this sort of semiradical Progressivism, Gates also pursued a gospel of reform through the arts. Imbued by an early immersion in John Ruskin's teaching that the shoddy art produced by industrial society was indicative of moral failure in suppressing the aesthetic production of the individual laborer, she took various steps to implement the philosophy of the Arts and Crafts movement through Hull House's programming. This included art classes, art and handicrafts exhibits, and the promotion of art education in the public schools, which led to her serving as president of the Public School Art Society. In 1897 she spent some time in London learning the art of bookbinding, followed by the establishment of the Hull House Bookbindery the following year. This attempt to educate immigrants in craftwork proved ironically unsuccessful as a means of promoting beauty for poor people, since the resulting products were too labor-intensive and expensive for any but elite patronage. "If I had thought it through," she lamented in later years, "I would have realized that I would be using my hands to create books that only the rich could buy."[67]

In 1883 Gates joined the Episcopal Church, thus parting religious ways with the more secular-minded Addams. During the early 1890s she became affiliated with the Society of the Companions of the Holy Cross, which had been founded by Emily Malbone, the daughter of a prominent Hartford family, in 1884. The original purpose of the society was to provide a spiritual connection for Malbone's invalid friend Adelyn Howard, who was otherwise isolated from the broader world. The practice of intercessory prayer—petitioning God for the well-being of particular individuals or groups—has remained a central devotional practice of the group into the present. The society grew rapidly, establishing branches across the nation and meeting annually for a retreat that in 1913 found a permanent home at "Adelynrood" ("Adelyn's cross") in Byfield, Massachusetts, a location chosen for its proximity to Boston churches and cultural institutions. Its members were women, primarily Episcopalians, from a variety of backgrounds, but most were academics and professionals. Several of them were settlement house residents, and Malbone tried for a time to make such houses centers for the society, helping equip some with the basic elements needed for Anglican daily worship. This venture proved unsuccessful, but the society flourished nonetheless among women dedicated to "plain living and high thinking," who shared a "search for the inner spiritual life; a deep interest in literature; communal worship; a dedication to social service and social justice; [and] the appreciation of a form of spiritual experience."[68]

Gates was active in the Chicago chapter of the society and received spiritual direction from its chaplain, James O. S. Huntington, the founder of the first Episcopal male religious order in the United States. She had always been under the strong influence of her aunt Eliza, however, who had in 1854 converted to Roman Catholicism, and Gates had been deeply impressed by a visit to the Benedictine Abbey at Monte Cassino she had made with Addams. Although she was put off by the Roman Catholic Church's opposition to socialism, she also grew disillusioned with what she saw as the excessively Protestant character of the Episcopal Church. In her later years and in deteriorating health, she left Hull House, abandoned her political activism, and died in a Catholic convent in upstate New York.[69]

In the extremely cold winter of 1912, the "Bread and Roses" strike broke out among the textile workers of Lawrence, Massachusetts. Drawn from fifty-one nationalities and heavily female, the strikers were coordinated by the radical International Workers of the World, led by "Big Bill" Haywood and Elizabeth Gurley Flynn. Hundreds of the strikers' children were sent to stay with sympathetic out-of-state families, a tactic that aroused both sympathy and howls of protest. Violence, mass arrests, and martial law ensued.

Speaking at a rally on the strikers' behalf was Vida Dutton Scudder, professor of English at Wellesley College and scholar of medieval English literature. (She pronounced her first name as "VEE-da.") Scudder urged nonviolent resistance and boycotts. She invoked the words of "a young Hebrew working man, later executed as a demagogue," who "said a strange thing: 'Blessed are ye when men should revile and persecute you.'" For her efforts, she was publicly denounced by the *Boston Evening Transcript*, which called for her resignation from Wellesley. The board of trustees, chaired by Bishop William Lawrence, rejected this demand, but did ask that Scudder temporarily suspend offering her course on "Social Ideals in English Letters."*[70]

Scudder (1861–1954) followed a career that was in some ways similar to that of Gates, although she remained both a socialist and an Episcopalian to her dying day. She was the daughter of a Congregationalist missionary who drowned during a mission in India while Scudder was an infant. She soon returned to Massachusetts with her mother, who belonged to a prominent Boston family and had been converted to the Episcopal Church by Phillips Brooks, who later confirmed Vida. Among her uncles were E. P. Dutton, the publisher quoted at this chapter's beginning; Horace Scudder, the editor of the *Atlantic Monthly*; and the somewhat eccentric Horace Dutton, a Christian social reformer who gave away his entire fortune. After spending much of her early life in Europe with family and becoming immersed in the history of art, she matriculated at Smith College in 1880, the year after its first class had graduated. After college she became one of the first American women to study at Oxford, where she heard John Ruskin's last course of lectures and became deeply influenced by his critique of industrial civilization. Her

---

*Bishop Lawrence, who is alleged to have remarked that "godliness is in league with riches," was the grandson of Amos Lawrence, after whom the city was named. He was also the cousin of Harvard president A. Lawrence Lowell, whose name included those of two family-founded mill towns.

early exposure to the thought of F. D. Maurice through her mother was now revived, and she became simultaneously aware both of contemporary issues of social class and the richness of the medieval Catholic heritage. Upon returning to Boston, she took a master's degree at Smith and declined an offer to teach at her alma mater in favor of Wellesley, where she remained for the rest of her forty-year career, living with her mother and various female companions.[71]

At Wellesley Scudder pursued a career as one of the nation's first prominent female scholars, writing prolifically on medieval literature, Christian socialism, and the Franciscan tradition. In 1887 she had a reunion with Smith friends Jean Fine and Helen Rand. Rand had been inspired by a visit to Toynbee Hall to establish a settlement house in this country. In cooperation with Scudder's Wellesley colleague Katherine Lee Bates (the author of "America the Beautiful") and other Seven Sisters alumnae, the trio founded the College Settlements Association. The first fruit of their enterprise was the Rivington Street Settlement in New York, which preceded the opening of Hull House by only two weeks, although Scudder's group had never heard of Jane Addams. In 1892 two more ventures opened under the group's auspices, the College Settlement in Philadelphia and Denison House in Boston. It was the latter that became thereafter a major focus for Scudder's life until she and her mother left Boston for Wellesley in 1912.[72]

Scudder found in settlement work an escape from the sense of isolation and unreality that had plagued her since childhood. Headworker Helena Dudley was able to achieve Scudder's vision of the settlement as a genuine community between the poor and the college women who staffed them. The South Cove neighborhood served by Denison House included a variety of immigrants, including Chinese, Irish, and Syrians, but Scudder was particularly attracted to the Italians, given her early exposure to Italian culture. Scudder presided as "La Bossa" over a large "Circolo Italo-Americano," even though her Italian was closer to that of Dante than of Boston's newcomers. (Unlike many settlement house workers, who encouraged immigrants to celebrate their heritages, Scudder became frustrated with peasant culture and aimed her programming instead at the elite.)[73] Exposure to these Italians, who as a community were conflicted between strategies of isolation and assimilation, gave her perspective on her own heritage. She contrasted what she characterized as the patience and hospitality of the poor with "hard self-respecting New England, insensibly dominated by the duty of paying one's debts, after which, if one had a fairly safe bank balance, the luxury of charity might be enjoyed."[74]

As the vignette that began this chapter dramatically illustrates, Scudder was also deeply involved in contemporary social issues, both in theory and in practice. In her 1912 *Socialism and Character* and numerous other writings on the subject, she attempted to develop a theological groundwork for a moderate Christian socialism that was neither utopian nor millennialist. She grew critical of the earlier Social Gospel as overly optimistic. She remained strongly influenced by the incarnationalist emphasis of Maurice and the social criticism of Ruskin, while finding value in more contemporary thinkers such as Tolstoy. In addition to participating in protests such as the Lawrence textile strike, she became involved in a variety of church-related organizations such as W. D. P. Bliss's Church of the Carpenter, and she was elected the first president of the Church League for Industrial Democracy in 1919.[75]

Scudder's activism was always informed by a spirituality that was a blend of Anglo-Catholicism, acquired in part through her association with Charles Henry Brent and St. Stephen's, and a devotion to Saint Francis that arose from her early immersion in Italy and the Middle Ages. She wrote of "my consecration to the effort to relate the history and teaching of the Poverello to modern needs, which has taken precedence over all other interests in my later life." She also found inspiration in the work of Saint Catherine of Siena, whose letters she translated, who "perfectly presents the perpetual paradox— supernatural life fostered and triumphantly revealed through a church which too often crucifies the holy ones to whom it gave birth." She was a longtime member of the Companions of the Holy Cross, serving for decades as supervisor of probationary members, and carried on a running argument with Emily Malbone by maintaining that the society should more closely follow monastic discipline. Her later work, such as the 1921 *Social Teachings of the Christian Year*, anchored her social thought firmly in Anglican liturgy. Despite her attraction to the Roman Catholic tradition, she maintained that "within my own Anglican Communion I have been able, once surrendered to its disciplines, to breathe the air I craved."[76]

Some Outliers

Like many prominent Episcopalians of the era, James Otis Sargent Huntington (1854–1935) came from a New England family that dated to early Puritan days. His father, Frederick Dan Huntington, had been a Unitarian minister and Harvard professor who converted to the Episcopal Church and became rector of Emmanuel Church in Boston's newly developing Back Bay.[77] The older Huntington had carried out extensive social outreach ministries in all of his posts, including service as bishop of Western New York. After graduation from Harvard, his son James, like George Hodges, attended Saint Andrew's Divinity School in Syracuse, which had been established by the senior Huntington. It was through his father that he acquired a deep saturation in the thought of Maurice, as well as experience at a mission to English and German mill workers near Syracuse.[78]

In 1880, during a retreat at the very Anglo-Catholic St. Clement's in Philadelphia conducted by the Cowley Fathers, the younger Huntington discerned a calling to a particular kind of religious vocation.[79] The Cowley Fathers (more formally known as the Society of St. John the Evangelist) were among the religious orders that had been springing up in Victorian England for the first time since monasticism had been suppressed by Henry VIII, who had seized the orders' extensive land holdings to reward his supporters. When Huntington now experienced a call to the monastic life, he decided against affiliation with Cowley or other English orders, which already had a presence in American Anglo-Catholic parishes such as Boston's Church of the Advent as well as, for a short period, St. Clement's. Instead, he and two like-minded young companions established the Order of the Holy Cross in New York City. Although the other two fell by the wayside, Father Huntington in 1884 made his final profession of vows of poverty, chastity, and obedience to Bishop Henry Codman Potter, with Bishop Huntington participating.[80]

Huntington's monastic enterprise, which seemed radical to many Episcopalians who affirmed the denominational identity implied by the now seldom-used name "Protestant Episcopal Church," was recognized by Potter and other Broad Churchmen such as Rainsford on the grounds that the work that they had been performing in Manhattan's East Side tenements was socially valuable.[81] Holy Cross shared the British Anglo-Catholic commitment to work among the poor, but was more democratic in structure and more centrally committed to its social mission than, for example, the Cowley Fathers. While continuing this social outreach, which included early versions of the parish house and settlement house, Huntington became increasingly involved in systemic reform. He gained considerable notoriety for his public support of the "Single Tax" program of Henry George, who maintained that social inequities could be corrected through a confiscatory tax on the value of land.[82] He joined the Knights of Labor, lectured widely on labor issues, and helped mediate a coal strike in Illinois in 1888 as well as other protests. Huntington was also, in 1887, the founder of the Church Association for the Advancement of the Interests of Labor (CAIL) (mentioned earlier in connection with Bishop Potter), an Episcopal society that worked with unions to promote the well-being of workers. CAIL grew rapidly, with most of the denomination's bishops becoming honorary vice presidents.[83]

The Order of the Holy Cross eventually decided that its outreach work in the slums was not proving very effective and that its inner-city location was not conducive to its growth. In 1892, against Huntington's wishes, it abandoned its urban social outreach and moved from New York to a property that had been donated to them in rural Westminster, Maryland. Having taken a vow of obedience and no longer the superior, Huntington was obliged to follow. The order's mission work was put into the care of the Sisters of St. John the Baptist, the group with whom Huntington and his associates had worked in their early years. The monks, who numbered twenty-three by the time of Huntington's death in 1935, conducted retreats—at Adelynrood, among other places—and made an impact especially as founders of boarding schools, including Kent in Connecticut and St. Andrew's in Tennessee. The order continues to this day at the monastery designed for it in 1904 by Henry Vaughan in West Park, New York, with branches in Santa Barbara, Toronto, and South Africa.[84]

If Huntington mounted a radical critique of the American political economy within an Anglo-Catholic framework, William Dwight Porter Bliss (1856–1926) represented, if anything, even more radical views within the theological context of the Broad Church movement. Bliss was born to missionary parents in Constantinople and began his career as a Congregationalist minister. After gaining firsthand experience of working-class life at a parish in South Natick, Massachusetts, Bliss joined both the Knights of Labor and the Episcopal Church in 1885; two years later he was ordained as an Episcopal priest and became the rector of the Grace Church Mission in Boston's South End, supported by the Episcopal City Mission. He read Maurice and Kingsley as well as Henry George and the utopian novelist Edward Bellamy, and was a charter member of the first Nationalist Club based on Bellamy's advocacy of the nationalization of industry and state ownership of capital.[85]

Bliss was drawn to the Episcopal Church partly because of the protection its polity afforded clergy from congregational control, but also because of the line of Anglican thought from Richard Hooker to Maurice that regarded church and state as dual aspects of a common community and clergy as "civil officers" responsible for the common good. Anglicanism's inclusion of a variety of theological persuasions also sat well with his ecumenical outlook. So did its sense of this-worldliness, expressed in the social reform programs blossoming within the Church of England. After becoming established in that communion, he embarked on a career as campaigner for his gradualist, rather Fabian socialist ideas, founded on the notion of an organic unity of society as opposed to laissez-faire individualism. With Huntington he was one of the founding members of CAIL in 1887; helped found the Society of Christian Socialists in 1889; and in 1891 became the organizing secretary and lecturer for the Church Social Union, which was modeled on an English predecessor, and in which Richard Ely and Bishop Huntington had been instrumental. He lectured extensively, edited a rather short-lived journal, *The Dawn*, and in 1897 published *The Encyclopedia of Social Reform*, a massive compendium of information on social issues.[86]

One of Bliss's more innovative ventures was the Mission of the Carpenter, which opened in Boston in 1890. The mission, incorporated two years later with Bliss as rector, aimed at social inclusiveness across class lines, ecumenical outreach through the downplaying of doctrine and creeds, and practical social action. This was supplemented by the Brotherhood of the Carpenter, a parish guild that tried to promote such action through means such as spotlighting employers with good records of dealing with labor and helping find employment for members in need. Relations between the mission and the brotherhood varied over the following years. Neither was a resounding success, and both came to an end in 1896 when Bliss turned his attention to lecturing. For a few years, however, these ventures provided a center for lively fellowship among reform-minded Bostonians, including Vida Scudder. Scudder later recalled that "we feasted on ham and pickles and hope for an imminent revolution" in a spirit of "true agape."[87]

A Worldly People

Bliss and his hopes for an inclusive, egalitarian society based on the teachings of Jesus and attained gradually without the conflict of social classes was a not very popular extreme of social thought among Episcopalians during the era. Sumner, in his Yale years, gave extreme expression to a laissez-faire position that continues to exercise a strong appeal in American society into the present day. At still another extreme was the medievalism of Ralph Adams

Cram, which had considerably more impact as a program for church building than for the reform of society, where Cram's copiously expressed ideas were largely ignored.

Although many prominent church members, such as J. P. Morgan and Henry Clay Frick, remained deeply conservative, there nevertheless did emerge a set of themes of reform that resonated widely among clergy, laity, and bishops. This reform-mindedness had a major impact in the committees that the national denomination began to create during the early twentieth century to investigate social issues and also informed much parish and diocesan programming. Although it had assumed the status of a denomination within the American context, the Episcopal Church had always retained in its collective memory the idea of establishment—that it had a destiny to serve as a national church on the model of the Church of England. As a "church" rather than a "sect" or "denomination," it had an obligation to the whole of society, not simply to its formal membership. This inclusivity had been part of the context for Toynbee Hall and the Anglo-Catholic slum missions that had arisen in London in the later Victorian era.

Such inclusivity had been given theological legitimation by Frederick Denison Maurice, whose work, as we have seen, had a pervasive influence among American Episcopalians of the Progressive era. For Maurice, the focus of Christianity was neither individual salvation nor sacramental piety; rather, it was the hastening of the Kingdom of Christ in the world of the here-and-now. Maurice's interpretation of the Incarnation—the Word become Flesh—as a sacralizing of the secular sphere provided a rationale for the attention of Christians to the needs of the casualties of the social upheavals that had given rise to the teeming industrial cities of the era. Although many Episcopalians lived out their worldliness in the sensual luxuries of what Thorstein Veblen labeled the conspicuous consumption of the "leisure class," others saw their mission as transforming the world that lay around them into one that took seriously Jesus's mandate to love one's neighbor as oneself.

The institutional church, which included many parishioners whose circumstances were often comfortable or better, provided immigrants and other urban poor with immediate physical relief as well as some social and cultural capital in the form of marketable skills, connections to employment, an enhanced work ethic, and knowledge of how to navigate the baffling world of the American city. Some of these same churches served as networking sites for Progressive reformers who were at times working at cross-purposes with other congregants who had a vested interest in maintaining the established political system. The settlement house served similar functions, bringing together well-educated and idealistic young people to work with immigrants and expand their own social and intellectual networks. Occasionally a more radical venture, such as the Church of the Carpenter, pursued the goal of transcending class lines, but did not fare as well as organizations in which those lines were in fact maintained.

Episcopal social reform took a variety of expressions, but tended toward what one might call "Progressive conservatism," grounded in an organic vision of society and a positive view of the possibilities of government. The underlying viewpoint was that of an upper middle class that sought to mediate between the perceived excesses of both the emergent upper class, which was prone toward the sins of political corruption, exploitation of the poor, and material indulgence, and the working class, especially immigrants, who could be tempted by various forms of immorality and radicalism. Although settlement house workers sought to instill in newcomers a sense of appreciation of the cultures they had brought with them, these cultures were sometimes perceived as those of the upper classes of their native lands rather than the folk arts of poor people. Almost all attempts at outreach were grounded, perhaps realistically, in a more basic sense that the poor, or at least their children, needed to acquire solid middle-class values such as hard work, honesty, and reliability, as well as a reasonable knowledge of English, if they were to survive in the American city. Many Episcopalian activists also sought to bring about reforms that would benefit working people, as well as stabilize the broader social order, in ways that merged indistinguishably with the activities of more secular-minded reformers as well as Social Gospel advocates of other denominations. Grounded in the teachings of John Ruskin, these reformers were just as apt to be critical of vulgar displays of new wealth as of the squalid circumstances to which the poor were often reduced.

CHAPTER FIVE

The Gospel of Education

The first "preppie" to make a widespread impact on the broad American consciousness was J. D. Salinger's angst-ridden Holden Caulfield, whom the reader meets as he is being expelled from "Pencey Prep." The theme of the exclusive boarding school as a setting for the unfolding of the painful drama of adolescence has continued from *The Catcher in the Rye* (1951) through John Knowles's *A Separate Peace* (1959), John Irving's *The World according to Garp* (1978), and Curtis Sittenfeld's *Prep* (2005), the protagonists of which are frequently social outsiders.[1] And, although it begins at Harvard, Erich Segal's best-selling *Love Story* (1970) has as its hero the evocatively named Oliver Barrett IV, dubbed "Preppie" by his ill-fated working-class sweetheart.

A further means through which the once-sequestered world of the private boarding school has entered the contemporary popular imagination is a best-selling work of nonfiction, Lisa Birnbach's *The Preppy Handbook* (1980), which wittily delineates from an insider's perspective the subculture of the prep school and its inhabitants and products.* Birnbach's book helped promote the merchandizing of a style of dress—khakis, button-down Oxford cloth shirts, deck shoes, and espadrilles—that had originally been the leisure attire of well-to-do northeasterners, to a mass market of middle-class Americans, most of whom had little personal contact with the world of boarding schools and their kindred institutions. Once purveyed to a local elite by regional stores such as Brooks Brothers and the original L.L. Bean in Freeport, Maine, the prep style is now marketed through mail-order firms such as Land's End, Talbots, J. Crew, and a vastly expanded national version of L.L. Bean.

---

*A less successful sequel, *True Prep*, by Birnbach and others followed in 2010, the jacket of which features two golden retrievers rampant. These amiable beasts have become totems of preppiedom, often adorned with bandanas while frolicking around the campus as mascots. Golden and Labrador retrievers, previously fancied primarily by prep school graduates and duck hunters, became the most popular dog breeds in the United States during the enthusiasm for all things "prep" in the 1970s and 1980s. The spellings "preppy" and "preppie"—the words function both as nouns and adjectives—are largely interchangeable with one another and with their shortened form, "prep." The term began to appear in American usage around the turn of the twentieth century, but does not seem to have become widespread until the 1970s.

That both alienation and conspicuous consumption should be associated with the prep school phenomenon in popular culture is profoundly ironic. As will become clear in this chapter, the men (and occasional women) who were leaders in the boarding school movement during its "golden age"—roughly the Civil War to the Great Depression—saw their goals as community rather than alienation, and as selfless service to a society that they denounced for its arrant materialism. Headmasters of prep schools were frequently priests of the Episcopal Church who saw their mission as the shaping of new generations of leaders who embodied all of the qualities they associated with the "Christian gentleman."* The preppies served up to the public by Salinger and Birnbach may be distortions of reality, symptoms of changing times, or ironic results of flaws in the original model that were invisible to the founders. Whatever the case—and it may involve all of these possibilities—the great Victorian founding headmasters such as Groton's Endicott Peabody and Henry Coit of St. Paul's would most certainly not have been amused.

Although Episcopalians did not invent the private boarding school in the United States, their relationship with it has been intimate. The earliest such schools—notably the academies at Andover, Massachusetts (1778), and Exeter, New Hampshire (1781), founded by members of the Phillips family—were established under Congregationalist auspices. Such private academies, whose students usually boarded with local families, were the main source of secondary education for the minority of Americans who received more than the basics at the local schoolhouse until the later nineteenth century. (Compulsory secondary education did not become widespread in many parts of the United States until the 1920s.)

The classic prep school, or "private family boarding school," at which students lived in residential units presided over by teachers called, on the English model, "masters," did not come into prominence until the decades following the Civil War.[2] It was during this phase of development that the Episcopal Church began to play a prominent role in the development of American education. For this to happen, a number of developments had to come into simultaneous play. The same age that gave rise to the Social Gospel produced, in counterpoint to the millions of immigrant urban workers who

*"Headmaster" and "rector" are more or less interchangeable terms in the Anglo-American private school context. American public school principals shared many of the administrative duties of headmasters, other than those associated with student residency, but lacked their mystique and moral authority. In most Episcopal schools, priestly ordination was a requirement for the headmaster position, and it remains so in some of these schools today.

manned the great new factories, a much smaller cohort of wealthy industrialists and financiers who benefitted from the labors of the toiling masses. This emergent *haute bourgeoisie*, which was attracted to the Episcopal Church in large numbers, was no longer satisfied with the residential and educational possibilities of the industrial cities that produced their wealth.

This new wealth—combined with some older money in established cities such as Boston and New York—was put to use not only for private aggrandizement, as manifested in the great mansions of Fifth Avenue and Newport, but also for the good of the (sometimes rather limited) public. Following the lead of lapsed Presbyterian philanthropist Andrew Carnegie and his "Gospel of Wealth," the newly rich invested in cultural institutions, such as those I describe chapter 6, which were intended both to civilize the masses and give their cities a cachet that might rival that of their much older European counterparts. They also supported a new set of deliberately exclusive institutions that would insulate themselves and their children from classes of people they considered undesirable. For adults, the downtown club, such as New York's Union League, and later the suburban country club were founded so that networking among the elite could take place in a refined atmosphere. In an age in which immigration restriction first became a pressing issue, these clubs often explicitly excluded ethnic and religious groups, particularly Jews and Catholics, whose members were perceived as insufficiently socialized into the mores of white Anglo-Saxon Protestant society.[3]

Consciousness of racial superiority and its defense on ideological grounds had, prior to the Civil War, been mainly focused on the relationship of those of European descent to enslaved Africans and their descendants. In the decades following that conflict, the concept of race was now applied to make distinctions among Europeans, so that Jews, Irish, and Italians were construed as constituting separate (and inferior) racial groupings who were potentially dangerous. Jews were seen as intelligent and ambitious, and as being able to muster the financial resources requisite for entrée into elite institutions; their reputation as sharp dealers and as "pushy," however, made them socially undesirable. In the process, an older generation of successful and highly assimilated German-speaking Jews, who had previously been reasonably welcome in polite society, were now lumped with their less domesticated Eastern European kinfolk as unacceptable. Irish, Italian, and Slavic Catholics, primarily working class, were seen as engendering criminality, labor organization, and political corruption, while their ecclesiastical leaders presented competing claims of moral authority. In contrast, the emergent elite embraced a new self-consciousness about the superiority of its Anglo-Saxon heritage and an Anglophilia that bestowed social cachet on all things English—including the Episcopal Church. This "racial" consciousness inevitably infected the project of educational institution building.[4]

The war with Spain in 1898 brought to a head a number of ideological currents that had emerged from the social tensions of the era. Catholic, monarchical, and imperial, Spain had long represented a contrast for Americans, with their own Protestant, republican society. The opportunity for war, however thin the justification may have been, appealed to Americans such as Theodore Roosevelt as an opportunity for national self-assertion in the international realm as well as for cultural and individual regeneration among old-stock Protestants. The increasing relegation of middle-class American males to indoor work, and the perceived feminization of the broader culture, especially of religion, helped shape a campaign to reassert masculine character in warfare, religion, and athletics. The quest for a "muscular Christianity" that spread across the spectrum of American Protestantism in this era manifested itself in a new drive for the evangelization of dependent peoples acquired through the war (especially in the Philippines), in the physical culture of the Boy Scouts and the YMCA, and, for the new elites, in the boarding school and its distinctively masculine ethos.[5]

The modern private boarding school achieved prominence during these years and was shaped in part by all of these social and cultural currents: the emergence of a new, moneyed urban elite; the self-segregation of that elite through new residential and social patterns; its inclination toward the patronage of new cultural institutions; its self-definition as a class through the exaltation of its British Protestant heritage and the exclusion of alien others; a new emphasis on masculine identity expressed especially through "muscular Christianity"; and the growing popularity of the Episcopal Church. It would, however, be a mistake simply to write off the boarding school as a means for the creation and perpetuation of a privileged WASP elite. The roots of these schools antedate the post–Civil War "classic" period of their flourishing and reflect serious attempts at educational reform in a rapidly evolving American society.

Origins

Episcopalians were not the first religious community to be involved in the shaping of an urban elite, although arguably they were the first to do so on a national scale. The Quakers had played such a role in eighteenth-century Philadelphia, and the Unitarians—the liberal wing of the old Puritan Congregational tradition—did so in nineteenth-century Boston. We can find the beginnings of the modern boarding school among the Unitarians. Although Unitarians focused their educational benevolence on Harvard College and relied on local academies and venerable public institutions such as the Boston Latin School for such preparation as it required, a remarkable pair of young Unitarian scholars—Joseph Green Cogswell and George Bancroft—turned their attention to the reform of education at the secondary level.[6] Cogswell and Bancroft had been among the first cohort of Americans to study in Germany at a time when American colleges offered little beyond the traditional classically based curriculum. Frustrated with their early careers at Harvard and inspired by their exposure to educational reform efforts in Europe, the two collaborated on a new venture, the Round Hill School, established in Northampton, Massachusetts, in 1823.[7]

Round Hill was influenced especially by the efforts of the Swiss educator Emmanuel von Fellenberg at Hofyl near Berne. Hofyl was distinguished by, among other things, a rural setting; a broad curriculum that included both classical and modern languages as well as science, mathematics, music, drawing, and physical education; an emphasis on moral education and character accompanied by religious exercises; a highly structured daily routine; and the common lodging of students and faculty in a shared residential setting.[8] Bancroft and Cogswell attempted to translate von Fellenberg's vision to an American setting in which the values of the New England Federalist and Unitarian traditions could become the basis for the formation of a new generation of leaders.[9] Round Hill, which incorporated all the previously mentioned features of Hofyl, was the first authentic American boarding school, and a remarkably progressive one by the standards of the day. Particularly important was its notion of community: Students and teachers lived together in a "total institution" in rural Massachusetts, and related to one another on a familial rather than an individualistic or authoritarian model. ("Total institutions"—monasteries, penitentiaries, mental hospitals—are ones in which the lives of their "inmates" are completely enclosed and shaped by a single complex of buildings.)[10]

After Bancroft lost interest and Cogswell proved a poor administrator, Round Hill closed in 1834. A similar enterprise, which was personally endorsed by Cogswell, was the Flushing Institute on Long Island. Its founder, William Augustus Muhlenberg, introduced in chapter 4 as the founder of the

Episcopal Church's first religious order, was immersed in the same waves of European educational reform that had inspired Round Hill; he had gained practical experience in education while serving simultaneously as the rector of St. James parish in Lancaster, Pennsylvania, and as secretary of that city's public school board. In this latter capacity he effectively ran the local schools, according to the (English) Lancastrian system, in which older students served as monitors and taught the younger. His resignation as rector of his next parish, St. George's in Flushing, in order to devote himself full time to his new pedagogical venture, was the beginning of the involvement of Episcopalians in the boarding school business.[11]

The Flushing Institute, which opened its doors in 1828, was organized along principles very similar to those of Round Hill. The school was located in a rural setting that effectively isolated students from their wealthy families in New York and Philadelphia as well as from corrupting urban influences, and students lived together with their mentors under a common roof in a controlled environment according to a uniform schedule. The curriculum was also similar, and included physical education. Like Round Hill, the Flushing Institute rejected the notion of competition in favor of a pedagogical and disciplinary philosophy that treated boys as individuals, each of whom needed to be nurtured according to his particular abilities. The school thus functioned ideally as a family—*in loco parentis.*[12]

The major difference between the Flushing Institute and its Unitarian-oriented predecessor was the emphasis that Muhlenberg gave to Christian nurture in his enterprise. While Round Hill began and ended each day with "devotional exercises" that actually incorporated Episcopal usages, Muhlenberg's school was saturated with his own distinctive take on the Anglican tradition.[13] Muhlenberg, who described himself as an "evangelical catholic," originally envisaged a school that would combine secondary, collegiate, and theological levels, and would help prepare "Cadets of the Church" on the model of West Point, as an Episcopalian vanguard against Roman threats to American religious integrity. Although this rather grandiose vision never fully materialized, the institute was firmly anchored in an earnestly Evangelical moral ethos and religious observance in the High Church manner. Although it may have shaped good Christians, the institute failed to produce many clergy.[14]

As his plans to expand his educational enterprise proved doubtful, Muhlenberg left the Flushing Institute—which had by then evolved into

St. Paul's College and Grammar School—in 1846 to assume the rectorship of the Church of the Holy Communion in Manhattan. His work inspired a number of bishops to pursue similar educational ventures, but most of these were short-lived. One partial exception was St. James College near Hagerstown, Maryland, founded in 1842 by Bishop R. W. Whittingham in consultation with Muhlenberg. Muhlenberg's protégé, James Barrett Kerfoot, headed the new school, and later became the first president of Trinity College in Hartford and then the first bishop of Pittsburgh. The Civil War forced the college to close, but it later reopened as a secondary school; its website describes it as "the oldest Episcopal boarding school founded on the English model in the United States" as well as one of the few still headed by an Episcopal priest.[15] Whether it was actually founded on "the English model" or on a combination of Swiss and American prototypes is worth pondering.[16]

Henry Augustus Coit and St. Paul's

Both Round Hill and the Flushing Institute contributed directly to the founding of the first of the schools in what would become humorously known as the "St. Grottlesex" complex of boarding schools. ("St. Grottlesex" is a conflation of St. Mark's, St. George's, St. Paul's, Groton, and Middlesex, all but Middlesex [nondenominational] founded under Episcopal auspices.) George C. Shattuck Jr. was a prominent and wealthy Boston physician and pioneer in medical education who had attended Round Hill. It was at his home that the Church of the Advent (discussed in chapter 2) was founded in 1844.[17] Eleven years later, Shattuck set about founding a school for his own sons that would be based on Round Hill principles, but centered on the High Church brand of Anglicanism to which he had become committed. He had himself visited several of the leading English "public" schools, and had been particularly impressed with their physical plants. St. Paul's, as the school was called, was to be located on Shattuck's summer estate in Concord, New Hampshire. The board of trustees was restricted to Episcopalians and consisted mainly of friends of Shattuck, including the rector of Advent and Carlton Chase, the bishop of New Hampshire.[18]

The search for a founding rector for St. Paul's proved difficult; as Bishop Chase observed, a propos of the candidate pool, the Episcopal Church's clergy included a fair share of "drones, hypochondriacs, and eccentric persons."[19] Eventually an offer was made to Henry Augustus Coit (1830–1995)—at twenty-five, a very young priest who had previously served as a missionary in upstate New York. He accepted and remained as rector of St. Paul's until his death in 1894 at the age of fifty-nine. He was the first of a long line of rectors, at St. Paul's and its many imitators, whose personality irreversibly stamped the ethos of the institution. He was indeed, as Bishop Chase had feared, eccentric, but his very eccentricity worked to good effect in shaping the school and its young charges. Coit was shy personally, but austere, intense, and charismatic in his institutional role. Phillips Brooks characterized him as "a curious man" and "a piece of the Middle Ages." Owen Wister, an alumnus who more or less invented the Western novel, observed that Coit's "marble effigy, recumbent in the School Chapel, is rightly clothed in a monastic robe." As James McLachlan observed, Coit was to become "the pattern and epitome of the American headmaster of the Victorian age."[20]

To head a school intended to be an Episcopal successor to the Round Hill tradition, Coit had the perfect lineage. He had attended Flushing Institute; served as a tutor at its offshoot, St. James College; and been deeply influenced by his mentor Muhlenberg in both his churchmanship and his educational philosophy. The goal of St. Paul's, which Coit had internalized and exemplified, was the shaping of Christian gentlemen. The isolated rural setting, curricular structure, and familial arrangement were all retained from the Round Hill/Flushing Institute model. If anything, St. Paul's was even more intensely religious, on High Anglican lines, than its predecessors. Most of the masters were ordained Episcopal clergy. Chapel observances were elaborate and included daily Morning and Evening Prayer, Sunday worship service, saints' days, and festivals of the liturgical year. Coit's presence informed the compulsory services, and his sermons were described by school historian August Heckscher as the "sustained elevation of a vision fixed on values beyond the day." One alumnus, however, remembers that his sermons were less memorable than his performance of the liturgy: "No other man ever seemed to me so perfect a living voice of the Prayer Book." Coit also conducted a semiannual catechetical examination in front of masters, visitors, and the bishop, where each boy was questioned by Coit, with the rector's "almost awful righteousness."[21]

It is not surprising that such an elaborate schedule of liturgical worship would require an appropriately ornate physical setting. An early (1858) chapel still stands and contains memorial windows, plaques, and tablets from the early days of St. Paul's. (This propensity for physical testimony to the institution's history became a standard technique of boarding schools, as well as colleges, for creating an almost instant sense of tradition.) A more imposing statement of the centrality of religion to campus life is the Chapel of St. Peter and St. Paul, designed by Henry Vaughan in 1886 and enlarged in subsequent years. This structure has been characterized by architectural historian John Coolidge as "the first American chapel"—figuratively, at least, in the sense of its status as a prototype for the monumental boarding school house of worship.[22]

St. Paul's Chapel intentionally evokes the "Oxbridge" fashion of building for collegiate worship in the monastic tradition—rows of stalls in the nave face one another—and more specifically reflects the design of Bodley's chapel at Queen's College, Cambridge. Its soaring tower—at 120 feet, almost as tall as the chapel is long—echoes fifteenth-century Perpendicular Gothic prototypes in England's West Country. Its many memorial busts and tablets include an effigy of Coit by Bela Pratt, the prominent sculptor whose work includes the bust of Phillips Brooks at Boston's Trinity Church as well as the personifications of Art and Science at the opposing Boston Public Library. The reredos, based on that at Winchester Cathedral, features paintings from the English firm of Clayton & Bell, who also did the chapel's stained glass, and wood carving by Johannes Kirchmayer. The overall style, according to Vaughan's biographer, is "a combination of scholarly historicism and Victorian Arts and Crafts sensibility." Vaughan became the official St. Paul's architect in 1902 and designed a number of other campus buildings in a combination of late Gothic, Jacobean, Georgian, and Anglo-Dutch modes.[23]

There were some things, however, that St. Paul's during the Coit years was not. Although its usages and architecture did have some English resonances, the fundamental conception of the institution was not based on English models, but rather stood in the Swiss-American lineage of Round Hill and the Flushing Institute. This was a period during which English and American boarding schools, as we shall see, were evolving simultaneously in similar directions. Nor was Coit particularly Anglophiliac. In addition, St. Paul's was not, at this stage, very much of a "prep" school. Coit had inherited from Round Hill's leaders an ambivalence toward the colleges of the day—especially Unitarian Harvard—as deficient and retrograde in their curricula and academic standards. (Coit had briefly attended the University of Pennsylvania as well as St. James, but favored Trinity College in Hartford over the Ivies because of its affiliation with the Episcopal Church.)[24] Only five of the first seventy graduates of St. Paul's attended college; many of the rest entered directly into the business world.[25] Finally, St. Paul's in the early years was not oriented toward "muscular Christianity" in a serious way, although gymnastics, on the Round Hill model, was present almost from the beginning. Coit himself was unathletic and generally unenthusiastic about sports. He did eventually give in to student demand for cricket, an enterprise he thought far more gentlemanly than the rowdy American pastime of baseball.[26] Rowing, similarly, was deemed acceptable because of its genteel associations. Team sports, however, remained intramural until well into the twentieth century.[27]

Another way in which Coit and the early St. Paul's challenged, to an extent, the popular narrative of the American boarding school was in the realm of wealth and social class. To be sure, the founders and trustees of the institution from its conception in Shattuck's mind had been men of wealth, and it was their sons and those of their peers who would constitute the large majority of the student body for decades to come. Muhlenberg had earlier voiced unease about the situation. "Alas," he had written to Kerfoot in 1851, "so long as church schools can receive only the children of the rich, they will be raising crops of weeds." Coit, himself the son of an Episcopal clergyman, shared his mentor's distrust of the effects of wealth and of the emergent industrial society that was producing it. His answer was not to close St. Paul's to the Mellons, Morgans, and Vanderbilts who sent him their children, whose loss would have been disastrous for the enterprise; rather, he enforced an almost monastic regimen upon these privileged lads, who slept in curtained cubicles in Spartan dormitories. St. Paul's graduates might have had great wealth thrust upon them, but Coit did his best to ensure that it would not corrupt the values of his Christian gentlemen.[28]

Coit, then, was the embodiment of the values of the school he helped establish: "For almost forty years, Henry Coit was St. Paul's school."[29] He thus became the prototype for a succession of protégés and imitators of "the founding headmaster," a new social and educational type that was rapidly emerging in this era. (Coit, for example, put the bee in the bonnet of Joseph Burnett to found St. Mark's School in Southampton, Massachusetts, in 1865.) A sort of "apostolic succession" of headmasters or rectors thus arose, in which a master at one school might be called to found or lead another.[30] It was in this context of an expanding market for elite secondary education on the St. Paul's model that a headmaster would emerge whose reputation was to eclipse even that of Coit's: Peabody of Groton.

Endicott Peabody and Groton

Endicott Peabody (1857–1944), known as "Cotty" to friends and family, and "the Rector" to generations of Groton students, shared much with Coit in his educational vision, but brought with him an entirely different heritage. His family (as well as that of his wife Fanny, who was his first cousin) traced back to the earliest Puritan era, and their mutual great-grandfather, Joseph, had been the foremost merchant of Salem in its heyday. Peabody's father Samuel made a crucial career move that was to have a major impact on his son's professional development. In 1870, when Endicott was thirteen, Samuel was invited by Junius S. Morgan—father of the great J. P. Morgan—to be his business partner, representing the firm in London. The next year, Endicott began a five-year academic career at Cheltenham, one of England's "public" (in American terms, "private boarding") schools.[31]

Peabody's Cheltenham sojourn evolved into one of the first direct linkages between English and American private secondary education, a connection that had been oblique at best for Coit. Cheltenham was one of the boarding schools newly founded in the mid-nineteenth century at a time when a wave of reform was dramatically changing its older counterparts, some of which dated to the later Middle Ages. Winchester, the oldest, had been established in 1382 by Bishop William of Wykeham for the education of "poor scholars." By the early nineteenth century it and its prestigious counterparts, such as Eton, Harrow, and Rugby, were serving a much posher constituency and had also become notorious for flogging—discipline by severe corporal punishment—and fagging, in which underclassmen acted as servants to seniors. "Reading over the literature of the period," McLachlan remarks, "one is often reduced to the somewhat lurid impression that when Regency students were sober enough they spent most of their time either beating or raping one another."[32]

Spearheading the reform of the English public schools was Thomas Arnold, who became headmaster of Rugby in 1828 and set about at once through the force of his personality to transform the school into a place of classical learning and moral uprightness. An influential early leader of the Broad Church movement in the Church of England as well as a master pedagogue, Arnold was determined to make his boys "vicars of righteousness," and left an indelible impression on Anglo-American education as well as on his immediate charges. His reputation on both sides of the Atlantic was greatly enhanced by the success of Arthur Penrhyn Stanley's *Life of Arnold* (1844) as well as Thomas Hughes's fictionalized *Tom Brown's School Days* (1857). (The

Endicott Peabody, founding rector of the Groton School. (Courtesy of Groton School)

latter was the first of a genre of novels set at public schools that continued in J. K. Rowling's "Harry Potter" series.)[33] Arnold was ultimately overshadowed by his literary son Matthew and skewered as an "Eminent Victorian" by the social critic Lytton Strachey.[34]

Perhaps even more influential in school reform than Arnold was Edward Thring, who served as headmaster of the Uppingham School from 1853 to 1887. Though nearly as old as Rugby, Uppingham had subsisted in obscurity until Thring—also ordained in the Church of England—transformed it into a model boarding school. The revitalized Uppingham emphasized the development of the "whole boy" together with a curriculum that balanced the traditional classical subjects with art, music, shop, and the first gymnasium in England. Thring was in agreement with Arnold that boys should be trained to be Christians, gentlemen, and scholars, in that order of emphasis. Thring also introduced at Uppingham the "cottage system," in which a cohort of thirty boys lived together with a master as a small Christian community. These notes of reform were in the air during Peabody's time in the English public school system; if Cheltenham was not in its vanguard, it was imbued with a strong spirit of public—that is, imperial—service, a note to which Peabody would return.[35]

After finishing at Cheltenham, Peabody matriculated at Trinity College, Cambridge, where he read law, rowed, and played cricket. Though his family had shared the Unitarian persuasion of their place, time, and class, he now became saturated with the ethos of Anglicanism, as many of his Cantabrigian friends were deeply invested in that tradition. "In the Church of England," his biographer wrote, "he found that warmth, color, and form which his soul needed." He also was exposed to the aegis of Charles Kingsley, who was recently departed, but made a serious mark on the Cambridge scene through his mixture of muscular Christianity, Broad Churchmanship, and a biting critique of the inhumanity of industrial society. Kingsley, like many Victorian social critics, contrasted the rampant individualism of his times with a nostalgic vision of a *gemeinschaftlich* Christian commonwealth they imagined that pre-industrial England had embodied. In McLachlan's words, "It was this complex of inchoate ideals and notions—of the Anglo-Saxon mission, of a lurking distrust for industrial capitalism, of a hope for an organic Christian community—that Peabody brought with him to State Street."[36]

State Street was the heart of Boston's financial district, to which "Cotty" returned after Cambridge to enter the family firm of Lee, Higginson, and Company. Business, however, was not to his liking; for vocational guidance he sought the counsel of Phillips Brooks. This encounter resulted in Peabody's enrollment at the Episcopal Theological School in Cambridge, a center for the emergent Broad Church movement in the United States. His studies there were interrupted for several months while he answered a somewhat improbable call to a ministerial presence in Tombstone, then in its wild and woolly frontier days. During his brief stay in that frontier outpost he established the first Episcopal Church in Arizona, having thoroughly impressed the rather rowdy locals with his particular embodiment of muscular Christianity.[37]

After returning to his theological studies, he did some preaching at St. Mark's School in Southborough, Massachusetts, the first prep school to have been founded on the model of St. Paul's. Approached about the headmastership, he was unable to accept, since he was not yet ordained. He also turned down a suggestion from Phillips Brooks that he teach at St. Paul's for a year for experience. Leighton Parks—earlier encountered in chapter 2 as the rector of St. Bartholomew's in Manhattan—soon afterward suggested to Peabody, who was serving as his assistant at Boston's Emmanuel Church, that he consider founding a school himself. His connections with the Lawrence family—like the Peabodys, pillars of Boston's "Brahmin caste"—led to an invitation to establish a school in rural Groton, where they volunteered to buy land near their estate for the purpose. (This turned out to be a ninety-acre farm, which they had had assessed by Frederick Law Olmsted, the leading landscape architect of the day, who found it worthy.) A board of trustees was assembled in February of 1884 that included Parks; William Lawrence, then dean of the Episcopal Theological School and later bishop of Massachusetts; J. P. Morgan; and assorted Endicotts, Peabodys, and Lawrences. Bishop Phillips Brooks served as president. McLachlan aptly describes this rallying of support by family, friends, and church connections as "setting Cotty up."[38]

The Preface to the Records of the Trustees read as follows:

> In the early part of 1883, Endicott Peabody, who had been five years at Cheltenham College, one of the newer schools of England, who had also graduated at Cambridge University, and at that time was a student in the Senior Class of the Episcopal Theological School, Cambridge, Massachusetts, wished to make an attempt to found a boys' school in this country somewhat after the manner of the Public Schools in England.
>
> As these schools, under the influence of the Church of England, have developed a kind of manly Christian character, he believed that a School, under the influence of the Protestant Episcopal Church, would do a similar work in this country.
>
> He was assured by men experienced in such matters that, owing to changes in methods of education and the rapid growth of the large cities, there was a demand for such an Institution.
>
> In the autumn of the same year he began the work of Foundation in earnest. A fine estate in Groton, Massachusetts, was promised, unexpected support in money was obtained and much interest in the scheme was expressed both in Boston and New York.[39]

Thus was Groton launched, in a fashion and on premises not very different from St. Paul's—with the exception of the open appeal to the English public school model, which by now resonated with an increasingly Anglophiliac and wealthy clientele. The rapid success of Groton depended in large measure on the same force that had powered St. Paul's: a charismatic headmaster whose overpowering personality seemed to incarnate the school's essence. Part of both men's charisma derived from a common sense of religious mission as Episcopal priests. Although Coit was Anglo-Catholic—in later years, he identified increasingly with the Cowley Fathers—and Peabody was Broad Church, both saw their mission to be the molding of Christian gentlemen.[40]

During the early years, Peabody was extremely successful in generating financial support and expanding Groton's campus rapidly. Peabody himself described the relationship of the campus's plan and fabric to his educational and moral vision in a Boston diocesan periodical in 1900:

> At one end of a large open quadrangle stands the chapel, which is still in the process of construction. Close by are the gymnasium and fives [an English version of handball] courts; opposite to these is the schoolhouse; between them on either side are the houses in which the boys live, and in the centre [*sic*] lies the playground. Such a plan seems to emphasize the unity as well as the comprehensiveness of the life of the boys. It is as natural for them to go to one place as another. The quadrangle represents to them the all-round man with learning and physical strength and home life and spiritual truth coming as a matter of course into his expanding nature. The chapel, when it is finished, will be the most beautiful of all the buildings and will dominate the group, as it is intended that the spiritual life shall dominate the development of the boy's character.
>
> The different buildings have been constructed at a large expense through the generosity of friends of the school. They have been planned with a belief that the "almighty wall," as a schoolmaster [Thring] has put it, plays an important part in moral training. The boys sleep in dormitories, which are divided into alcoves, or cubicles, each boy having a separate alcove simply furnished. The dormitories are large; they are easily ventilated and afford opportunities for that publicity which is the best safeguard of the moral life, at the same time giving the boy sufficient privacy.[41]

Peabody goes on to discuss other matters, such as the importance of masters with long-term vocational commitments to the institution. A number of themes present themselves, however, in simply this brief excerpt. First is the holistic view of education that Peabody had inherited through both the Swiss-American and English lineages of private education, in which academics, sports, and religious and moral formation all played complementary roles.

The importance of the built environment—"the almighty wall"—in shaping the educational experience is notable, especially the centrality and physical dominance of the chapel which, like that at St. Paul's, was designed by Henry Vaughan.[42] Another theme is the importance of generous and deep-pocketed donors, without whose support the rapid erection of such an impressive physical plant would have been impossible. Further, the internal arrangement of the dormitories was both austere and lacking in the privacy that might have permitted the sorts of adolescent naughtiness that Peabody also sought to combat through a rigorous, highly structured regimen that led to physical near-exhaustion by the end of the day. (Groton and other American schools did not import the old English system of fagging, which had encouraged sexual as well as physical abuse.)

Although Peabody's Groton did not differ dramatically from Coit's St. Paul's, it did represent some changes in emphasis that partly reflected Peabody's own personality and agenda, and partly the changing times. One was the centrality of athletics. Coit, as we have seen, encouraged physical development and gentlemanly sports, but was not himself a "jock." Peabody was. A sportsman since his English student days, Peabody hired masters in his mold, and rector, masters, and students together participated in team sports in the early days before standardization of rules. He was especially fond of football, which he believed promoted such manly Victorian virtues as honesty, courage, self-control, and unselfishness. Jesus, for him, was not a "poor, delicate, rather effeminate person who has no appeal for red-blooded men"; rather, "he was a strong man physically, muscular, sinewy, enduring." As an article in *Newsweek* observed on the occasion of Peabody's retirement in 1940, "he elevated exercise almost to the status of a sacrament."[43]

Another realm in which Groton represented a change in the ethos of "prepdom" was its relationship to colleges, especially what would later become known as the Ivy League.[44] Coit was originally suspicious of these schools on religious grounds, and Peabody maintained an ongoing antagonism toward Harvard because of what he regarded as its neglect of traditional morality with the coming of scientist Charles William Eliot to its helm in 1869. (Peabody corresponded relentlessly with his alumni, and chastised those whose conduct had come to his attention as contrary to the values instilled in them at Groton.)[45]

The clash between the values of a Harvard that increasingly valued professional expertise and the personalistic and character-based ethos of Groton became apparent when the Harvard University School Examination Board paid a visit to Peabody's domain in 1893. The committee was not amused by

Henry Vaughan, St. John's Chapel at Groton School, 1899–1900.
(Courtesy of Groton School)

either the curriculum or the quality of instruction, which they found to be amateurish and verging on the incompetent. Harvard's dean of Men, LeBaron Russell Briggs, noted the "British character of the school in language and dress" and archly commented that "the truly English urbanity of the Masters becomes in the submasters . . . a kind of artificial language . . . a suburbanity." Paradoxically, however, the committee concluded that, despite the apparent mediocrity of the instruction, Groton nevertheless delivered an excellent education.[46] Whatever Peabody's hesitations, Groton students, like those of similar schools, headed for Harvard, Yale, and Princeton in overwhelming numbers, a phenomenon modified only somewhat by the meritocratic revolution in college admissions that began in the 1950s.[47]

Another area of apparent paradox was that of social values. On the one hand, Groton's students were drawn heavily from the ranks of what would eventually become known as the "East Coast Establishment." (Jews and Roman Catholics were not so much actively excluded as self-excluding.) In its early years, 90 percent of Groton students came from families in the *Social Register*, a percentage that declined, though not dramatically, with the passage of time. Once at Groton, however, both Roosevelts and scholarship students (who existed, but were not publicized) were subject to the same regimen of cold showers and tin washbasins. Theodore Roosevelt, a close friend of Peabody's and a Groton parent, offered helpful advice to Groton students when he urged them not to take Champagne and butlers with them on camping trips in the Adirondacks. Peabody himself, in a 1908 letter to the editor, denounced "the idle rich—who are, speaking in the large, the vicious rich—are on the whole the most harmful element in our community."[48]

Peabody's connection with the Roosevelt family was indicative of another feature of his evolving set of values. Where Coit, though not oblivious to the plight of the poor, demonstrated little interest in politics, Peabody became increasingly allied with the Progressive cause—he regarded the first Roosevelt as an exemplary public servant—and made sure that Groton students were exposed to contemporary issues. Jacob Riis, the Danish-born reformer who exposed the dreadful conditions of slum life in New York City, became a good friend of Peabody and a frequent guest speaker at Groton, praising the school for its stress on personal character. Peabody also endorsed a number of the causes of the Social Gospel movement, such as the consumers' leagues that CAIL (Church Association for the Advancement of the Interests of Labor) had been promoting; in a public address in Boston in 1897 he sharply criticized in particular the plight of exploited shop workers, calling on consumers to unite to bring pressure on merchants for better conditions for their employees. Although he voted for Hoover in 1932, he soon converted to the New Deal of Franklin Delano Roosevelt (Groton '00), who had managed to avoid strenuous athletic activity by becoming manager of the baseball team. Many Groton "old boys" would play prominent roles in FDR's administration, especially in the State Department.[49]

Like his mentor Phillips Brooks, Peabody embodied the quality of Personality: like Coit at St. Paul's, he *was* Groton for the fifty-six years of his reign. Also like Brooks, he preached Character, the components of which were as much Victorian as Christian and more bourgeois than aristocratic. If Coit had been like a medieval saint, Peabody was, in the words of seminary classmate Bishop Julius Atwood, "the last of the Puritans." He little valued abstract ideas in theology or elsewhere, and felt the same way about the arts. "I am not sure I like boys to think too much" is a Peabody observation that captures his attitude. Peabody was more concerned with right action than deep thought, and Groton aimed at turning out the sort of boy who would translate Groton's values into everyday life more than one who would question the eternal verities.[50]

The Type and the Varieties

By the turn of the twentieth century, a formula or typology for the private family boarding school had developed and become highly successful in the Northeast. The ingredients included the following:

1. A charismatic headmaster—often an Episcopal priest who either founded the school or easily adapted to the specifications of the founding trustees.
2. A wealthy and well-connected board of trustees who were able to provide funding for the venture as well as create a network of prospective students.
3. A student body drawn partly from established families but primarily from the ranks of the newly wealthy, with a small number of scholarship students.
4. A rural location, self-contained and isolated from urban dangers and temptations.
5. A physical plant that included classrooms, athletic facilities, dormitories, and a prominent chapel.

6. Resident "masters" who also served as sports coaches and, when unmarried, lived with and supervised the students.

7. A rigorous daily routine of studies, sports, and other activities that left students little free time or energy for individualistic pursuits or sexual mischief.

8. Rituals and regalia, often of very recent origin, designed to instill a sense of tradition and continuity with the English public schools.

9. A classical curriculum that gradually expanded to include the sciences and other "modern" subjects.

10. A vigorous program of athletics, especially team sports, often justified in the language of "manliness" and "muscular Christianity."

11. An overall emphasis on traditional, middle-class Protestant morality and character formation.

12. A pipeline to Ivy League colleges, from which graduates would then have ready access to positions in business, government, and the professions.

13. The maintenance of close ties with alumni, who would continue to support the school financially, enroll their children (often at very early ages), and occasionally return to become masters.

Variations on this theme occurred as well. Military schools predominated in the South, with a small mixture of both military and prep schools in other parts of the country. (Michigan's Cranbrook, which makes an appearance in chapter 6, is a preeminent example of a combination of boarding and day school in the Great Lakes region.) The country day school movement, both church-sponsored and nondenominational, arose in the early twentieth century, and emulated the boarding schools in most aspects except student residency.

Another variation on this theme was the founding and operation of boarding schools by religious orders.[51] In the Episcopal Church, the Order of the Holy Cross, though small in numbers, made an impact in the field through its establishment of what were originally two very different institutions, St. Andrew's on Tennessee's Cumberland Plateau and the Kent School in western Connecticut. As described in chapter 4, the order, which had arisen through the combination of Anglo-Catholic and Social Gospel influences on James O. S. Huntington and a few like-minded individuals in the early 1880s, soon left behind both its base in New York City and its fervor for social reform, and the attention of the small core of members turned toward, among other things, education.[52]

The order's first opportunity for an educational venture was at "the Domain" of the University of the South—better known as "Sewanee"—which had been established in 1857 under the leadership of Leonidas Polk, the Episcopal bishop of Louisiana who died in battle as a major general in the Confederate Army. Sewanee was intended to be a distinctively southern, as well as Episcopal, alternative to the Ivy League. Its growth following the Civil War gave rise to a variety of primary and secondary educational ventures, including the Fairmount School for Girls, a sort of family enterprise of the theologian William Porcher DuBose; a vocational school for local girls operated by the Sisters of St. Mary; and the Sewanee Military Academy.

Still another school came into being when the Diocese of Tennessee requested the Holy Cross Order to staff what in 1905 became the St. Andrew's Industrial and Training School for Boys. Two members of the order took over the operation, which began with eight very poor boys between the ages of nine and fifteen drawn from the local farming community. Students had to farm and do other work at the school, and were charged only a nominal tuition. No single personality dominated the operation, and personnel rotated frequently. For some time St. Andrew's continued its populist mission, but eventually joined both the military academy and St. Mary's in taking on the trappings of the preparatory school. In 1968 St. Mary's closed down, with some of its students initiating coeducation at St. Andrew's. The Holy Cross Order gave up control of St. Andrew's in 1970, and the following year the academy abandoned its military character. The three institutions each represented variants on the boarding school theme: the cooperative, the military school, and the girls' school. They combined in 1981 to form St. Andrew's-Sewanee, which is very much in the family boarding school tradition and is still headed by an Episcopal priest.[53]

The Kent School, founded on Connecticut's Housatonic River in 1906, was another story. Kent's founder, Frederick Herbert Sill OHC (fondly known as "Pater") was very much in the mold of Peabody and, especially, Coit, given his monastic identity and Anglo-Catholic proclivities. (Novelist James Gould Cozzens '22 observed that "Kent had been Kent because Pater had been Pater.")[54] Though always a member of the Holy Cross Order, Sills in fact functioned as an independent entrepreneur, distancing himself from the order's supervision while remaining in sufficiently good standing to retain the support of Huntington, a frequent campus visitor. Sill started the school from scratch, renting an old farmhouse and employing a farm family as help. When the latter rapidly proved incompetent, Sill himself cooked dinner and had his students perform the chores, thus beginning a tradition of the self-help system in keeping with the school's mission of providing an elite education at reasonable cost.[55]

Unlike Coit and Peabody, Sill had to scramble hard to raise financial support, but Kent soon prospered and took on many of the aspects of the family boarding school. Costs were kept low and social barriers minimized through the self-help system, which included farm work. Athletics were important— Sill had been coxswain of the Columbia crew—but Sill and Kent were more accommodating to those students who were drawn to creative pursuits than some of Kent's counterparts. The school's High Church orientation was visible in its holidays, which included the feasts of St. Michael and All Angels, All Saints, the Purification, and Ascension. In 1929 an elaborate chapel in the Norman style was erected, with stained glass windows dedicated to various saints—including the school's patron, St. Joseph—and a set of bells for change ringing in the English manner. Kent, in short, was a variation on what had by then become a well-established theme, and "Pater" Sill took his place in the lineage of founding headmasters. If Coit had been a medieval saint, and Peabody the last Puritan, Sill was characterized by one alumnus as a Norman abbot. He also became a posthumous subject for *The Reader's Digest* feature "The Most Unforgettable Character I've Ever Met."[56]

Most of the schools established in the nineteenth and early twentieth centuries were single-sex, with the large majority for males. (Most would become coeducational in the later twentieth century.) A notable geographical outlier was the Annie Wright Seminary. What are now the Annie Wright Schools were founded in 1884 in Tacoma, Washington, by the railroad magnate Charles Barstow Wright in collaboration with James Adams Paddock, missionary bishop of what was then the Washington Territory. The school's first principal was Henrietta Wells, the wife of the rector of St. Luke's Episcopal Church (which had also been founded by Wright). The school's mission was "to provide education for the rising generation of daughters of the pioneers, children who will lay a firm foundation for the great state that is to be, a state which will require them to have kind, not callous hearts; joyous, not pampered spirits; broad, not petty minds; refined, not tawdry tastes; direct, not shifting speech—women who will meet wealth with simplicity, and poverty with dignity, and face life with quiet strength—developing from strength to strength; contributing to the righteous up-building of this great country." It flourished, attracting girls from the Pacific Northwest as well as British Columbia and Hawaii.[57]

More squarely in the Episcopalian heartland, Rosemary Hall in Connecticut was founded in 1889 by Mary Atwater Choate, whose husband, Judge William Gardner Choate, would soon thereafter establish the Choate School for boys.[58] She soon engaged an English feminist, Caroline Ruutz-Rees, the sole respondent to Mrs. Choate's newspaper advertisement for a headmistress. Ruutz-Rees (pronounced R-treece) went on to serve in that role for over forty-eight years, implementing an ideal of female education that differed considerably from Mrs. Choate's desire for a school that would train girls in "domestic arts." The school's St. Bede's Chapel, consecrated by the bishop of Connecticut in 1909, offered daily candle-light services and the chanting of the Psalms. Ruutz-Rees herself was more a moralist than a catechist, and prescribed for her students a blend of rigorous academics, muscular Christianity, and character building with a feminist twist. "You are to be brave and upright and cheerful, and not sentimental," she enjoined her girls in her letters during a sabbatical year abroad. They were to be "builders and doers in the world instead of destroyers and consumers." Her motto was "No rot."[59]

Episcopalians did not invent the boarding school, nor did they ever hold a monopoly on it. They did, however, dominate it during a crucial period in its emergence on the American scene, as administrators, teachers, trustees, donors, parents, and students. Church and school became closely allied as parts of the nexus of institutions that were developing among a nascent upper class, largely nouveaux riches, concentrated in the Northeast, but present in the Great Lakes and Pacific Coast regions as well. Boarding schools became the vehicles that would socialize and credential the children of families who had attained or were aspiring to membership in this national elite.

But it was not quite that simple. The great founding headmasters of these schools were profoundly ambivalent about their roles as gatekeepers for a sector of American society whose values and practices they often found odious. Whether monks or muscular Christians, they valued service above profit, and lamented that so many more of their charges went on to careers on Wall Street rather than the Episcopal Church. The boarding school was an alternative paradigm of organic community that contrasted sharply with the "rugged individualism" of the world of business. But school leaders did not have the realistic option of admitting more than a handful of students whose families could not afford the substantial tariff that elite education required, nor the influence that could make most of their charges swerve from the career paths that had been ordained for them. The result was that same tension and contradiction exemplified in the career of Social Gospel advocate Bishop Henry Codman Potter, who presided at society weddings while arbitrating labor disputes. The boarding schools would adapt and thrive, but the church itself would not be able to sustain the tension indefinitely.

CHAPTER SIX

The Gospel of Wealth and the Gospel of Art

"Taste is not only a part and an index of morality; it is the ONLY morality. . . .
Tell me what you like, and I'll tell you what you are."
—John Ruskin, *Traffic* (1864)

During the decades that followed the Civil War, a major shift in the economic basis of American society was taking place that had profound consequences for Episcopalians. The so-called Gilded Age was one in which fortunes on a scale previously unknown in the United States were being accumulated by men—and a few women—who profited enormously from the expansion of the American economy and its communications, transportation, and financial infrastructure on a transcontinental scale. Prior to the introduction of a graduated income tax in 1913, there were few constraints on the ways in which the wealth accumulated by the Carnegies, Rockefellers, Morgans, and their counterparts was utilized.

But people of great wealth were not entirely exempt from moral constraints. Andrew Carnegie, a Scotsman who had abandoned his ancestral Presbyterianism, became a self-appointed apostle of what came to be called the "Gospel of Wealth." Carnegie called upon his fellow "Robber Barons" to put their money to work to help shape a society in which the industrious and able would be able to transcend the adverse conditions into which they might have been born. They were to be aided and encouraged in this endeavor through such means as Carnegie's famous endowed chain of libraries, and thereby rise into positions of social and economic leadership.[1] Most religious denominations also encouraged benevolence, although exactly what form such giving might take varied from group to group and within each group. The Episcopal Church had no firm policy on such matters but, like many other churches, was entering a period of considerable and often heated debate as to what form charitable giving might best take and who, if anyone, was responsible—individuals, churches, private benevolent societies, government agencies—for the plight of the poor. The Social Gospel movement, in which Episcopalians participated actively, was one major theological and institutional response to these questions.

Another, less contested, philanthropic issue of the day was the provision of cultural institutions for America's rapidly emerging cities. Prior to the Civil War, museums, libraries, and the like were largely in private hands in the forms of individual collections; associations maintained by small, usually elite groups; and proprietary enterprises maintained by entrepreneurs such as P. T. Barnum for their own profit.[2] By the 1880s, however, a major paradigm shift had taken place among the leaders of older cities such as Boston and newly prosperous ones such as Chicago. Among the nouveaux riches, such as the Rockefellers, the patronage of cultural and educational activities helped provide an aura of cultivation, respectability, and authority. For already established families, such as the Morgans, the collection of objects of art and specimens of natural history was simultaneously a means of private recreation and enjoyment and a way to advance the cultural status of their local and national communities. Museums, libraries, symphony orchestras, and the like could uplift an uncultivated citizenry, many of whom were recent immigrants, while instilling civic pride in the wealthier classes and impressing the snobs of what one twenty-first-century government official contemptuously referred to as "old Europe."[3]

This was also an age in which, perhaps not entirely coincidentally, the Episcopal Church enjoyed a social cachet above virtually all other religious groups (with the possible exception, in some areas, of the Presbyterians). Philadelphia Quakers and Boston Unitarians, once dominant in their respective cities, now began to desert their families' ancestral faiths and enlist in the Anglican vanguard. To be sure, Episcopalians had held sway for some time in bastions such as Manhattan, where Grace and Trinity Churches were joined by St. George's, St. Thomas's, St. Bartholomew's, and St. James's as dispensers not only of sacramental grace but of social acceptance. The names of fashionable families who were already Episcopalian, like the Morgans, or those, like the Fricks, who now became so, goes on interminably: Aldrich, Astor, Biddle, Booth, Brown, Du Pont, Firestone, Ford, Gardner, Mellon, Morgan, Procter, Taft, Vanderbilt, Whitney. Episcopalian branches of the Baptist Rockefellers and Jewish Guggenheims even appeared on these family trees.[4]

It is also probably more than coincidental that most of these families were also involved in the emergent world of art collecting, whether in the accumulation of private collections—which might someday be turned over to public institutions such as the Metropolitan Museum of Art; the support of nascent public museums like "the Met"; or the creation of private museums, such as the Frick and the Morgan in New York and the Gardner in Boston. The collection of works of art—especially those of European provenance—had never been extensive among Americans prior to the Civil War. Fortunes had not been as great, European travel not as extensive, and the pictorial, material, and decorative arts had never enjoyed the cachet they would acquire in subsequent decades. When James Jackson Jarves tried to sell his pioneering collection of Italian "primitive" paintings—work by Giotto, Duccio, and the like—to an American art museum in the late 1850s, he was unsuccessful, and finally obtained a paltry $22,000 from Yale in 1871.[5]

Something of a paradigm shift seems to have taken place beginning in the 1880s, when both the private and public collecting of European art emerged as a major activity among the well-to-do and the pioneers of a distinctive American urban culture, who were frequently one and the same. This shift involved a new premium placed on physical beauty, particularly as exemplified in artistic creation. The Puritan-founded culture that had shaped American sensibilities until then had been firmly logocentric, and had privileged "the word"—which had, after all, been the means of communication between God and humanity—over pictorial or material representation of sacred knowledge. Words did not necessarily now lose their luster, but were complemented in their centrality by the beautiful *objects* that Americans now sought to possess, or at least to behold. This shift was mediated by the thought of John Ruskin in England and his American disciple, Charles Eliot Norton, in the movement sometimes called the "Gospel of Art." And, although the details lie beyond the scope of this study, the "canonization" of classical music that took place during this era added another dimension to the legitimation of the role of the various senses in the religious and cultural realms.

Episcopalians were not unique among American Christians in discovering the religious potential of the material world; Sally Promey, among other scholars, argues that liberal Protestant spokesmen such as Horace Bushnell and Henry Ward Beecher were active in the legitimation of especially the visual arts among their followers.[6] Episcopalians, however, by virtue of their wealth and the taste culture that their denomination helped shape through its sacramental practices, were particularly well positioned to play a leading role in the process. What follows are six accounts of significant instances of cultural philanthropy, centered on the careers of representative individuals. Four were laymen: William Cooper Procter, J. P. Morgan, George Gough Booth, and Henry Ford. One, Isabella Stewart Gardner, was a laywoman. The final figure treated here, as a sort of coda, was a clergyman, W. A. R. Goodwin, who successfully sought lay backing for his Williamsburg project. All save the last were wealthy, and all sought to create public exhibits they hoped would be of benefit in various ways to their fellow citizens. At the end, we will return to see what, if any, significance for these careers lay in the fact that all were, at least after a fashion, Episcopalians, and what role the Episcopal Church as an institution may have played in this cultural transition.

William Cooper Procter

For William Cooper Procter (1862–1934), soap making and Episcopalianism were equally part of the family tradition. Procter, the third in his line to bear the name "William" and known instead as "Cooper," was also the third (and last) Procter to head the venerable Cincinnati firm of Procter and Gamble. During his tenure, Procter, while deeply suspicious of unions, brought about significant innovations in working conditions by introducing sickness and death benefits, profit sharing, and "guaranteed employment," protecting workers against layoffs. He was also a pioneer in research and development and market research.[7]

Procter was a lifelong member of Christ Church in Glendale, Ohio, a parish established in 1865, which was built initially using $1,000 contributed by Procter's father.[8] Glendale, which lies directly north of Cincinnati, was arguably the nation's first planned commuter suburb, and was a stop on the path of the Cincinnati, Hamilton, and Dayton railroad line.[9] The senior Procter also funded a handsome, large stone rectory at Christ Church after his daughter Olivia married the rector, Cleveland K. Benedict, in 1895.[10] The Procters later became more seriously involved in the Episcopal Church through the marriage of another sister, Elsie, to the Reverend Paul Matthews, later bishop of New Jersey. Bishop Matthews's sister Eva was the founder of the Community of the Transfiguration, an Episcopal religious order whose mother house is still located in Glendale.[11]

Christ Church would be a major focus in the life of William Cooper Procter, who married Jane Eliza Johnston there in 1889 and later served as a vestry member for forty-five years as well as both junior and senior warden. He was elected delegate to the General Conventions of 1907 and 1910, and then again in 1931. At the 1910 convention, which was held in Cincinnati, Procter was named chairman of the Executive Committee, an office that carried with it the power to appoint the other two committee members as well as the heads of all other committees. In addition to numerous gifts and bequests to Christ Church on the parts of William and, after his death, Jane, the couple was responsible for the endowment of the diocese with a fund that now renders the bishop of Southern Ohio the most highly paid member of the American Episcopate. The diocesan retreat center in Madison County is named after Procter, who also served as president of Cincinnati's Episcopal-affiliated Children's Hospital for many years, and endowed its research foundation and home for nurses.[12]

Procter's philosophy of benevolence was clearly expressed in a 1908 letter to his niece Mary, who was then a student at the National Cathedral School in Washington. "You have been given more gifts than you realize, but they carry correspondingly greater responsibilities. We are all here primarily for the purpose of helping God bring about THE KINGDOM OF HEAVEN upon earth, and to some it is given to do much more than others."[13] Procter was also impressed with Charles Kingsley's dictum that religion is not primarily about our own salvation, but rather that service is what is essential.[14] True to these Victorian sentiments, Procter devoted his formidable energies not only to the welfare of the local and national manifestations of the Episcopal Church but to a variety of other causes as well. As chairman of the Graduate School Committee at his alma mater, Princeton, he was instrumental in thwarting then president Woodrow Wilson in his plans for siting the school's new Graduate College, and was later awarded an honorary LL.D. for his various services and benevolences.[15] During World War I he commanded a regiment of the Ohio National Guard and served as a member of the National Defense Council. He also chaired at various times Cincinnati chapters of the Red Cross, the Community Chest, and other local charitable agencies.[16]

Procter's involvement with the arts was typical of a man of his stature in his day and included membership on the boards of the May Festival Association—Cincinnati's legendary spring community choral extravaganza—and the Cincinnati Symphony Orchestra. His own musical practice was confined to singing in the Christ Church choir. His observations on meeting with a noted musician offer some insight into the way in which he related to the artistic world. "On my way home, we were introduced to [Fritz] Kreisler, the violinist . . . It was the first time I ever saw him, and I like his looks. He is a manly looking fellow, but I don't think one would pick him up as a great artist. I understand he is working very hard and saving every penny he can to send back to Austria. He has even quit his gambling, where, I have been told, all his earnings formerly went."[17]

Procter's genial admission of bourgeois propensities in relating to the arts is further illustrated in a letter dated December of 1913:

> Last night we had the Harrison's [*sic*] together at the Club and then went to see the Russian dancer, Pavlova. I am afraid I cannot interpret Art, not even in dancing. I thought her dancing wonderful and part of it very beautiful, but I could not read any meaning into it. What does a dance interpret? The music, the feeling produced by the music itself? I don't know. Any how, no matter how dumb I may be, it took a plain, ordinary everyday tango such as I dare say hundreds of those present with little practice could do, to get the only encore of the evening. I wonder what Pavlova thought?[18]

Despite his affectation of insensitivity, Procter's questions were probably more perceptive than those that might have occurred to his fictional counterpart, George F. Babbitt. (It has been suggested that Cincinnati was Sinclair Lewis's primary model for "Zenith.")[19] The role of such a man as Procter vis-à-vis the arts is perhaps best illustrated in still another epistolary anecdote/observation: "Wednesday I had meetings of the May Festival Association and the Symphony Orchestra Board. It sounds absurd—my being on musical boards. I have tried to get off several times, but just at present I am some use just as mediator between the two. In some ways I believe I can help smooth matters out better than some of the others."[20]

Procter can be looked upon as a sort of prototype of one particular kind of wealthy Episcopalian who found himself involved in the arts. In the realms of religion, culture, and the civic and political orders, he found himself driven not so much by aesthetic pleasures but rather by a profound, latter-day Victorian sense of virtue and duty shared by other well-to-do Protestants of his day. One spent time on arts boards not so much because one enjoyed the arts—although Procter apparently did, to some degree—but more importantly because here was an area in which a talented and influential man could be of service. "Money left in large amounts to individuals, unless some real sense of stewardship is taught, is a curse and not a blessing," he wrote in yet another letter.[21] But Procter was a churchman as well as a moralist. In expressing satisfaction over the success of a campaign to establish his city's Children's Hospital, he expressed this thought: "This assures the material or financial side, and if we can just develop the spiritual side, there be no question but what we can give to the Church and Cincinnati an institution of great value and service."[22]

J. P. Morgan

When J. Pierpont Morgan (1837–1913) died, he was one of the richest men in the world and also one of the most influential laymen in the Episcopal Church. His last will and testament began as follows:

> I commit my soul into the hands of my Saviour [*sic*] in full confidence that having redeemed it and washed it in His most precious blood He will present it faultless before the throne of my Heavenly father; and I will entreat my children to maintain and defend, at all hazard, and at any cost of personal sacrifice, the blessed doctrine of the compete atonement for sin through the blood of Jesus Christ, once offered, and through that alone.[23]

Morgan was not new to wealth—the family fortune started with his grandfather and continued with his father, Junius—nor was he new to religion. On his mother's side, the Pierponts, he was related to Jonathan Edwards's wife Sarah; James Pierpont, one of Yale's founders; and Timothy Dwight, one of its presidents.[24] His mother's father was the Reverend John Pierpont, whose tenure at the Old Hollis Street Church in Boston was continually threatened by his vigorous abolitionism. It was at this Congregational church that Pierpont's parents were married and at which Pierpont himself was baptized in 1837.[25] While resident in Hartford in the 1840s, however, Junius transferred his allegiance to the Episcopal Church, and son Pierpont followed suit. The latter was educated briefly at the Episcopal Academy in Cheshire, Connecticut, and later at various schools in Boston, Switzerland, and Germany.[26]

The Pierpont Morgan who began his career as a financier in New York City in 1857 had been to the manner born, at least in American *haut bourgeois* terms—he was a member, as biographer Jean Strouse puts in, of both old and new elites.[27] He met through business connections his first wife, Amelia Sturges, whose father Jonathan had been a business partner of Luman Reed, one of New York's first prominent art collectors. In an odd bit of oedipal rivalry, Junius Morgan invited Amelia on a European trip even as Pierpont was courting her. The Morgans and Sturgeses reinforced one another's cosmopolitanism and status as burgeoning connoisseurs through their association, and were rather precocious by American standards in their appreciation of the Continental artistic heritage.[28] Amelia, sadly, died within a year of her marriage to Pierpont, who subsequently married Frances Tracy, daughter of a vestryman at St. George's Church, in 1865.

Throughout his subsequent career, Morgan lived three interconnecting lives: financial baron, art collector, and churchman. Soon after his arrival in New York he began attending St. George's in Stuyvesant Square during the noted Evangelical Stephen Tyng's rectorship, and he remained a faithful member, warden, and convention delegate for the remainder of his life. The enormous wealth that he accumulated during his career was key not only to his art collecting but also to his role as an Episcopal layman. His benefactions to St. George's and to a wide variety of Anglican causes are breathtaking. During much of the time of Morgan's membership at St. George's, the rector was William Rainsford, with whom Morgan was so impressed that he agreed to hire Rainsford on the latter's own terms. Even though Morgan, not surprisingly, was something of a political conservative, he never withdrew his backing from Rainsford thereafter, as bemused as he must have been by the latter's campaigns for social reform.[29]

Morgan's benefactions to St. George's were legion. Among them were a parish house, built in memory of his father-in-law, which included lodgings for four clerical staff members; a Sunday School room with an organ; a gymnasium; men's and women's clubrooms; baths for both sexes; and accommodations for a wide variety of other institutional church-style activities.[30] For a five-year period in the early 1890s he matched every donation made to the parish, for a total of fifty thousand dollars.[31] His largesse was more than parochial, however. He was elected a member of the Board of Trustees of the Cathedral Church of St. John the Divine in 1886. The following year he became treasurer, a position he would hold for the next decade, and he also helped conduct the cathedral's architectural competition. He subscribed ten thousand dollars toward an endowment for the bishop of New York after the election of Henry Codman Potter the following year, and he privately supplemented Potter's salary to the tune of twelve-and-a-half thousand dollars annually.[32] In 1891, in a very Episcopalian gesture, Morgan sent Connecticut's Bishop Williams a case of whiskey, together with a check for two thousand dollars, to be used for his "personal comfort."[33] Although his own son attended St. Paul's, Morgan contributed to the support of Groton and St. George's as well.[34] He also made substantial contributions to non-Episcopal causes such as the YMCA, and he was a founding member of the New York Society for the Suppression of Vice.[35]

Morgan's role as an Episcopal layman, however, was by no means confined to his financial munificence. In 1869, he attended his first diocesan convention as a delegate from St. George's; in 1882, he represented not only St. George's but also Holy Innocents Church in Highland Falls, New York, where he was also a vestryman. This arrangement continued for many years.[36] In 1886, he attended the General Convention in Chicago as a delegate and was appointed to the committee, chaired by William Reed Huntington of Grace Church, to revise the *Book of Common Prayer*. Morgan immersed himself in the task, becoming an authority on the subject and buying rare editions of the *Prayer Book* for the committee's use.[37] When the new volume was adopted by the Convention in Baltimore in 1892, Morgan had privately printed copies distributed to each delegate, with a special edition on vellum given to bishops and select libraries. One especially handsomely bound copy was given to the Episcopal Church as the standard edition.[38]

Participation at the General Convention became something of an addiction for Morgan. Strouse observes that "in his Hartford youth, Pierpont had followed the proceedings of these conventions and collected autographs of the bishops. As an adult, he attended the conventions and collected the bishops."[39] It became his custom to travel to these triennial events in a private railroad car accompanied by three or four of these dignitaries—mainly from New York and New England—together with their wives, and put them up in the host city at lavish quarters he had engaged for the occasion.[40] His role at the General Convention was on one occasion musical. When the debate over one issue at the Richmond meeting in 1907 had become particularly heated, Morgan rose during the vote counting and began to sing "O Zion, Haste, Thy Mission High Fulfilling." Other delegates gradually joined in, and the atmosphere had grown markedly calm by the time the result was announced—a defeat for Morgan, who had introduced the resolution himself.[41]

Herbert Satterlee's chronicle of his father-in-law's life reveals an interesting pattern of personal devotion that emerged in tandem with his church involvements. As the Richmond anecdote suggests, Morgan was very fond of hymns, and from early in his New York days spent Sunday evenings with friends who liked to gather for a hymn-sing after dinner.[42] His favorites included "Blest Be the Tie That Binds," "I Need Thee Every Hour," "Rock of Ages," "Jesus Lover of My Soul," and "Nearer My God to Thee." He disliked novelty in hymnody, and was especially stirred by hymns that recalled his childhood.[43] He also attended and supported the 1876 revival staged in New York by Dwight L. Moody and Ira D. Sankey, names strongly associated with sentimental Victorian Evangelicalism.[44] For a period, every Christmas was celebrated at St. George's with solos by Harry Burleigh, the African American musician and arranger who held a place of eminence on the parish's musical staff.[45] Although Morgan's musical and devotional sensibilities were more "down-home" than sophisticated, and his theological bent was clearly Evangelical, he nevertheless balanced these proclivities with a religious tolerance—illustrated in his relationship with the Social Gospeller Rainsford—and a cultural sophistication that seemed at odds with other aspects of his personality.[46]

Morgan's propensity for collecting things first manifested itself during his youth, when he began to accumulate both episcopal autographs and fragments of stained glass from the churches and cathedrals of the Europe he had explored as an adolescent.[47] His alliance with the Sturges family had exposed him to a far more sophisticated knowledge of European art than that available even to wealthy American contemporaries. His collecting propensities took two directions, which ultimately became one: personal and institutional. In the former capacity, Aline Saarinen has characterized him as "the most prodigious private art collector of all time."[48] His collection eventually included "not only Old Master paintings and drawings but sculpture, majolica, tapestries, Regency furniture, bronzes, jewelry, watches, ivories, coins, armor, portrait miniatures, seventeenth-century German metalwork, Carolingian gold, rare books and illuminated manuscripts, Gutenberg Bibles, Medieval reliquaries, Limoges enamels, Gothic *boiserie*, Chinese porcelains, ancient Babylonian cylinder seals, Assyrian reliefs, and Roman frescoes from Boscoreale."[49] His fascination with "sacred places and objects" informed his extensive travels in Europe and Egypt, which were continual buying expeditions, and may help explain his particular interest in things medieval, such as his collection of 630 medieval and Renaissance manuscripts.[50]

The first venue for Morgan's collection was his home, a tasteful brownstone on Madison Avenue at the corner of 36th Street. Morgan also kept a house in London, described by Bishop William Lawrence in his biographical sketch of his sometime benefactor: "I doubt whether there was ever a private dwelling house so filled with works of the richest art. . . . It was this atmosphere of domesticity in the midst of the richest of treasures that made Prince's Gate unique; everything in the house was a part of the house, and the house was the home of its master."[51] Morgan's homes in both New York and London were periodically open to the public for viewings of his collections.

As Morgan's collections began to overflow his Manhattan house's capacity, he devised an alternate scheme for their care by employing Charles Follen McKim of the architectural firm of McKim, Mead and White to design a library suitable for a "Renaissance prince"—an archetype of artistic patronage often associated with Morgan. (McKim and his firm have been credited with revolutionizing Manhattan architecture through their lavish use of the Renaissance palatial style.) With Morgan's assent, and at considerable extra expense, McKim employed the ancient Greek technique of "dry masonry," with minimal use of mortar, to build the library. The interior was adorned with sculpture and murals created for the occasion by contemporary artists. The result, in the words of architectural historian Wayne Andrews, was "one of the great achievements of American interior decoration." For Morgan, this was not simply a repository for his artistic holdings but also a working space. The first two groups of visitors to the sumptuous West Room were the Purchasing Committee of the Metropolitan Museum and the vestry of St. George's Church, two of Morgan's favorite organizations.[52]

Morgan also followed his father's lead as a patron of the great cultural institutions that were beginning to spring up in American cities, especially New York, during the later decades of the nineteenth century. He was one of the original trustees of the American Museum of Natural History, and a participant in the founding of the Metropolitan Museum of Art in 1871.[53] Morgan invested much of his time and wealth throughout the rest of his life to the Metropolitan Museum, becoming determined that the "Met" would contain "an undreamed-of collection of art so great and so complete that a trip to Europe would be superfluous" for Americans.[54] To this end, Morgan, who was elected president of the museum in 1904, took an aggressive role in managing the institution, recruiting the best European and American curators to direct and staff it and expand and professionalize its operations.[55] He himself set an example in connoisseurship, amassing a much-read collection of art history monographs and having his own collections catalogued in a highly scholarly manner.[56] When, after his death, the entirety of his collection was displayed at the Met in 1913, the effect on the museum-going public was profound. About 40 percent of his collection was given to that institution, and a new wing had to be built to contain it.[57] Morgan's vision of a museum worthy of an America aspiring to equality with Europe as a locus of culture was well on its way to being realized. As Aline Saarinen put it, "the Morgan collection represents the most grandiose gesture of noblesse oblige the world has ever known."[58]

How are we to interpret these various aspects of Morgan's personality and career? One insight is provided by Francis Henry Taylor:

Main Room, J. P. Morgan Library (Photograph by Samuel H. Gottscho. Courtesy of
Library of Congress Prints and Photographs Division, LC-G613-79642)

Unlike other captains of American industry who adorned their success with the emblems of a past glory in order to buy a measure of security in the closing years of this life and a doubtful immortality in the next, Pierpont Morgan enjoyed the pleasures of the present for their own sake, knowing full well that in the hands of his Redeemer a final accounting would take place. In this respect he was always Church and never Chapel. Uncompromising and self-indulgent though he may have been, he accepted both material and spiritual gratification in the spirit of a *grand seigneur*. He never whined nor concealed his motives with the tight-lipped phrases of the Covenanter.[59]

Although this observation says much about Morgan, it is probably better to read him as a transitional, at times paradoxical or contradictory figure, than as embodying either side of a dichotomy. After all, Morgan's piety did have something of the "chapel" about it. His inclinations were toward the sentimental Evangelicalism represented by Stephen Tyng, but he was able to embrace Tyng's successor, William Rainsford, fulsomely, although more on grounds of character than theological or social program. The somewhat blurred lines that separated home and museum in his domestic life are indicative of his own posture toward the larger world, where he resented accusations that his own personal word on matters of public finance might be anything less than absolutely reliable (and accurate). Though "princely" in lifestyle, he hewed to a very bourgeois notion of personal honor and integrity, and judged people according to these criteria. Further, in contrast to both of these *mentalités*, his approach to connoisseurship and museum administration aligned him with a Progressivist inclination toward specialized expertise rather than the informed amateurism that governed his own collecting impulses.

Morgan was, finally, the embodiment of Establishment: the notion that there was an institutionalized set of touchstones of belief, behavior, and taste that were embodied in the proper sort of individuals and could serve as a beacon for a nation in profound social transition. The Episcopal Church, the cultural and education institutions he patronized, and Morgan himself were all part of the outward and visible face of this Establishment, of which, in his mind, the democratic republic was sorely in need.

Isabella Stewart Gardner

Fenway Court, the house-museum that Isabella Stewart Gardner (1840–1924) built—or, more evocatively, created—at the turn of the previous century,

is one of the most extraordinary monuments to American cultural philanthropy in an era rife with such monuments. Gardner came from New York
"new money" but, when she married John Lowell "Jack" Gardner at Grace
Church in 1860, she acquired a connection with one of the most established
of New England families.[60] The couple's only son died young, and the Gard-
ners carried on their lives by building a house on fashionable Beacon Street
and traveling extensively in Europe and Asia. Although "Mrs. Jack" became
notorious for her (alleged) dalliances with a variety of artistic young men—
most especially the novelist Francis Marion Crawford—her husband was
remarkably tolerant, only occasionally reigning her in when her social and
financial ventures seemed excessive, even by his generous standards. After
both the death of her husband in 1898 and that of her father seven years earlier
left Gardner free of oversight and in possession of a very substantial fortune,
she turned her attention completely to the creation of her masterwork: her
own house.

In addition to her extraordinary personality, three factors combined to
make up the Gardner legend: religion, art, and money. We have already accounted for the money. In terms of religion, Gardner was a "cradle" Episcopalian, her family having been members of the Grace Church in Manhattan
at which she was married.[61] Her serious involvement in Anglicanism began
in the 1870s, with the establishment by the new monastic order, the Cowley Fathers, of two Anglo-Catholic enclaves on Beacon Hill: the Church of
St. John the Evangelist on Bowdoin Street and the Church of the Advent
on Brimmer Street. Gardner ardently embraced the Cowley establishment,
donating, among other things, high altars by Ralph Adams Cram for both
churches, and helping finance a mission church for African Americans,
St. Augustine's, on Beacon Hill.[62]

One of the many legends about Gardner's eccentric and, at times to proper
Bostonians, shocking conduct is that concerning her publicly washing the
steps of the Church of the Advent in atonement for her grievous, presumably
sexual, sins.[63] The actual story is more interesting and revealing. Gardner,
the head of the altar guild, did in fact talk the Cowley Fathers into reviving
the Maundy Thursday custom of washing the stripped altar (not the church
steps) with a mixture of vinegar, salt, and water. Gardner carried out this
ritual ablution with the aid of two other women of the parish, all shod in
Franciscan-style sandals and dressed in special blue habits of Gardner's own
design.[64] The combination of love of ritual and tradition, classic liturgical
spirituality, and a sense of style that asserted itself even in the context of an

ostensible act of self-abnegation is important in understanding the highly complex Gardner persona.

It was during the 1880s that Gardner also began to emerge as a figure in the world of art collecting, instructed by Charles Eliot Norton and abetted by a sometime-protégé of Norton's, Bernard Berenson.[65] Berenson's remarkable career began with his coming to Boston as a child with his Lithuanian Jewish parents, acquiring an education at Boston University and, under Norton's tutelage, at Harvard. He subsequently emerged as one of the premiere art connoisseurs, historians, and brokers on the American scene. (Berenson was actually converted to Christianity and baptized an Episcopalian by Phillips Brooks. Whether this decision was motivated primarily by religious conviction or social advantage is not clear. In any event, the baptism did not stick, and he later lapsed into agnosticism.)[66] In collaboration with Berenson, her point man in Europe, Gardner proceeded to amass one of the most remarkable collections of European—especially Renaissance—art in the United States.

It is important to remember that the canon of art, especially painting, was only now becoming established. Prior to the 1880s, what are now considered the "Old Masters" enjoyed nothing like the normative status they do today. Gardner and Berenson, with J. P. Morgan, were part of a coterie of collectors, connoisseurs, scholars, and brokers who were instrumental in establishing the canon that is perpetuated through such vehicles as the names inscribed on the frieze of the Boston Public Library. As collectors like Gardner acquired cachet, and connoisseurs like Berenson gained authority, the value—both cultural and financial—of the works of Rembrandt, Titian, and their like began to soar, as wealthy Americans, from a mixture of aesthetic appreciation and a desire for cultural legitimacy, began to exploit the willingness of European families with lengthy pedigrees but little cash to "deaccession" their heirlooms. The wishes of Americans to establish legitimacy for a culture short on pedigree but long on cash were played out in the success of Gardner, Morgan, and others in importing, often through legally dubious means, a good chunk of Europe's cultural heritage into the private and public collections of Americans.[67]

Although Gardner's collection of art, mostly European but also containing American and Asian specimens, was quite spectacular in its individual components (over 2,500 in number), the whole was, and remains, greater than the sum of its parts. (Gardner's will, which made the museum public, stipulated that its contents and their arrangement never be altered.)[68] During her lifetime, however, Fenway Court was anything but static. Gardner was an active patron (and, perhaps, manipulator) of any number of young artists, and the court's halls were perpetually alive with exhibits and recitals. Artists of various sorts inhabited the guest suite, Anglican liturgies were conducted in the chapel, horticultural shows took place in the sculpture garden, and musical recitals and plays were staged in the commodious quarters the court provided. Such varied dignitaries as the governor of Massachusetts, the Roman Catholic cardinal, and philosopher William James might have been in attendance on any particular occasion.[69] Gardner broke from accepted Brahmin practice in opening her doors to Catholics, Jews, gays, African Americans, and, in creative as well as sponsoring roles, women.[70] In biographer Douglass Shand-Tucci's terms, she was indeed more a "Bohemian" than a "Brahmin" in a society in which her pedigree had always been suspect.

Fenway Court was not simply a building that housed an art collection, but a creative work of bricolage itself. The museum is in the form of a Venetian palazzo turned inside out. Its walls, of the sort one might expect on the exterior, face inward to frame an interior court that combines horticultural profusion with Roman, Byzantine, Romanesque, Gothic, and Renaissance architectural and decorative elements, most of them purchased in Venice in 1897.[71] The rooms and passageways that make up the second and third levels are generally themed, often by place and time rather than genre, and combine paintings with sculpture, wood carving, tapestries, textiles, architectural elements, autographs, and other decorative genres in a manner that illustrates the motto of Gardner and her museum: *C'est mon plaisir*. The Spanish Chapel, for example, which was dedicated to Gardner's departed son, displays, among other items, Zurbarán's painting *The Virgin of Mercy*, and a tomb figure of a Spanish knight.[72] As Aline Saarinen remarked, "It is impossible to say where objects leave off and building begins for they are all one and the same . . . . It is a Bostonian's dream of Italy."[73]

Two rooms on the third level—the fourth level was set apart for Gardner's personal lodgings—are worthy of particular note. The chapel is dominated by a large fragment of French High Gothic stained glass from Soissons Cathedral, which was called to Gardner's attention by one of her circle, Henry Adams, the author of *Mont-St.-Michel and Chartres*.[74] It is here that the Cowley fathers still celebrate a Requiem Mass for Gardner every year on April 14, her birthday, in remembrance of her generosity to the order.[75]

The final room on the third level, which was never open to more than family and a few intimates during her lifetime, is the "inner sanctum"—what Henry James might have called the *penetralia*—of Fenway Court.[76] This

Gothic room features an altarpiece representing the "Holy Kinship," a carved and gilded wood triptych in late Gothic style and of early sixteenth-century German provenance, and a host of other religious objects.[77] Dominating the room is a "great iconic image" of Gardner in the form of her notorious portrait of 1887–88 by John Singer Sargent. This was inspired by the same artist's portrait of Mme. Gautreau ("Madame X") that had caused considerable scandal upon its public exhibition because of the subject's décolletage.[78] Hilliard Goldfarb, chief curator of the Gardner Museum in the early twenty-first century, describes the Sargent thus:

> The painting portrays her as a pagan deity in a hieratic pose, as the contemporary press noted (Henry James characterized the picture as a "Byzantine Madonna"), with her head surrounded by a mandorla created from an enlarged version of a Renaissance fabric now in the Long Gallery. She is simply presented in a black dress, and Sargent accentuated the features for which she was known—her fine complexion and her figure—by placing her flesh in relief to the darkness and tying a black shawl tight about her hips. Her pearls and rubies highlight the portrait (one critic called the rubies on her slippers "drops of blood"). Gardner confronts the spectator directly, uncompromising, as if assessing the beholder.[79]

WHEN THE NEW PORTRAIT was exhibited as *Woman—An Enigma,* at the St. Botolph Club in Boston, however, Gardner's décolletage and idol-like presentation, as well as her suggestive stance (actually, a standard model's pose) and ostentatiously placed jewelry, sparked controversy. The negative comments so upset Jack Gardner that he asked that the portrait not be exhibited publicly during his lifetime.[80] Gardner had, however, in Anne Higonnet's words, "canonized herself as the patron saint of the museum."[81]

When Gardner died in 1924, she had already scripted plans for the laying-out, funeral, and burial. Her coffin was placed beside the Spanish Chapel and covered with a purple pall and white roses. (She had also specified violets, if they were in season, which they were not.) "There was a mirrored door at the foot of the coffin which was covered with a linen sheet against which a black crucifix was hung." A Cowley priest read the Prayers for the Dead, and two sisters from Anglican orders stayed with the body until the time of the funeral. Masses were said at Fenway Court each morning until the funeral took place at the Church of the Advent four days after her death. She was

John Singer Sargent, oil portrait of Isabella Stewart Gardner (1888), founder of the Renaissance palazzo as the private home that would later become the Gardner Museum. (© Isabella Stewart Gardner Museum, Boston, MA, USA / Bridgeman Images)

buried in Mount Auburn Cemetery in Cambridge, together with most of the eminent deceased of Victorian Boston.[82]

Gardner's role in the history of American art collection and exhibition was, to say the least, impressive. She was a major player in the transition of art collecting from a private hobby into a cultural project at once academic, commercial, philanthropic, and public. In her goal of public edification, she was modeling the Ruskinian strain of piety with which her mentor, Charles Eliot Norton, had imbued her.[83] She was, however, not simply anyone's disciple. In her patronage of contemporary artists she rejected the conservative, Barbizon-inclined tastes of contemporary Boston, and instead favored more avant-garde figures such as Henri Matisse and Paul Manship.

Most distinctive of all, however, was the Fenway Court project in which Gardner combined her own tastes and sensibilities with an extraordinary array of objets d'art to achieve a unique synthesis. With her own Sargent-painted image as Fenway Court's tutelary deity, the house became not only her home but the site for a myriad of creative activities from contemporary music to Anglican liturgy. As Anne Higonnet points out, Gardner's individualistic approach to the arrangement of her galleries went against the emergent conventions that were shaping such institutions as the Museum of Fine Arts in Boston and the Metropolitan in New York. Gardner rather tried to evoke a sense of the organic character of the cultures and epochs her rooms represented and thereby involved the viewer in an empathetic relationship with those cultures. To do so involved intuition as much as connoisseurship, helping bridge the gap between the gendered "masculine" public and "feminine" private realms that characterized the "separate spheres" ethos of Victorian society. In doing so, Higonnet argues, Gardner had proven herself not only a formidable patron of the arts but also a pioneer in exerting cultural authority.[84]

A final dimension of Gardner's achievement that is not usually dwelt upon by scholars is the religious. Gardner was deeply involved in Boston Anglo-Catholic life, and Fenway Court not only contains a remarkable collection of religious art—the dominant genre, in fact—but also several chapels or chapel-like spaces that were on occasion used for religious rituals. Gardner's unconventional life and not-too-savory reputation, however, created something of a paradox in her character. It is certainly possible to view her as a self-contradicting hypocrite, using her wealth to purchase spiritual favors from the Cowley Fathers. One must grant, of course, the colossal egotism, perhaps bordering on narcissism, that drove the Fenway Court project. More plausible, though, is to see her admittedly flamboyant lifestyle and personality as compatible with a view of religion more aesthetic than the preaching-centered observance characteristic of both Puritans and of Unitarian Boston. Fenway Court, in this view, can be seen as a domestic and a museum space and also a sacramental locus. In addition to Gardner holding explicitly religious rituals at Fenway Court, we can view her as being an exponent of the Gospel of Art that was being preached in more conventionally Bostonian terms by the post-Unitarian Charles Eliot Norton (whose father, Andrews, had been known as the "Pope of Unitarianism" in his day).

For Gardner, though, art was not simply useful in promoting good taste and proper Ruskinian morals. Fenway Court can be taken as a whole, in the Wagnerian sense, as a *Gesamtkunstwerk*, a total work of art. As such, it presumably had, in Gardner's vision, a sacramental character—an outward and visible sign of the divine grace that is revealed through beauty. Whatever else she may have been, Gardner does seem to have been sincere in holding this view, which was singularly consistent with certain strains of Anglicanism.

George G. Booth

One of the least known of our six subjects is George Gough Booth (1864–1949), a highly successful Detroit newspaper publisher and founder of the Cranbrook institutions in nearby Bloomfield Hills. Booth's artisan grandfather had left his native Cranbrook in Kent, England, for Canada, where he and his son, Henry Gough Booth, pursued a variety of trades as well as an array of Dissenting denominations. Henry became an Anglican after meeting his wife, whom he married at Christ Church, Toronto, in 1858. He later became involved with the Reformed Episcopal Church and, with son George, moved to Detroit to expand his erratically successful enterprises. The younger Booth worked at a variety of trades and eventually fell in with James E. Scripps, publisher of the Detroit *Evening News*, whose daughter he had met at the Reformed Episcopal Church of the Epiphany and married in 1887. The following year, Scripps, eager to turn his attention to art collecting, turned over the *News* to his son-in-law.[85]

As Booth made his fortune in the newspaper business, he also became involved in the same worlds of art collecting and cultural philanthropy as his father-in-law. Booth had made his fortune in Detroit, the quintessence of the new industrial culture, whose arts institutions had been described by a contemporary writer as "the outward and visible sign of an inward and spiritual salesmanship."[86] His first cultural venture was the founding of the Cranbrook Press in 1900, the first such enterprise to bear the revered name of the fam-

Albert Kahn, Cranbrook House, 1908, the Arts and Crafts style home of publisher George G. Booth, founder of the Cranbrook institutions. (From Jervis Bell McMechan, *Christ Church Cranbrook* [1979]. Courtesy of Christ Church Cranbrook)

ily hometown in England. The enterprise operated in Arts and Crafts style, using a handpress with type designed by William Morris.[87] Booth himself spoke about Morris at the Second Annual Exhibition of Arts and Crafts at the Detroit Museum of Art in 1905. The following year, the Detroit Society of Arts and Crafts, modeled on Boston's, was founded, with Booth as president. Nine years later, Booth donated the property on which the society would build a picturesque complex of artists' shops and studios.[88]

The Arts and Crafts philosophy also informed Booth's emergent personal lifestyle. In 1904, he purchased the 174 acres that would become the site of the Cranbrook complex. He commissioned Albert Kahn, soon to achieve fame as the architect of the Ford industrial empire, to build him an English Arts and Crafts style house, a project that continued into the 1920s.[89] Integral to the Arts and Crafts ideology was the integration of handcrafted decorative arts with the architectural frame, and Booth's house fulfilled this ideal. It contained, among other things, sculpture by Paul Manship; ceramic tiles by Mary Chase Stratton of Detroit's art pottery center, Pewabic Pottery; wood carving by Johannes Kirchmayer; and metalwork by Samuel Yellin and Frank Koralewski, all exemplars of the crafts modes that flourished during the early twentieth century.[90] Booth's home, now a museum, was, in a modest way, a version of Gardner's—a "total work of art"—although the emphasis here was on contemporary design that consciously revives archaic Anglo-American forms rather than on the resurrection of a European past in a New World context.

The Booth house was only the beginning of the larger Cranbrook project. Booth, in collaboration with his wife and architect son, was developing a vision of an educational and cultural complex that would combine art, science, and religion in one harmonious whole. In the words of Booth's (somewhat uncritical) biographer, "His often expressed aim, 'to make good citizens,' called for training students morally, religiously, intellectually, in the midst of beauty. The schools, physically the best available, were to be enhanced by works of art and craftsmanship from all parts of the ancient, medieval, and modern world, and by gifts from collections already gathered in years of travel."[91] This was an educational vision that differed substantially from that of Endicott Peabody, who had always viewed the arts implicitly as conducing toward decadence.

Booth—determined, in his own words, to "die poor"—endowed the newly established Cranbrook Foundation with twelve million dollars in 1927. This organization, largely composed of like-minded friends of the Booths, included the Reverend Samuel Marquis (also a major player in Henry Ford's enterprises), who guided the development of the project until its reorganization in 1973.[92] The Cranbrook complex began with what is now known as the Brookside School for Boys, built between 1926 and 1928. Its designer was the Finnish architect Eliel Saarinen, who had recently come to the United States to compete in the *Chicago Tribune* competition, in which his memorable entry placed second. Booth's son Henry met Saarinen while an architecture student at the University of Michigan and recruited him to help fashion the new campus.[93]

Saarinen and his family—which included his weaver wife, Loja, and his architect son Eero—became central to the project in a number of ways. The elder Saarinen brought to the task of campus design a vision that complemented, improbably but effectively, the elder Booth's Anglophiliac nostalgia. Saarinen's aesthetic vision had been shaped by the Finnish equivalent of the Arts and Crafts movement, which in that country had been intimately linked with a drive toward nationalist cultural recovery.[94] Harmonious with the broader ethos of his time, Saarinen's style combined elements from Arts and Crafts with the streamlined classicism of the Art Deco exhibited so gracefully in downtown Detroit's skyscrapers, as well as the regional modernism of Frank Lloyd Wright.[95] At first glance, the Cranbrook campus evokes a vision of an idyllic English collegiate or public school campus, a model that Booth certainly had in mind. However, on closer inspection, the style and carefully integrated ornament are unique—reminiscent, in their eclectic transformation of traditional forms, of Bertram Grosvenor Goodhue, Ralph Adams

Cram's longtime partner and founder of the architectural firm that would be chosen to design the neighboring Christ Church Cranbrook.

Just as Saarinen's design began in, but by no means ended with, English Victorian precedent, so did the complex of institutions that Booth envisaged and brought into being. Art was central to this vision, both in its integrated presence in every aspect of campus design as well as in formal instruction. Booth, who was keenly interested in and supportive of the arts, decided that his optimal contribution to their well-being would consist neither in the collection of old masters nor contemporary work, but rather in the creation of an educational setting in which artists-in-residence would live together with their students in an organic communal setting. To implement this vision, Booth in 1932 recruited Saarinen, who was already deeply engaged in the design of the complex, as first president of the Cranbrook Academy of Art. Many of the original faculty were friends of Saarinen, and represented not only the traditional "fine arts" of painting and sculpture but a whole range of crafts, such as ceramics, weaving, silversmithing, and bookbinding, as well. A Cranbrook Institute of Science was the final educational component incorporated into the Cranbrook project.[96]

The other member of the Cranbrook institutional complex, which is no longer directly connected with the other constituents, is Christ Church Cranbrook. Booth's holistic vision of education included religion as well as the arts and sciences. Christ Church was founded by Booth with the intention that it be an Episcopal parish in the Diocese of Michigan—at some point he had departed from the Reformed Episcopal Church of his younger days—as well as a chapel for his envisioned school and a community church for the growing Bloomfield Hills settlement. To this end, Booth recruited Samuel Marquis, then rector of St. Joseph Church on Woodward Avenue in Detroit. Booth had become impressed with Marquis after they had successfully resolved an altercation over a sermon Marquis had preached at St. Paul's Cathedral, of which he was then dean, attacking Detroit's newspapers.[97] Invitations to compete for the design of the new church, which the Booth family intended to pay for in full as a gift to the community, were extended to the now-separate firms of both Ralph Adams Cram and Bertram Grosvenor Goodhue. After Cram had withdrawn from the competition, and Goodhue had unexpectedly died, the commission went to Oscar H. Murray of Bertram Grosvenor Goodhue Associates.[98]

Trinity Church in Boston's Copley Square is often regarded as the first American church, Episcopal or otherwise, in which artists and artisans of the highest quality came to collaborate on a *Gesamtkunstwerk*, a unified work of

Bertram Grosvenor Associates, Christ Church Cranbrook, 1928.
(Courtesy of Peggy Dahlberg, Christ Church Cranbrook)

art.[99] Christ Church Cranbrook has been called the last in this tradition.[100] Inspired by the churches of the Kent countryside, it is built in the English Gothic revival style and situated in a rural setting across from the Cranbrook campus. Its tower contains one of the first carillons in the United States. The interior, however, is what sets Christ Church apart. The artisans were selected by the Booth family who, as we have seen, were aficionados of the Arts and Crafts movement. The arts represented include woodwork, glass, frescoes, sculpture, mosaics, tapestries, and metalwork. In addition to the work of contemporary artists, a variety of objects acquired by the Booths during their European travels are sited in the church, including a fifteenth-century bishop's chair from the vicinity of Amiens and a terra-cotta relief of three singing angels by Italian Renaissance artist Giovanni della Robbia.[101]

Particularly interesting is the inclusion of women, both as craftspeople and as subjects of iconography. Among the former were Katherine McEwen, a founder of the Detroit Society of Arts and Crafts, who executed the colossal chancel fresco with the theme of the building of the church throughout the world, and tile mosaics by Mary Chase Perry Stratton of Detroit's Pewabic art pottery firm. The west window is dedicated to the theme of womankind and consists of sixteen panels, each of which contains three figures representing a particular female calling. In addition to biblical and medieval figures, more contemporary women represented include Sarah Bernhardt, Mary Lyon, and Harriet Beecher Stowe. This inclusive pantheon of scriptural and latter-day saints echoes both the encyclopedic purposes to which glass was often put in medieval cathedrals, as well as similar commemorations of religious and secular exemplars in the National Cathedral in Washington, D.C., and Grace Cathedral in San Francisco. In the same vein, the north window represents craftsmen throughout the ages, including Johannes Kirchmayer, who himself crafted the reredos. Carvings in the medieval manner on the bottoms of the misericords—props to reduce the stress of prolonged standing—in the choir stalls include humorous images of donor Booth and architect Murray.[102]

George Booth's legacy has proved enduring. The Cranbrook complex includes a school that ranks among the finest private schools in the region, one of the most impressive examples of the export of the boarding school model beyond the Northeast. The Academy of Art similarly enjoys a very high reputation. Booth's career was that of a self-made man, rising from a family of artisans and small businessmen of mixed success to become head of a regional newspaper empire. Religiously, he moved from the Evangelical milieu of his family, in its last incarnation in the Reformed Episcopal Church, into the "mother" denomination in a church of his own building much more in keeping with Anglo-Catholic aesthetic norms. Booth's rhetoric, as recorded in a number of his speeches and essays, was very much that of Victorian America, more moralistic and idealistic than overtly theological, and imbued with the principles of the Arts and Crafts movement, in which art and morality were inseparable. ("The architect," he once informed a group of members of that profession, "is a seeker after truth, a servant of a better life for all . . . a servant of the Goddess of Truth and Beauty.")[103] His emphasis on service as the goal of education was very much in harmony with the ideals of Endicott Peabody and other leaders of the Episcopal-affiliated independent school movement. As such, he was a representative Episcopalian of his time and class, finding in the world of material beauty a source of moral inspiration for his own generation and for generations to come.

Henry Ford

Henry Ford (1863–1947) was one of the richest and most influential men of the twentieth century. It is less well known that Ford was also a lifelong Episcopalian—though of a rather peculiar sort. Ford was born into an Anglo-Irish family that had settled in the Detroit area in the 1840s.[104] His parents were easy-going Anglicans, teaching their children that how they lived was more important than what they believed.[105] Henry was confirmed by Bishop S. S. Harris at Christ Church in Dearborn in March of 1888, a few weeks before his marriage to a rural neighbor, Clara Bryant, who had herself been confirmed by the same bishop.[106] Although Henry would remain a nominal Episcopalian until his burial from Detroit's St. Paul's Cathedral in 1947, it was Clara who would do the ecclesiastical heavy lifting throughout their lengthy years of married life.[107]

Henry's own faith—that is, what we can reconstruct of it—was seemingly of a piece with his broader character, and consisted of what one of his many biographers disparagingly characterized as "his own oddly radical ragbag of beliefs and allegiances."[108] Henry had little formal education, and what he (and Clara) received in rural schools was based primarily on the McGuffey series of *Eclectic Readers*.* Henry instead was a natural tinkerer, and was far

---

*Neil Baldwin, in his *Henry Ford and the Jews: The Mass Production of Hate* (New York: Public Affairs, 2001), argues that these readers may have laid the groundwork for the anti-Semitism that characterized Ford's later life, especially in his publication of the vitriolic *Dearborn Independent* during the 1920s. See Baldwin, chapter 1 ("McGuffeyland").

happier working with machinery than with words or ideas. (And far better at it, as subsequent unfortunate incidents in Henry's life would demonstrate.) His father, William, had been simultaneously a warden at the local Episcopal church and, according to the same biographer, a Freemason and "something of a free thinker."[109] Henry was strongly affected by his own reading of Ralph Waldo Emerson, to whose work the naturalist John Burroughs had introduced him.[110] Emerson's Transcendentalism, which had been influenced by that worthy's explorations in Asian traditions, harmonized with Ford's enthusiasm for the doctrine of reincarnation, a belief that would be part of his religious baggage most of his life.[111] Henry also became a 33rd degree Mason, an honor he pursued to express his indignation at his grandson Henry II's conversion to Roman Catholicism upon his marriage to a Catholic.[112] Ford's anti-Semitism, expressed virulently for several years in his *Dearborn Independent*, is perhaps the best-known blot on his reputation.[113]

An interesting perspective on Ford is provided by Samuel S. Marquis, who was the dean of Detroit's St. Paul's Cathedral when Ford hired him as head of his Sociological Department in 1915, in which capacity he remained until his "resignation" six years later.[114] This branch of the company, later renamed the Educational Department, was charged with the supervision of the personal lives, habits, and characters of current and potential Ford employees, to ensure that they were becoming middle-class Americans of good values.[115] Although Ford, who met Marquis through his wife Clara, is reputed to have told the dean that he wanted him "to put Jesus Christ in my factory," Marquis does not confirm this precise anecdote.[116] He was, however, deeply impressed with Ford's distinctive philanthropic spirit and characterized the enterprise during its best days as "a great experiment in applied Christianity in industry."[117]

According to Marquis, "Mr. Ford hates the word charity, and all that it stands for."[118] By this, Marquis meant that Ford regarded a benevolent attitude toward his workers as both morally correct and fiscally prudent. Workers who were healthy, earned a "living wage," and enjoyed proper home lives were far more likely to be loyal and productive workers than those who simply subsisted on the margins of existence. Ford would therefore help a man to acquire the skills to become a worker, but refused to give anything to those who were unwilling or incapable of such work. The Progressive-minded Marquis generally agreed, although he was troubled that Ford was blind to the possibility that "until the millennium arrives we need a few people of means who will accept our modern organized charity as one of the necessary evils and will give it their support" to care for those who were simply unable to become agents of the new industrial order.[119]

Marquis's remarkably balanced appraisal of Ford, which nevertheless led to the subsequent shunning of himself and his wife by Clara Ford, finds in his sometime employer a moral enigma. He lauds Ford for his pattern of clean, unextravagant living and lack of conspicuous vices. Although Ford was his parishioner, he was "not a churchman in the sense that he attends church with regularity, enters into its worship, sacramental or other, is interested in the extension of its work, and contributes to its support in a manner commensurate with his means."[120] He was not "a diligent reader of Scripture," although he once commissioned a new vernacular translation of the New Testament. (On this enterprise, probably never actually begun, Marquis remarked wryly that Ford "agrees with St. Peter that Brother Paul wrote many things hard to be understood. Perhaps a new translation would go toward clearing up Paul's thought."[121]

It was not Ford's religious unconventionality that troubled Marquis so much as the man's seemingly inexplicable dark side. Ford's most grievous offense, in Marquis's view, was his abandoning the benevolent policies of the mid-teens, such as the five-dollar day, which earned Ford so much renown, in favor of a reliance upon men of doubtful, even sadistic character during the economic downturn of 1920.[122] (Harry Bennett, whose linkages with the underworld were employed in the heyday of Ford's battles with organized labor in the 1930s, was presumably the prototype of this lot.) The result was Ford's unceremonious and mean-spirited scrapping of the best of his executive talents along the way.[123] "There seems to me no middle ground in his make-up," Marquis lamented, in a seemingly futile attempt to reconcile the high-minded altruist with the childish bully.[124]

Marquis's summary judgment on Ford was the following:

> Henry Ford has his faults, but they are not those of Dives. And I cannot think of him as finally going where Dives is. Neither can I quite picture him with Lazarus on the bosom of Abraham, in view of what he has recently been saying about Abraham's descendants. It seems to me the situation would be mutually embarrassing. I think St. Peter will pass Mr. Ford at the gates, but following that I fear that he and Abraham will have to iron out some personal misunderstandings.[125]

In the realm of philanthropy, much of the Ford fortune went during his own lifetime to what would become the Henry Ford Hospital in Detroit and, after his death, to the enormously well-endowed Ford Foundation.[126] In the realm of the arts, Henry's son Edsel, whose considerable talents were largely squelched by his father's dominance, was by far the more important figure; his support for the Detroit Institute of Arts (DIA), and his resolute backing of Mexican artist Diego Rivera in his creation of the controversial "Detroit Industry" murals at the DIA, was central to that institution's rise to eminence under its entrepreneurial director, the German-born William Valentiner.[127]

Henry Ford's major work in the realm of what broadly might be construed as cultural philanthropy was his creation of a unique piece of Americana. The Henry Ford Museum and Greenfield Village were twin projects commenced in 1925 and that continue to be popular attractions in Ford's own Dearborn. These two contiguous institutions reflect two sides of the Fordian psyche. The museum is now a state-of-the-art collection focused on the history of American transportation. It reflects what we might call "Ford the Futurist," the man who claimed to have invented modernity. Greenfield Village, on the other hand, is a highly personalized look backward at an earlier America, nostalgically distorted in Ford's imagination as the seedbed of national virtue. Like Old Sturbridge Village in central Massachusetts, Greenfield Village is an assemblage of buildings from a variety of different communities, rather than, like Historic Williamsburg, a restored community that had actually existed. Unlike either, Ford's creation consists of real buildings chosen for their resonance in Ford's historical imagination and assembled in a fashion he found pleasing rather than according to any plausible historic configuration. Among them are the birthplaces of Thomas Edison and William Holmes McGuffey, as well as the Wright Brothers' bicycle shop and the Ford homestead itself. The result was intended not so much to be faithful to the sort of past that professional historians try to re-create but rather to evoke materially a didactic and morally instructive past, rather like that which one might assemble from McGuffey's *Readers*. (The Fords collected these readers, which were used in the Greenfield Village school.)[128] Ford may have observed that history is more or less bunk, but he had no compunctions about having a go at it himself—on, of course, his own terms.[129]

One particularly interesting building in Greenfield Village is the Martha-Mary Chapel, named after the mothers of Henry and Clara and built out of bricks from Clara's family home.[130] This Greek revival structure, which was also reproduced at the Ford estate in Richmond Hill, Georgia, is rather generic in appearance and presumably designed as an iconic evocation of the piety of an earlier and simpler era. Even though Clara was a committed

Episcopalian, there is little Anglican in these structures; an order of worship for the Georgia version is generally Protestant, with little hint of the *Book of Common Prayer*.[131] After the Fords' deaths, a million-dollar endowment from Clara's estate financed the building in 1952–53 of St. Martha's Episcopal Church, a small "modified Gothic" structure sited next to the Ford Cemetery in northwest Detroit, where Henry and Clara are buried.[132]

Despite Henry's eccentricities, the pattern of the Ford family with regard to cultural philanthropy was not that unusual for the time. The bulk of Ford giving went to institutionalized medicine, and Clara especially was active in a variety of organizations such as the League of Women Voters.[133] Clara was also the only member of the family to lead a conventionally religious life in any serious way. Son Edsel, deeply but ambiguously involved in the family business, was the real cultural patron, and his involvement was crucial for Detroit's emergence as a major center of the arts. Henry's major contribution to the cultural realm was in the Dearborn historical museum complex, which can be read both as a monument to himself as well as an attempt at putting his vast financial resources to work at the task of exercising cultural authority after various previous efforts—the Peace Ship, the *Dearborn Independent*, a run for the United States Senate—all went nowhere. Greenfield Village today is more of a curiosity than a genuine aid to historical understanding, and contrasts sharply with the Colonial Williamsburg project, which is our final topic. Perhaps Samuel Marquis was right in asserting that Henry Ford's fundamental error—one common to the successful—was believing that his expertise in one realm of life qualified him to act as an expert in others in which he possessed neither training nor genius.[134]

W. A. R. Goodwin

As a coda to this discussion of wealthy Episcopal laity and cultural philanthropy, it seems useful to add one not-very-wealthy clergyman to our list, the Reverend William Archer Rutherfoord Goodwin (1869–1939) of Williamsburg, Virginia, as an example of the role clergy occasionally played in this arena.[135] Goodwin was born on a Virginia farm to a family poor in cash but rich in clergy.[136] He attended Roanoke and Richmond Colleges, and studied for the ministry at the seminary in Alexandria on a scholarship provided by a sympathetic Richmond woman.[137] (He would later compile a history of the Virginia Theological Seminary.)[138] In 1894 he became rector of St. John's Church in Peterborough, Virginia, and simultaneously joined the faculty of the Bishop Payne Divinity School, for which he also worked as fundraiser and financial secretary. His attitude toward African Americans, whose clerical education he promoted at the latter institution, was one of benign but paternalistic concern.[139]

Goodwin first came to Williamsburg in 1903 as rector of Bruton Parish Church. Williamsburg was at the time a rather sleepy southern backwater, where only the beginnings of an interest in restoring its past as a colonial capital had been kindled by the Association for the Preservation of Virginia Antiquities.[140] Goodwin took the first steps toward the restoration of Bruton Parish Church during this rectorship. The church had been drastically remodeled in 1839 when, among other things, part of the interior was remade into Sunday school classrooms, the chancel moved to the center, and the lower tower turned into a coal bin. Goodwin's aim, which he largely achieved, was to restore Bruton to its 1769 state, before various Revolutionary-era secular uses and later religious transformations had turned it into a liturgical monstrosity.[141]

In 1909, Goodwin left Williamsburg to accept a call as rector of St. Paul's, a well-to-do parish in Rochester, New York. Here he built up a reputation as an administrator, and, in 1916, published *The Church Enchained*, in which he demonstrated the spirit of the Progressive era by proposing a new model for parochial organization based on the military, called the "Group System."[142] This concern with efficiency and expansion, combined with an aggressively Broad Church theology, got him into trouble with his Anglo-Catholic bishop, William D. Walker, who took considerable umbrage when Goodwin sponsored a resolution at the General Convention to authorize the Board of Missions "to cooperate with other Christian people in the extension of the Kingdom of God through conferences."[143] Walker's successor was Charles Henry Brent, now the former missionary bishop of the Philippines, who took a shine to Goodwin, made him head of the diocesan department of missions, and employed him in other positions of trust as well.[144]

Goodwin returned to Williamsburg in 1923 as professor of Philosophy and Social Services at the College of William & Mary, and eventually became chair of what later became its Department of Biblical Literature. He was also appointed director of the college's endowment campaign. Three years later, he also again became rector of Bruton Parish Church.[145] It was in this new vocational context that he conceived of a plan far beyond that of restoring his own church. His vision of a restored Williamsburg was rooted at least partially in a sense he shared with many of the old-stock Americans of his day: that the recent flood of immigration had created a need for a revival of knowledge of the values that had supposedly reigned when the nation had been a more ethnically and religiously homogeneous society.[146] A re-creation of the capital town ("city" seems too strong a word) could have this kind of repristinating effect by making it possible for contemporary Americans of all backgrounds to visualize and experience the physical environment in which their spiritual, if not genetic, forefathers had lived.[147]

To do this, however, would require means far beyond those of an impecunious country parson. Goodwin therefore began to seek out the aid of the philanthropists who abounded in his era. His first, rather ill-advised approach was to the Ford family, whose sympathy he attempted to gain by pointing out that the Ford automobile was a principal factor in the erosion of the fabric of the traditional Virginia landscape. Even though Henry and Clara had already purchased the Wayside Inn in Massachusetts as an adventure in historic restoration, the Fords were unmoved by Goodwin's perhaps less than tactful strategy and, unsurprisingly, gave him the cold shoulder.[148]

Goodwin had better luck with another family whose name had become synonymous with fabulous wealth and profuse philanthropy: the Rockefellers. Baptists in an ocean of Episcopalians, John D. Rockefeller and his children were also motivated by a sense of obligation to restore something to the society that had made them almost uncountably rich. John D. Jr. especially was sensitive to the numerous journalistic characterizations of his father as an economic predator and was eager to make amends through cultural projects of redeeming social importance. The younger Rockefeller shared Goodwin's sense that a restored Williamsburg could be salutary for a nation that had lost its moral moorings, a complaint as prevalent in the twenties as it has been in more recent decades. After Rockefeller had made up his mind, he commissioned Goodwin to sell the town on the project and to buy up properties without mentioning the name of the philanthropic dynast who was putting up the money. During the ensuing decades, the Colonial Williamsburg that emerged underwent a variety of ideological glosses, from filiopietism to patriotism to a sense that the colonial past could not be fully comprehended until the roles of women and black slaves, as well as those of white patricians, had been satisfactorily addressed.[149]

Goodwin seemingly had a sacramental view of his enterprise. His secretary observed that he "often said that the city should be made a sacrament, an outward and visible sign of spiritual truth and beauty, through which the lives of visitors to the place would be inspired and enriched."[150] John Ruskin also played an important role in shaping Goodwin's sense of the enterprise. His parishioners at Rochester had given him a copy of *Modern Painters*, one passage from which Goodwin memorized and later invoked frequently: "It is my own duty to preserve what the past has had to say for itself, and to say for ourselves those things that shall be true for the future."[151]

A more extensive early take on this enterprise is revealed in the volume he assembled from his own writings and the sermons of others involved in the restoration and rededication of Bruton Parish Church in 1907. The writings that make up the book provide a counternarrative to the traditional northern account of Anglicanism in the South. One theme that winds through these essays and sermons is the essential continuity of religious life represented by Bruton Parish's history. The "ruthless innovation" that supposedly had characterized other strains of Christianity was absent here; rather, an uninterrupted execution of Anglican worship had persisted from the founding of the colony at Jamestown through the Revolution and Civil War to the present. Only minor adjustments had ever been necessary, such as the altering of the prayers in the *Book of Common Prayer* for the monarch to invoke divine blessings to be directed instead for the guidance of the president or, during the "late unpleasantness," the governor of Virginia.[152]

Several other important themes run through this work. First, Goodwin emphasizes that the founding of Virginia was an essential chapter in the transmission of English civilization to the New World, a civilization that was subsequently nurtured by the Episcopal Church and its colonial antecedents. In his sermon at the church's restoration, the Reverend B. D. Tucker observed that "It is the church . . . of the men who, while here as representatives in the Virginia House of Burgesses, helped to lay the foundations of our Anglo-Saxon civilization in this republic, who were the pioneers of this great nation."[153] Goodwin echoes this theme in his "Historical Sketch" of the parish, where he observes that "the county road which ran by the church yard, marking the inward and outward march of English civilization, now rose to the dignity of the Duke of Gloucester Street."[154]

Other central themes here are the notions that the colonial Anglican ministers in Virginia were for the most part highly honorable and capable men; that colonial and antebellum Anglicans had served the colony's and state's African slaves well; and that colonial Anglicanism, and Bruton Parish Church in particular, had helped shape the notions of liberty that resulted in American independence. Virginia colonists recognized that the law of God was the fundamental basis of human legislation, and consequently turned their attention first to establishing the legal foundations for the church in the colony.[155] The vast majority of Virginia's colonial leaders were church-men and vestrymen, and it was, ironically, while serving in the latter capacity that they came to realize the need to resist encroachments on their liberties by the Church of England. As for the slaves, Goodwin writes that "in these homes around these altars the negro servants received the best instruction and richest spiritual blessing which has ever come into the lives of these people now emancipated from slavery, and self-exiled from these high and holy spiritual privileges. We confidently believe that there is more of genuine spiritual good which has come to them as an inheritance from this social and religious tutelage than has since been acquired by them, or imparted to them, along independent lines."[156]

Like Henry Ford, Goodwin believed that the actual physical fabric of the past, if properly preserved and presented, could play an important didactic role in bringing to life salient aspects of that past in a way more vivid than the usual fare served up in school texts. Unlike Ford, he was far more sensitive to the necessity of restoring and, when necessary, re-creating that fabric in a manner as faithful as possible to the way it had actually been experienced by contemporaries. Where Ford, however, presumably did not care for the opin-ion of professional historians and followed his own eccentric lights, Goodwin, who did care, was nevertheless oblivious to aspects of the past that did not fit into his own culturally bound scheme of interpretation, such as the impor-tance of African Americans in the Williamsburg scene. Nevertheless, his con-tribution to the quest for the physical, as well as verbal, conveyance of history and its didactic possibilities has earned him a place as one of the founders of the modern historic preservation movement as the initiator of an enterprise in architectural and cultural recovery that is still creatively evolving.

The Legacy

What does this exercise in collective biography suggest to us that might be useful in understanding the Episcopal Church and its relation to American culture? For one thing, all but the last of these sketches highlight the role that the laity have played in the shaping of a distinctively American Anglican ethos. Virtually all clergy have cautionary tales about difficult and strong-minded wardens. As we have seen, the ranks of the latter have included J. P. Morgan, George G. Booth, and William Cooper Procter, as well as Har-vey Firestone, Henry Francis Du Pont, and many others.[157] Add Isabella

Stewart Gardner as head of the Church of the Advent's altar guild, and we can conjure a picture of formidable lay leadership indeed. The impact of such leadership, especially by the wealthy, on the life of the church at the local and national levels deserves further consideration.

Second, it is clear enough that many wealthy Episcopalians were deeply attracted by the arts, especially those expressed in material media such as painting, sculpture, and the various decorative arts. It would not be difficult to name quite a few other Episcopalians—Gertrude Vanderbilt Whitney, Henry Clay Frick, Henry Francis Du Pont, and Andrew and Paul Mellon, to cite some prominent examples—who were founders of major museums, or private collectors and donors to established museums. Not all such collectors, to be sure, were Episcopalians, but a remarkable number were.

Third, there does not seem to be a significant correlation between Anglo-Catholicism and Episcopal involvement in the arts. On the one hand, it is obvious that Anglo-Catholic churches such as Advent and All Saints Ashmont in Boston did foster the liturgical arts by practicing rituals in ways that involved and even depended on elaborate material accoutrements. As Douglass Shand-Tucci's studies of "Boston Bohemia" further demonstrate, many of the artistically inclined in fin-de-siècle Boston were attracted to Anglo-Catholicism.[158] However, only Gardner among our subjects had explicit Anglo-Catholic affiliation. All of the active laity, including Gardner, came from Low Church backgrounds; none save she explicitly repudiated them, although none remained dogmatically Evangelical. The impulse toward material artistic expression, which had roots both in the Ecclesiological movement of the 1840s and in the Broad Church context of Phillips Brooks and his Trinity Church in the 1870s, seems to have transcended the lines of theological division that infected the American Anglican community during these decades.

Fourth, Christian theology in general, and Anglican religious thought in particular, do not seem to have overtly shaped the discourse about art in these circles. To be sure, John Ruskin, whose writings were enormously influential in the United States, had originally studied for the ministry in the Church of England, but in his later career he veered away from institutional Christianity. As Ruskinianism was propagated on American shores by agents such as Charles Eliot Norton at Harvard and the votaries of the Arts and Crafts movement in Boston and beyond, it usually took the form of high-minded dicta about the relationship between "Art," "Beauty," and "Morality." Many of Ruskin's proponents, including Norton himself, remained unchurched. Even Episcopalians like George Booth, who were deeply involved in the Gospel of

Art movement, tended to speak in terms of generalized Victorian virtues such as "Service" and "Duty" rather than in specifically Christian language. This reinforces the notion that Episcopalians have traditionally been a "worldly" people who, like Phillips Brooks, have tended to emphasize the continuities between church and culture rather than their disjunctions.

Fifth, although Episcopalians spoke and, presumably, thought in terms of the moral and intellectual currents of the day, one sort of discourse seems lacking here, that of capitalism. Obviously the art-collecting phenomenon that emerged with such strength during these decades was based on a firm economic infrastructure. Wealthy collectors such as Gardner and Morgan practically created the international art market that has pervaded the aesthetic world ever since (as regular accounts of art auctions in the "Arts" section of the *New York Times* reveal each week) and turned artworks into commodities that could be bought and sold like automobiles and refrigerators. On the other hand, few of these collectors seemed interested in collecting for profit. Morgan, for example, had no need of enhancing his social status or wealth and was therefore free to indulge in art both for personal gratification and for loftier social aims. For the fin-de-siècle elite—as opposed to upstarts such as Bernard Berenson—the arts constituted a realm set apart from the profane world of commerce, even though that world had made the acquisition or enactment of these arts possible. This was part of the process that Lawrence Levine has described as the "sacralization" of the arts in American life during this period, a process reflected in the temple-like structures erected to house them.[159] Susan Pearce put it suggestively when she described the museum as "a kind of material heaven" in which apotheosized objects duly decreed as canonical leave the secular world to enjoy a sort of eternal status as "priceless," that is, beyond the reach of market forces.[160]

Why, then, collect? Pearce is also illuminating in this regard. Collecting is a way of representing and re-creating the self: "collections are material autobiographies." When carried out with the goal of making a gift to society, collecting also can be a means of acquiring social power, especially by a woman like Gardner, whose access to the reins of Boston society was otherwise constricted by gender and social origin. Further, even for Americans like Morgan, whose family had already accumulated considerable social as well as financial capital, altruistic collecting could make possible a status denied Americans, that is, nobility. "Collections are undertaken in order to impress contemporaries, to arouse admiration and amazement, and to secure an immortal place for the collector through the building of the collection as his monument . . . pictures have the art of turning base metal into fine gold, of transforming money acquired in trade into nobility in every sense of the word."[161]

What, then, of folk like Henry Ford, who aggressively depicted themselves as commoners rather than trying to emulate the Renaissance nobility and church dignitaries with whom Gardner and Morgan implicitly identified? What unites them is a quest for cultural authority at a time and place in which that quality was up for grabs. With what had once been an Evangelically based common culture rapidly disintegrating with the influx of new immigrants, the proliferation of religions, and the sharpening of distinctions among social classes, figures from the world of business now began to lay claim to the sort of moral leadership that had previously been the province of the clergy. Although, perhaps paradoxically, the Episcopal Church was much more hierarchical in structure than most of its Protestant competitors, the sharp distinction that had once divided Puritan clergy and laity or that continued to divide Roman Catholic priest and parishioner was largely absent in other than Anglo-Catholic circles. Morgan both cultivated and implicitly patronized his church's bishops when he entertained them during the General Convention, and when he and his counterparts on vestries across the nation wielded great influence over policy through the power of the purse. Similarly, Ford attempted to enhance his authority as the sage of the common man by utilizing his enormous wealth to buy, transport, and rearrange numerous historic sites to serve as "outward and visible" teaching devices to instruct Americans in what he saw as the basic values, of which they needed continual reminding.

Sixth, it seems evident that the Episcopal Church of this time both aspired to and in fact achieved to some degree the status of a quasi-national, or semi-established, church. Washington's National Cathedral, itself an assemblage of the arts and a tribute to the history of the entire nation, was conceived by Henry Yates Satterlee during this era as a "house of prayer for all people," and has in fact functioned since as a sort of common national pulpit. More broadly, Episcopalians such as Morgan, W. A. R. Goodwin, and, in his own peculiar way, Henry Ford, were all concerned with the exercise of cultural authority, and this exercise often implicitly involved the authority of the church itself. It would be more accurate here to speak of the Episcopal Church not only as a religious institution but as the institutional center of a broader and more diffuse elite culture. This culture manifested itself in the building of churches and cathedrals and also in the activities of people like those described here, for whom the church's ethos and their sense of their own roles as movers and shakers on the broader cultural landscape inevitably interpenetrated one another.

Seventh, and finally, it is arguable that the Episcopal Church played an important role in the cultural transformation that was taking place during these years through legitimizing the realm of the material in religious, moral, and cultural life. Jeanne Kilde has shown how the "auditorium church" model favored by the more Evangelical denominations manifested the symbiotic relationship between religion and the theater during this era.[162] Even here, however, the emphasis was on the preached and sung word rather than on material objects themselves as mediators of sacred knowledge and power. Although stained glass began to appear in such churches, it was either purely ornamental or confined, in Protestant fashion, to biblical scenes. A few Protestant liberals, such as Henry Van Dyke of New York's Brick Presbyterian Church, emphasized the possibilities of color and ornament in worship, but their lead was not to be followed widely for several decades, if at all.[163] William Leach has written that "especially in Protestant cultures, both color and light were viewed with deep suspicion, their use perceived as ethically dangerous and demonic and as an engenderment to longing and desire."[164] The Roman Catholic Church boasted at least an elaborate a material culture in the realm of worship and devotion, as did its Anglican counterpart, but its cultural influence was largely restricted to its own, predominantly immigrant and working-class community.

It would be overreaching to claim that the Episcopal Church itself created a major change in the relation of Americans to the sensual and material worlds; rather, it would be more accurate to state that there was an "elective affinity," to borrow the phrase Max Weber borrowed from Goethe, between Episcopalian taste and practice and the direction in which the broader, secular society was heading. Leach notes that, just as aniconic Reformed tradition had viewed color and light with a doubtful eye, it was exactly these sensual stimuli that were now becoming a part of the material makeup of the emergent American urban commercial culture:

> From the 1880s onward, the application of color, glass, and light
> spread rapidly throughout the domain of popular entertainment and
> consumption. Opera houses, ballet companies, restaurants, hotels,
> department stores, and amusement parks, as well as fairs and (later)
> museums, incorporated them into exterior and interior design. Similar
> "architectural hocus-pocus" amplified the "atmospherics" of movie

and vaudeville houses, inviting customers into "another system of aesthetics." No single institution could have achieved this, but several, interlinked and cross-fertilizing one another, endowed the display aesthetic with a secure life of its own.[165]

Significant also is the fact that the department store, a new urban phenomenon that was instrumental in promoting the new ethos of consumerism, relied for advertising in part on lavish displays, including churches and cathedrals among their Christmas settings. "The cathedral was but one of a whole succession of mythical worlds, each of equal value, that Wanamaker and other department stores merchants installed in store interiors."[166] The boundaries among hitherto distinct social institutions were beginning to blur as new aesthetic and commercial canons reversed the priorities that generations of Puritan suspicion of material excess had imposed on American culture.

The Episcopal Church has often come under Evangelical suspicion as the church of the worldly—hence the moniker "Whiskeypalians"—who rejected the constrictions that generations of Protestants had imposed on various forms of behavior deemed incompatible with rigorous biblical norms. During the period under consideration here, this suspicion was not without foundation: Many Episcopalians did reject cautions against worldliness and embraced the material and sensual world, often with the approval of certain clergy who frowned neither on material success nor sensual display. Beginning with the creation of Boston's Trinity Church in the 1870s for that "Prince of the Pulpit" Phillips Brooks, the arts were now welcome in the realm of Christian worship, even in the home church of a cleric suspicious of the Gothic as too popish, but who wanted above all else to have a central pulpit from which his eloquence could be proclaimed to his multitude of followers.

A more useful way of characterizing the Episcopal Church during this time is to see it as an institutional mediator of cultural transition. By encouraging the arts and incorporating them into its very fabric, the church provided a way through which the impulse toward self-glorifying material accumulation could be channeled into activities that were religiously and culturally edifying. This was the age of church and cathedral building on a grand scale, in which architects such as Ralph Adams Cram, Henry Vaughan, and Bertram Grosvenor Goodhue lavished attention not only on exterior design but also on the ornate interiors, which were executed by the finest craftspeople of the age. For individual collectors and museum founders such as Booth, Gardner, and Morgan, the sturdy Protestant virtues of "Honor" and "Service" could be combined with an appreciation of "Beauty," all of which could be embodied in cultural institutions that, in their eyes at least, helped transfigure an otherwise crassly commercial urban culture. Still others, such as Ford and Goodwin, attempted, according to their respective lights, to restore the material fabric of an American past that had much to teach later generations. This is not to say that the great collectors of the era were saintly philanthropists; their characters embodied the mix of virtues and vices to which the rich and powerful are subject in varying proportions. Nevertheless, the culture of urban America was manifestly enriched by their benevolences under the aegis of a church that had room for both the prophetic judgments of the Social Gospel and the sensual opulence of the Gospel of Art.

Epilogue
The Irony of American Episcopal History

The Episcopal Church prospered during the decades between the Civil War and the Great Depression, with the number of communicants soaring from slightly over two hundred thousand in 1870 to more than a million and a quarter in 1930.[1] The number of churches and missions also grew impressively, from 2,605 to 8,253. Most dioceses built cathedrals, and, following the centralizing impulses in the broader culture, diocesan bishops as well as the presiding bishop grew in authority. As the nation filled out between the coasts, so did the Episcopal Church grow into a national denomination, serving a constituency that was predominantly urban, well educated, and prosperous.

Parallel and related to the rising fortunes of the Episcopal Church was the rise of an elite that was also gaining a national character. A number of social institutions emerged during the era that helped standardize the culture of this group: private boarding schools, Ivy League colleges, urban and country clubs, the boards of cultural institutions. Many law firms, corporate boards, and government agencies, especially the State Department, also served as networking sites for this reasonably porous elite, in which newcomers might gain acceptance through the acquisition of wealth, social skills, and connections as well as intermarriage. One prerequisite that could never be legitimately acquired, though, was northwest European Protestant origin. It was to this emergent "East Coast Establishment" that the Episcopal Church served as a sort of chaplaincy.

The Episcopal Church was in fact an agent of social stratification. Many of its churches had become not simply houses of worship but social gathering places useful for networking. They often served also as cultural institutions bestowing grace and legitimacy on the new American cities. Even though African American Episcopalians mainly belonged to parishes of their own, these stood at the upper end of the hierarchy of black denominations.

On the other hand, the institution did contain within itself agents of change. Its polity, derived from that of England's national church, in which "parish" had both religious and social dimensions, implied the church's responsibility for the well-being of the entire community, not simply its active membership.

Social settlements, of Anglican provenance, and the distinctively American institutional church were two responses to urban crisis closely aligned with the Episcopal "project" of social and cultural leadership, as was the movement toward the abolition of pew rentals. The Christian Socialism of F. D. Maurice and Charles Kingsley and the critique of industrialism central to the thought of John Ruskin and William Morris provided theoretical grounding for a campaign to ameliorate, if not abolish, the runaway capitalistic individualism that many Episcopal leaders saw as corrosive of what they envisioned as an organic society informed with Christian principles of harmony and community. Senior Warden J. P. Morgan and his untamable rector, William Rainsford, represented a sort of dyadic dynamic that drove St. George's, an institution that embraced seemingly contradictory but often surprisingly harmonious impulses.

Even apparently elitist programs could be construed as promoting these social goals. In the minds of their leaders, private boarding schools existed not only to train a national cadre of business and political leaders, but also to imbue this emergent elite with Christian values, including social awareness and responsibility. Cultural projects such as art museums, musical programming, and historic preservation were often presented as gifts to the community, whose members were to be edified by exposure to the sublime and the instructive. The goal for all except a few outliers such as Bliss was a harmonious society in which Episcopalians would play a role of benevolent, if sometimes paternalistic, leadership. Although growth was welcome, indecorous Evangelistic campaigns such as those of Billy Sunday were usually not. Episcopalians for the most part tacitly accepted the rightness of a hierarchical denominational system, in which they stood at the apex in terms of social prestige. Serving as the nation's unofficial "established" church was not incompatible with a measure of de facto exclusiveness.

The stock market crash of 1929 and the onset of the Great Depression slowed down but did not halt the Episcopal campaign of church growth, institutional expansion, and cultural and social influence. Some expensive enterprises did have to be curtailed, such as cathedral building, plans for which came to naught in Philadelphia as well as in Olympia, Washington, where meager beginnings were subjected to the indignity of foreclosure. Work continued on St. John the Divine but eventually succumbed to the exigencies of wartime, leaving it in seeming perpetuity with the moniker "St. John the Unfinished." Church membership continued to increase at a healthy rate, but the numbers of clergy diminished as parishes and dioceses became hard pressed to support them. The boarding schools were less affected by financial hard times than by the war, in which masters and other staff were conscripted and students had to assume many maintenance tasks.[2]

The Depression brought to the fore a man who embodied as much as had Henry Codman Potter the internal contradictions within the Episcopal community. Franklin Delano Roosevelt was a graduate of Groton ('oo) and Harvard ('04), and served as senior warden of his familial parish of St. James in Hyde Park, New York. Roosevelt was, in short, the embodiment of the "East Coast Establishment," in which Episcopal identity played a central role. Roosevelt, however, rapidly incurred the displeasure of many of his fellow WASPs, who labeled him a "traitor to his class" as he abandoned the laissez-faire economics of his Republican predecessors and publicly denounced what he called "malefactors of great wealth." Although many members of his government were old stock Americans, Roosevelt broke with this customary repository of talent to appoint significant numbers of Jews and Roman Catholics to cabinet positions and the federal judiciary. His opposition to Prohibition and his endorsement of the Twenty-first Amendment undoing that unfortunate social experiment further put him at odds with the majority of Evangelical Protestants, although most Episcopalians presumably breathed a sigh of relief when the repeal arrived. They continued for the most part to constitute "the Republican Party at prayer," although such quintessentially "Establishment" leaders as Secretaries of State Dean Acheson and Cordell Hull served under Democratic presidents.[3]

In 1952, a crisis occurred at the Episcopal seminary at the University of the South in Sewanee. During the previous year, the bishops of the region had mandated that the church's theological schools in the South be open to students of all races. (The Bishop Payne Divinity School in Virginia, which had been established in 1884 to educate African American clergy, was absorbed into its parent institution, the Virginia Theological Seminary, in 1949.) Sewanee's trustees rejected their bishops' mandate on allegedly practical grounds, arguing that the legal and social climate of opinion at that time did not permit racial integration, while also fearing that such action would alienate wealthy donors. All but one of the seminary's ten faculty members threatened to resign, and soon did so. James Pike, then dean of the Cathedral of St. John the Divine, publicly declined the offer of an honorary degree from Sewanee. The following year, the trustees reversed their decision, but the hornet's nest of race had been poked, and the Episcopal Church would become progressively more implicated in the ensuing civil rights struggles over the next decades.[4]

The election of John Fitzgerald Kennedy as president of the United States in 1960 illustrated another shift in the relationship between religious identity, social status, and political power in the American scene. Kennedy was the grandson of two prominent Boston Irish political leaders and the son of a multimillionaire Harvard graduate, who became Franklin Roosevelt's ambassador to Great Britain. Educated at Choate ('35) and Harvard ('40), Kennedy rose to national political prominence as the epitome—with his wife Jacqueline—of social grace and sophistication.* Kennedy remained publicly faithful to his ancestral Catholicism, even though it became a major issue during the 1960 campaign. The election to the nation's highest office of a Roman Catholic who embodied many of the distinctive characteristics of the Eastern Establishment was an indication that Protestant identity was no longer a necessity for national political success. Nor—as subsequent elections would dispute—was Establishment culture yet a liability.

The 1950s and 1960s were also a period in which another aspect of Establishment mores would be challenged. The "St. Grottlesex" complex of boarding schools had been founded mainly under Episcopal auspices, and their constituency from their beginnings had been the wealthy Protestant families of the Northeast. The Ivy League schools, though varied in religious origin, had by the 1920s begun to adopt, often covertly, policies that strictly limited the number of students of Jewish and Catholic origin. "Character," a somewhat elusive quality cultivated by Groton and its peers in their students, now trumped academic achievement as the prime desideratum for Ivy admissions. By the 1950s, however, Harvard's president James Bryant Conant and others began to advocate a policy based more on "merit," as demonstrated by the SAT and other standardized tests. This policy shift resulted in the admission of considerably more Jewish students in particular. (Catholics, suspicious of institutions of Protestant origin and committed to their own alternative educational system, arrived in growing but proportionately lower numbers.) The notion of a "meritocracy" based on ability and achievement rather than descent and "breeding" thus further eroded the claims to social

*Jacqueline Bouvier Kennedy Onassis had attended Miss Porter's and Vassar, among other schools. Her stepfather, Hugh D. Auchincloss, was a cousin of novelist Louis Auchincloss, the chronicler of WASP life in novels such as *The Rector of Justin* (1954).

hegemony that had been part of the "Eastern Establishment" mystique. This erosion continued as selective colleges and boarding schools began in the 1970s to actively recruit students coming from a diversity of social and ethnic backgrounds.[5]

The high-water mark of Episcopal Church growth was 1965, when overall membership exceeded 3.5 million.[6] This date was not an accident. The civil rights movement, in which many Episcopal clergy had taken part, had been successful but divisive, alienating many southern members. The Vietnam War was in the offing, and the polarization of the nation that ensued further exacerbated tensions within the church. Most traumatic, however, was the controversy that took place within the denomination over responses to de-mands made by minority spokespersons in the struggle over "empowerment," a term reflecting the goals of the civil rights movement after its legislative triumphs of mid-decade. Episcopalians were not alone: Other "mainline" denominations experienced the same conflict between social witness and fiscal prudence, exemplified in the confrontational appearance of activist James Forman at Manhattan's Riverside Church in 1969. His "Black Mani-festo," demanding a half-billion dollars in reparations for the damage caused by slavery, put mainline churches in an awkward position. The Episcopal Church funded a number of local projects for community development and empowerment, some of which turned out to have been of doubtful propriety. Increased tensions between denominational leadership and grassroots parish constituencies often resulted.[7]

The Episcopal Church also suffered from contention over internal prob-lems during the 1970s. The American version of the *Book of Common Prayer*, which provided the central liturgical texts for the common worship shared by Anglicans of all persuasions, had last been revised in 1928, and still re-tained many of the Calvinist-tinged formulations of its sixteenth-century antecedents. The 1979 edition, which provided both modified archaic texts and more modern renderings, drew the wrath of traditionalists attached to Archbishop Cranmer's stately diction. Even more provocative was the ordination of women to the diaconate and priesthood, beginning on an au-thorized basis in 1976. Twelve years later, a woman—an African American woman—was elected bishop for the first time.

The fury of opposition raised by conservatives to these steps into moder-nity resulted in a number of defections, mainly to splinter groups that arose out of these controversies. These groups proved too fragmented to have a great deal of staying power. Tempers rose again in 2003, when the House of Bishops elected Gene Robinson, who was living in a publicly declared homosexual relationship, as bishop coadjutor of New Hampshire; he became bishop in his own right the following year. (A bishop coadjutor is an assistant bishop who automatically succeeds the reigning bishop upon his or her retirement.) This too galvanized opponents. The most vocal of these was Pittsburgh's Robert Duncan, who became one of several bishops to try to lead their dioceses out of the Episcopal Church and into an affiliation with more conservative branches of the Anglican Communion in the developing world. Attempts by these breakaway dioceses to retain their property have always been legally challenged, usually without success on the part of the dissidents.[8] The Episcopal Church was both experiencing and reflecting what Daniel T. Rodgers has called America's "age of fracture," in which a shared sense of belonging to a large whole now gives way to a plethora of fragmented and continually shifting communities of identity.[9]

One result of these quarrels and schisms has been a significant loss of membership, coupled with substantial confusion, legal fees, and an atmosphere of contentiousness in many parts of the church. Membership, which had dipped below the two million mark by the second decade of the twenty-first century, was also affected by the same demographic patterns that were having an impact on other mainline denominations. The widespread use of artificial birth control correlates particularly with educational levels. Since Episcopalians have always ranked among the best-educated of American religious groups, it should not be surprising that their birth rate has been low. And, unlike more conservative denominations, they have generally failed to put a great emphasis on socializing their children into the faith, with a corresponding high attrition rate among the younger set. These losses have been partially offset by an influx of members, primarily older adults, from other traditions.[10]

Another marker of the fortunes of the "Episcopal project" in retaining social power has been illustrated in the political realm. Episcopalians have generally been represented on the U.S. Supreme Court in disproportion to their numbers; however, as of 2010, that august body was composed entirely of justices of Jewish or Roman Catholic background (although all had attended either Harvard's or Yale's law schools).* The role of Episcopal affilia-

---

*Episcopalians on the high court begin with John Jay and John Marshall and in recent years have included Thurgood Marshall, Sandra Day O'Connor, David Souter, and Byron White. Chloe Breyer, the daughter of Stephen Breyer, is an Episcopal priest and the author of *The Close*

tion in presidential politics is also illuminating. For earlier presidents such as Franklin Roosevelt and Gerald Ford it was not an issue, although Ford was forced by the press to address the question of whether he had been "born again." George H. W. Bush, a "cradle" Episcopalian who had briefly attended a Presbyterian church in his adopted state of Texas, remained in his birthright faith while publicly identifying himself with Baptist evangelist Billy Graham. His son and eventual successor, George W. Bush, shared his father's academic pedigree of Andover and Yale, but distanced himself from his family heritage in his adoption of a more Texan public persona. This reinvention included a "born again" religiosity; he joined his wife's Methodist church, as his brother Jeb followed his own spouse into Roman Catholicism.

Among other presidential candidates, Barry Goldwater, who unsuccessfully challenged Lyndon Johnson in 1964, was an Episcopalian of Jewish background. His family history illustrates the role of Episcopal Church membership in the assimilation of American Jews into upper-class American life noted in passing in earlier chapters. John McCain, an Arizona senator and the 2008 Republican presidential nominee, had been a longtime Episcopalian, but somewhat ambiguously identified himself during the campaign as a Baptist. It seems clear that any advantage that the Episcopal "brand" may have possessed politically has substantially eroded, especially among Republicans seeking Evangelical votes. McCain, who had attended the Episcopal High School in Virginia, and the younger Bushes also present themselves as examples of their imperfect socialization into the denomination of their youth.[11]

Similar patterns can be found in other areas of American public life. Ivy League universities have in recent years all had high administrators of Jewish as well as other once inadmissible ethnic backgrounds. The succession of the Yale presidency from men with names such as A. Whitney Griswold and Kingman Brewster to Giamatti, Levin, and Salevy speaks for itself.[12] Although by no means all of the Ivy leaders of earlier generations were Episcopalians, they were almost universally male and Protestant, and usually of more prestigious denominations such as Congregational, Presbyterian, and Unitarian. By the 1970s, religious identification of any sort was becoming

---

(2000), an account of her training at General Theological Seminary. Clarence Thomas, who had been raised as a Baptist, belonged to the Episcopal Church for several years before becoming Roman Catholic. As of 2015, 35 of 108 justices—nearly one-third—have been Episcopalians. See http://www.adherents.com/adh_sc.html.

increasingly irrelevant to leadership in educational and other cultural institutions lacking a denominational affiliation—an illustration of what sociologist Phillip Hammond has called "the third disestablishment."[13]

Other examples abound. In years past, the Episcopal Church enjoyed considerable prestige in the military (especially the Navy), and membership was a mark of status as "an officer and a gentleman." In more recent years, Roman Catholics and Evangelicals have proliferated in the officer corps, and protests have been made over what has been perceived as coercive evangelism, especially at the less tradition-bound Air Force Academy.[14] On another front, marriage notices in the *New York Times*, a sign of social recognition, have grown noticeably more inclusive over the decades. In 1947, 58 percent of such notices involved Episcopalians. No Jews were included.[15] In recent years, notices of Jewish unions outnumber those of Episcopalians, as do secular ceremonies and those presided over by ministers of the "Universal Life Church," which provides free, instant, online ordination for such purposes. Roman Catholics are amply represented, as are Hindus and Muslims in growing numbers. (Evangelicals are much less visible.)

Was the Episcopal project of social and cultural leadership successful? In some ways it has been. Most American cities of a certain size are still graced by Gothic or Romanesque churches and cathedrals that give texture to the urban scene and often reveal dazzling interiors. Others are lost, endangered, or put to new uses, especially in smaller cities where the old local elites have dwindled and their descendants either dispersed or disengaged. The Gothic revival style largely died with Ralph Adams Cram, displaced by modernist approaches and a new version of the colonial revival. The complex of "St. Grottlesex" boarding schools flourishes, often still under clerical leadership, although their student bodies and faculties are manifestly diverse, as is their architecture.[16] Most cultural institutions founded through the philanthropy of wealthy lay Episcopalians prosper. The religious impulses that underlay such foundations remain ineluctably diffused in the interplay among benevolence, narcissism, aesthetics, sacrality, and economics that such institutions represent.

In the realm of social reform, the Episcopal project was successful in the way that David Hollinger has argued that the mainline—or, as Hollinger calls them, "ecumenical"—Protestant denominations have been successful: as "halfway houses to secularism." Although some Anglo-Catholics argued for the superiority, or even necessity, of their way as a path to salvation, ecumenically minded Broad Churchmen saw the possibilities of grace not only in other Christian denominations but in the workings of the larger social and cultural realms. The settlement houses and institutional churches were devices to help realize Maurice's Kingdom of Christ through the redemption of the material realm when succor for the urban poor was hard to come by. As Roosevelt's New Deal agencies began to take over these functions, Episcopalians such as his old "rector" Endicott Peabody cheered to see the government become involved in the work of this-worldly redemption. These "secular alliances" blurred the boundaries between the eleemosynary functions of church and state and lessened the urgency of church membership.[17]

As the institutional churches outlived their day and were razed or converted to other uses, Episcopalians have continued local outreach projects such as soup kitchens and counseling services, as the denomination has reached out through agencies such as Episcopal Relief and Development. As governmental aid to the poor has attenuated under conservative regimes, these church-sponsored endeavors have became even more central to the Episcopalian self-understanding of its mission. Although the denomination includes members across the social spectrum, Episcopalians overall continue to be among the wealthiest and best-educated American religious communities; they and the Presbyterians have been joined in recent years by Jews and Unitarian-Universalists, all united in their progressive social outlook.[18] Although many Episcopalians continue to vote Republican—laity in greater numbers than clergy—they can no longer be plausibly dubbed "the Republican Party at prayer." Rather, they have more aptly been characterized as the National Public Radio audience assembled for worship. Socially liberal, culturally conservative, a progressively oriented taste culture, twenty-first-century Episcopalians have often been nurtured in other traditions and found the denomination a comfortable home that does not insist on strenuous doctrinal commitments or draw sharp lines between its own territory and that of the broader Christian and secular communities with which it shares many values and concerns. The loss of conservative-minded members, clergy, parishes, and even entire dioceses, beginning in the 1970s, has led to a further homogenization of denominational culture and narrowed the ideological spectrum represented in its discourses.

While sociological studies document the maintenance among Episcopalians of many of the markers of elite social status, they do not address as clearly issues of social power and influence. When, for example, did Episcopal bishops begin to lose their role as quiet behind-the-scenes movers in the urban social and political scene?[19] When did Episcopal parishes begin to shed their cachet as markers of elite status and their role as convenient social and professional networking sites? These observations must be couched with a caution that these phenomena have become muted, but have by no means disappeared—many wealthy parishes in urban and suburban elite enclaves still flourish and carry on as usual.

The answer is most likely that this process began during the 1960s and accelerated during the following decade of social, political, and cultural turmoil, as a befuddled Gerald Ford and George H. W. Bush watched their denomination's quiet influence yield to that of the strident Religious Right, and Catholics, Mormons, and Evangelicals claimed leadership roles, especially within the Republican Party. Through both internal renewal and visible participation in national dramas of social change, the Episcopal Church had thrown off its aspirations to serve as an informal national "established" church in favor of a more prophetic role as advocate for social justice. The "yang" of J. P. Morgan, which for some decades had been in the ascendant, had now become eclipsed by the "yin" of William Rainsford.

The history of the Episcopal Church during the twentieth century can perhaps best be characterized as ironic. This irony is somewhat different, though, from that invoked by Reinhold Niebuhr in his 1952 classic, *The Irony of American History*. Niebuhr recalled the definition of irony manifest in Greek tragedy, in which a hero is brought short through hubris, a hidden flaw that undercuts his powers and produces an outcome opposite to that to which he had aspired. Although many have lamented the decline of the Episcopal Church in numbers and prestige since its heyday, these changes are hardly the stuff of Greek tragedy. Irony, though, is built into the very fabric of Anglicanism, a religious tradition improbably rooted in the political and personal machinations of the infamous Henry VIII.

The precipitous loss of membership by the Episcopal Church and other mainline denominations beginning in the 1960s has been attributed in part to a growing gap between the Episcopal and clerical leadership and the views of congregants, who began to respond to their church's social involvements and internal changes by withholding support and, in some cases, leaving entirely. The church is, however, governed by a polity in which laypeople have an active voice at all levels. It could have avoided the alienation of a minority of its laity only at the cost of maintaining the apolitical, implicitly conservative social role it had played through the century's middle decades. This in turn might have alienated many others, as the social upheavals of the 1960s and 1970s made neutrality an untenable position. As the social establishment it had represented began to dissipate, its continued role as the church of that establishment rapidly lost relevance. The ironic—but by no means tragic—outcome is that the prophetic strain that had been nurtured in the years of the Social Gospel has now reemerged and carried the day, as gay men and women can be married at its altars and even preside over its dioceses. Such is the irony of American Episcopal history.

Notes

Preface

1. See, for example, Sven Beckert, *The Monied Metropolis: New York City and the Consolidation of the American Bourgeoisie, 1850–1896* (Cambridge: Cambridge University Press, 1993); Rebecca Edwards, *New Spirits: Americans in the "Gilded Age" 1865–1905* (New York: Oxford University Press, 2011); Jackson Lears, *Rebirth of a Nation: The Making of Modern America, 1877–1920* (New York: HarperCollins, 2009).

2. Peter W. Williams, "A Mirror for Unitarians: Catholicism and Culture in Nineteenth Century New England Literature" (Ph.D. diss., Yale University, 1970).

Introduction

1. Amanda Mackenzie Stuart, *Consuelo and Alva Vanderbilt: The Story of a Daughter and a Mother in the Gilded Age* (New York: HarperCollins, 2005), 1–7, 144–47; Louis Auchincloss, *The Vanderbilt Era: Profiles of a Gilded Age* (New York: Scribner's, 1989), 105–11.

2. On Potter, see Michael Bourgeois, *All Things Human: Henry Codman Potter and the Social Gospel* (Urbana: University of Illinois Press, 2004).

3. Examples of such denominational histories include E. Clowes Chorley, *Men and Movements in the Episcopal Church* (New York: Charles Scribner's Sons, 1948); Raymond W. Albright, *A History of the Protestant Episcopal Church* (New York: Macmillan, 1964); David L. Holmes, *A Brief History of the Episcopal Church* (Valley Forge, Pa.: Trinity Press International, 1993); Robert Prichard, *A History of the Episcopal Church* (Harrisburg, Pa.: Morehouse, 1991, 1999, 2014).

4. See James F. White, *The Cambridge Movement: The Ecclesiologists and the Gothic Revival* (Cambridge: Cambridge University Press, 1962); and Phoebe M. Stanton, *The Gothic Revival and American Church Architecture: An Episode in Taste, 1840–1856* (Baltimore, Md.: Johns Hopkins University Press, 1968), for definitive accounts of this phenomenon.

5. See Everard Upjohn, *Richard Upjohn: Architect and Churchman* (New York: Columbia University Press, 1939).

6. This was Bishop Levi Silliman Ives of North Carolina. In England, John Henry Newman, the Tractarian leader, not only defected to Rome but was later made a cardinal.

7. Their official name was the Society of St. John the Evangelist. The religious orders had been suppressed after the English Reformation by Henry VIII, who coveted the

monasteries' rich land holdings, and were not revived in England until the 1860s. Episcopal parishes such as the Church of the Advent in Boston, St. Clement's in Philadelphia, and St. Mary the Virgin in New York City continue to represent this tradition.

8. Thomas Hughes, 1857.

9. Quoted in Albright, *Protestant Episcopal Church*, 302.

10. Ibid., 306.

11. Eric Homberger, *Mrs. Astor's New York: Money and Social Power in a Gilded Age* (New Haven, Conn.: Yale University Press, 2003), 116–19. For more on Brown, see William Rhinelander Stewart, *Grace Church and Old New York* (New York: E. P. Dutton, 1923), 177–79.

12. Homberger, *Mrs. Astor*, 113.

13. Ibid., 114–15.

14. Cleveland Amory, *The Proper Bostonians* (New York: E. P. Dutton, 1947), 179.

15. Albright, *Protestant Episcopal Church*, 310.

16. Stewart, *Grace Church*, 184–85.

17. Elizabeth Moulton, *St. George's Church New York* (New York: St. George's Church, 1964), 39; Stewart, *Grace Church*, 191.

18. Stewart, *Grace Church*, 183; Homberger, *Mrs. Astor*, 115.

19. Moulton, *St. George's*, 74.

20. Homberger, *Mrs. Astor*, 182–85; Sven Beckert, *The Monied Metropolis: New York City and the Consolidation of the American Bourgeoisie, 1850–1896* (Cambridge: Cambridge University Press, 1993), 59–60.

21. Rima Lunin Schultz, *The Church and the City: A Social History of 150 Years at St. James, Chicago* (Chicago, Ill.: The Cathedral of St. James, 1986), 12–13, 123; Frederic Cople Jaher, *The Urban Establishment* (Urbana: University of Illinois Press, 1982), 467, 518.

22. See Ronald Story, *The Forging of an Aristocracy: Harvard and the Boston Upper Class, 1800–1870* (Middletown, Conn.: Wesleyan University Press, 1980), esp. 8, 96.

23. Barbara Cross, ed., *The Autobiography of Lyman Beecher* (Cambridge, Mass.: Harvard University Press, 1961), II, 82. Beecher's autobiography was compiled and interpolated by Harriet and others of his many children.

24. Amory, *Proper Bostonians*, 104–5. See also Jaher, *Urban Establishment*, 101–2.

25. E. Digby Baltzell, *Philadelphia Gentlemen: The Making of a National Upper Class* (Glencoe, Ill.: The Free Press, 1958), 240.

26. Baltzell, *Philadelphia Gentlemen*, 227–28, 241–45.

27. Nathaniel Burt, *The Perennial Philadelphians* (Boston: Little, Brown, 1963), 75.

28. Ibid., 32.

29. Baltzell, *Philadelphia Gentlemen*, 244.

30. Ibid., 252.

31. Quoted in ibid., 252–53.

32. Ibid., Table 22, 248.

33. Ibid., 74–75; Amory, *Proper Bostonians*, 107.

34. Burt, *Perennial Philadelphians*, 566.

35. See, e.g., Cynthia Gensheimer, "Annie Jonas Wells: Jewish Daughter, Episcopal Wife, Independent Intellectual," *American Jewish History* (July 2014): 83–125.

36. John N. Ingham, "Steel City Aristocrats," in *City at the Point: Essays on the Social History of Pittsburgh*, ed. Samuel P. Hays (Pittsburgh: University of Pittsburgh Press, 1989), 266–67.

37. Ibid., 276; Francis G. Couvares, *The Remaking of Pittsburgh: Class and Culture in an Industrializing City 1877–1919* (Albany, N.Y.: SUNY Press, 1984), 31.

38. Ingham, "Steel City Aristocrats," 269. "By mid-nineteenth century, the Pittsburgh elite had created a strong, tightly knit local aristocracy which evidently managed to integrate the older mercantile elite with a newer manufacturing group."

39. James Parton, "Pittsburgh," *Atlantic Monthly*, January 1868, 17–36, quoted in Couvares, *Remaking of Pittsburgh*, 34.

40. Couvares, *Remaking of Pittsburgh*, 37.

41. Ibid., 98–104.

42. *The East Liberty Presbyterian Church* (Pittsburgh, Pa.: East Liberty Presbyterian Church, 1935); *Centennial History Calvary Episcopal Church 1855–1955* (Pittsburgh, Pa.: Calvary Episcopal Church, 1955).

43. Couvares, *Remaking of Pittsburgh*, 98.

44. Seth Low, Columbia University president and mayor, first of Brooklyn and then New York City, was, with other St. George's members, such as Robert Fulton Cutting and Nicholas Murray Butler, active in the reform-minded Citizens Union. Moulton, *St. George's*, 70–71.

45. Keith A. Zahniser, *Steel City Gospel: Protestant Laity and Reform in Progressive Era Pittsburgh* (New York: Routledge, 2005), esp. 1, 10.

46. Julia Shelley Hodges, *George Hodges* (New York: The Century Co., 1926), 82; *Steel City Gospel*, 69.

47. Ingham, "Steel City Aristocrats," 281.

48. Couvares, *Remaking of Pittsburgh*, 96.

49. Lawrence W. Levine, *Highbrow, Lowbrow: The Emergence of Cultural Hierarchy in America* (Cambridge, Mass.: Harvard University Press, 1988) is the classic study of the emergence of taste cultures in the United States during this period.

50. See Alice Chandler, *A Dream of Order: The Medieval Ideal in Nineteenth-Century English Literature* (Lincoln: University of Nebraska Press, 1970).

51. Andrew Carnegie, "Wealth" (1889), published as "The Gospel of Wealth" with other essays in *The Gospel of Wealth*, ed. Edward C. Kirkland (Cambridge, Mass.: Harvard University Press, 1962), 14–49.

Chapter One

1. I am indebted to my colleague Mary Kupiec Cayton, herself an Irish American, for this observation.

2. Louis Auchincloss, "Augustus St.-Gaudens," in *The Vanderbilt Era: Profiles of a Gilded Age* (New York: Charles Scribner's Sons, 1989), 137–42. See also John H. Dryfhout, *The Work of Augustus St.-Gaudens* (Hanover: University Press of New England, 1982), 162–66, 222–29, 189–93, 283–87, 299–300.

3. The current King's Chapel, designed by Peter Harrison in 1749–54, houses the first American congregation to adopt a Unitarian theology, although it has always continued to use a modified Anglican liturgy. Christ Church remains an active parish in the Episcopal Diocese of Massachusetts, while doubling as a tourist attraction on Boston's "Freedom Trail."

4. Bettina A. Norton, ed., *Trinity Church, The Story of an Episcopal Parish in the City of Boston* (Boston: Wardens and Vestry of Trinity Church, 1978), 9–16.

5. George L. Blackman and Mark J. Duffy, "The Tradition of Massachusetts Churchmanship," in *The Episcopal Diocese of Massachusetts 1784–1984*, ed. Mark J. Duffy (Boston: Episcopal Diocese of Massachusetts, 1984), 5.

6. Norton, *Trinity Church*, 17.

7. Rt. Rev. William Lawrence, "Phillips Brooks," in *Trinity Church in the City of Boston, Massachusetts: 1733–1933* (Boston: Wardens and Vestry, 1933), 67–68.

8. As Blackman and Duffy point out, congregational identity was so strong among Massachusetts Episcopalians that it never occurred to the proprietors of Trinity that there might be a problem in relocating within a few blocks of potential rival Emmanuel. Duffy, *Episcopal Diocese*, 2.

9. Rt. Rev. William Scarlett, ed., *Phillips Brooks: Selected Sermons* (New York: E. P. Dutton, 1950), 7.

10. John F. Woolverton, *The Education of Phillips Brooks* (Urbana: University of Illinois Press, 1995), 12, 68, 69.

11. Ibid., 13.

12. See Daniel Walker Howe, *The Unitarian Conscience* (Cambridge, Mass.: Harvard University Press, 1970).

13. Henry Adams, *The Education of Henry Adams* (New York: Random House/Modern Library, c. 1918, 1931, 1946), 54. Brooks was most likely the model for the clergyman in Adams's novel *Esther* (1884); the eponymous heroine seems to have been based on Adams's wife, Marion "Clover" Hooper, whose memorial was later wrought by Augustus St.-Gaudens. Raymond W. Albright, *Focus on Infinity: A Life of Phillips Brooks* (New York: Macmillan, 1961), 180.

14. Woolverton, *Education*, 64.

15. Ibid., 14. Andover was the first postgraduate institution designed specifically for clerical education in the nation. Harvard Divinity School, as a distinct institution separate from Harvard College—until then the locus of ministerial education—was established in 1816.

16. Ibid., 13–17; Albright, *Focus*, 14–15, 93.

17. Blackman and Duffy, *Episcopal Diocese*, 3.

18. Ibid., 1.

19. Woolverton, *Education*, 66–70.

20. Ibid., esp. 57, 72, 75, 87.

21. Albright, *Focus*, 53–111.

22. Woolverton, *Education*, 105–6.

23. Albright, *Focus*, 171.

24. Gillis J. Harp, *Brahmin Prophet: Phillips Brooks and the Path of Liberal Protestantism* (Lanham, Md.: Rowman & Littlefield, 2003), 23, 122–28.

25. Woolverton, *Education*, 107.

26. Scarlett, *Phillips Brooks*, 7. See also Albright, *Focus*, 200, 387; Harp, *Brahmin Prophet*, 215.

27. Albright, *Focus*, 386.

28. Ibid., 160, 393–95.

29. Ibid., 301, 358–68; Harp, *Brahmin Prophet*, 191–93.

30. Phillips Brooks, *Letters of Travel* (New York: E. P. Dutton, 1893), 329–35; Albright, *Focus*, 214, 253, 281.

31. Brooks, *Letters of Travel*, 298, 303; Albright, *Focus*, esp. 279.

32. Albright, *Focus*, 254.

33. Ibid., 92–93.

34. Harp, *Brahmin Prophet*, 152–53.

35. Albright, *Focus*, 120.

36. Ibid., 259.

37. Harp, *Brahmin Prophet*, 154; Albright, *Focus*, 165–66, 200, 274.

38. See Elisa Tamarkin, *Anglophilia: Deference, Devotion, and Antebellum America* (Chicago: University of Chicago Press, 2008), especially chapter 4 ("The Anglophile Academy").

39. Albright, *Focus*, 259–60.

40. Ian Tyrrell, *Reforming the World: The Creation of America's Moral Empire* (Princeton, N.J.: Princeton University Press, 2010), 14.

41. Selected letters from his travels were published as *Letters of Travel* (New York: E. P. Dutton, 1893).

42. James Turner, *Religion Enters the Academy: The Origins of the Scholarly Study of Religion in America* (Athens: University of Georgia Press, 2011), esp. 50–51, 56.

43. Albright, *Focus*, 113, 235.

44. Brooks, *Letters*, 320, 313, 311–12, 101, 103–4.

45. Ibid., 228, 265, 238.

46. Albright, *Focus*, 131–32.

47. Brooks, *Letters*, 69–70.

48. Ibid., 87–89.

49. Daniel Walker Howe, "Victorian Culture in America," in *Victorian America*, ed. Daniel Walker Howe (Philadelphia: University of Pennsylvania Press, 1976), 3–28.

50. Brooks, *Letters*, 183; see also Albright, *Focus*, 144, 145, 149, 192, 216, 226, 270, 293, 298.

51. Howe, "Victorian Culture," 12.

232 Notes to Pages 39–44

52. Ibid., 22, 24, 25. See also Harp, *Brahmin Prophet*, 108–9, 127–28, 181, 184.

53. Howe, "Victorian Culture," 24; Mary Kupiec Cayton, "The Making of an American Prophet: Emerson, His Audiences, and the Rise of the Culture Industry in Nineteenth-Century America," in *Ralph Waldo Emerson: A Collection of Critical Essays*, ed. Lawrence Buell (Englewood Cliffs, N.J.: Prentice-Hall, 1993), 84; David Riesman, *The Lonely Crowd: A Study of the Changing American Character* (New Haven, Conn.: Yale University Press, 1950).

54. Cayton, "American Prophet," 183.

55. Albright, *Focus*, 341–42.

56. "The Duty of the Christian Businessman," in *Phillips Brooks' Addresses* (introduction by Rev. Julius H. Ward) (Boston: Charles E. Brown & Co., 1893), 71–96; quoted passages from 73 and 81.

57. Norton, *Trinity Church*, 30, 17; Alexander V. G. Allen, *Life and Letters of Phillips Brooks* (New York: E. P. Dutton, 1901), ii, 268.

58. Brooks, "The Episcopal Church," in *The Memorial History of Boston*, ed. Justin Winsor (Boston: James K. Osgood, 1881), iii, 464.

59. Oscar Handlin, *Boston's Immigrants* (New York: Atheneum, 1969), Table IX, 246.

60. Brooks helped established Trinity missions on West Cedar Street, North Charles Street, and Chambers Street during the 1870s and 1880s. Albright, *Focus*, 146, 225, 306.

61. Heather D. Curtis, "Visions of Self, Success, and Society among Young Men in Antebellum Boston," *Church History* 73, no. 3 (September 2004): 613. Curtis here studies attempts by young male "in-migrants," many working at entry-level business positions such as clerks or tellers, to improve themselves in the context of Evangelicalism.

62. Albright, *Focus*, 90, 122, 149.

63. Ibid., 79, 177, 225.

64. Ibid., 176, 275, 327, 335; Harp, *Brahmin Prophet*, 133.

65. Harp, *Brahmin Prophet*, 134.

66. Theodore E. Stebbins Jr., "Trinity Church at 125," in *The Makers of Trinity Church in the City of Boston*, ed. James F. O'Gorman (Amherst: University of Massachusetts Press, 2004), 14.

67. Phillips Brooks, "Henry Hobson Richardson," *Harvard Monthly* 3, no. 1 (October 1886): 1.

68. Susan Southworth and Michael Southworth, *A.I.A. Guide to Boston* (Chester, Conn.: Globe Pequot Press, 1987), 217.

69. Kathleen Curran, *The Romanesque Revival: Religion, Politics, and Transnational Exchange* (University Park: Pennsylvania State University Press, 2003), xxv, xxvi, 210–11, 215.

70. Kathleen Curran, "The Romanesque Revival, Mural Painting, and Protestant Patronage in America," *Art Bulletin* 81, no. 2 (December 1999): 693–722, passim. See also William H. Pierson Jr., "Richardson's Trinity Church and the New England Meeting-house," in *American Public Architecture: European Roots and Native Expressions*, ed. Craig Zabel and Susan Scott Munshower, vol. 5 of *Papers in Art History from the Penn-*

sylvania State University (University Park: Pennsylvania State University, 1989). Pierson cites Harvard's Appleton Chapel and Boylston Hall as other Romanesque revival structures likely to have influenced Richardson, especially his Brattle Square Church.

71. Southworth and Southworth, *A.I.A. Guide*, 253–54.

72. Allen, *Life*, II, 251–53; Southworth and Southworth, *A.I.A. Guide*, 220; Milda B. Richardson, "Chancel Remodeling: Charles D. Maginnis (Maginnis & Walsh)," in O'Gorman, *Makers*, 175–91.

73. Paine, a childhood friend of Brooks and a man of great wealth, was much more of an activist than Brooks in addressing the needs of Boston's poor. Thomas M. Paine, "Chairman of the Building Committee: Robert Treat Paine," in O'Gorman, *Makers*, 32–59.

74. Albright, *Focus*, 167–88, 230–32; Allen, *Life*, 255; Keith N. Morgan, "Introduction" in O'Gorman, *Makers*, 4–5.

75. Southworth and Southworth, *A.I.A. Guide*, 219–20; Allen, *Life*, 254.

76. Jeffrey Karl Ochsner, "H. H. Richardson," in *American National Biography Online* (New York: Oxford University Press, 1990). See also Ochsner, *H.H. Richardson: Complete Architectural Works* (Cambridge, Mass.: MIT Press, 1982, 1984), 114–23; and Margaret Henderson Floyd, *Henry Hobson Richardson: A Genius for Architecture* (New York: Monacelli Press, 1997), 44–51.

77. Southworth and Southworth, *A.I.A. Guide*, 220.

78. New Old South (Congregational; Cummings and Sears, 1874–75) is the institutional successor to the Old South Meeting House (1729), still located in the Washington Street district and preserved as an historic site on the "Freedom Trail" of Boston Revolutionary War monuments. New Old South was most memorably presided over by George Angier Gordon (1853–1929), a Scottish-born "Prince of the Pulpit" whose message in many ways paralleled that of Brooks.

79. Southworth and Southworth, *A.I.A. Guide*, 226–28.

80. Brooks, "Henry Hobson Richardson," 4, 5.

81. Keith N. Morgan, "Introduction," 4; David B. Cheseborough, "Client: Phillips Brooks," 28; and Keith Bakker, "H. H. Richardson's Furnishings," 82–103. All in O'Gorman, *Makers*.

82. Virginia Chieffo Raguin, "Decorator: John La Farge," in O'Gorman, *Makers*, 119, 122, 123–25, 134. See also Helene Barbara Weinberg, "John La Farge and the Decoration of Trinity Church, Boston," *Journal of the Society of Architectural Historians* 33, no. 4 (December 1974): 323–53.

83. Norton, *Trinity Church*, 38–29.

84. Allen, *Life*, II, 256; Lyman Abbot, *Henry Ward Beecher: A Sketch of His Career* (Hartford, Conn.: American Publishing Co., 1887), 199–201.

85. Albright, *Focus*, 191; Norton, *Trinity Church*, 44; Erica E. Hirshler, "Women Artists at Trinity: Sarah Wyman Whitman and Margaret Redmond," in O'Gorman, *Makers*, chap. 10.

86. Later Gothic revival Protestant churches such as Second Presbyterian in Indianapolis and Fourth Presbyterian in Chicago would include figural representations

of historic figures such as John Calvin. See also Harp, "A New Protestant Aesthetic," *Brahmin Prophet*, 8–89.

87. Allen, *Life*, II, 250.

88. Ibid., 257–58.

Chapter Two

1. John T. Maltsberger, *The Church of the Advent, First Years* (Boston: Church of the Advent, 1986), 51–52.

2. Ibid., 52, 66–67.

3. Diana Hochstedt Butler, *Standing against the Whirlwind: Evangelical Episcopalians in Nineteenth-Century America* (New York: Oxford University Press, 1995), 113; George Franklin Smythe, *A History of the Diocese of Ohio until the Year 1918* (Cleveland, Ohio: The Diocese, 1931), 246–47.

4. On the growing popularity of "Catholic" ornament in American Protestant churches during the mid-nineteenth century, see Ryan K. Smith, *Gothic Arches, Latin Crosses: Anti-Catholicism and American Church Design in the Nineteenth Century* (Chapel Hill: University of North Carolina Press, 2006).

5. The standard work on the Ecclesiologists is James F. White, *The Cambridge Movement: The Ecclesiologists and the Gothic Revival* (Cambridge: Cambridge University Press, 1962).

6. William H. Pierson Jr., *American Buildings and Their Architects: Technology and the Picturesque: The Corporate and Early Gothic Styles* (Garden City, N.Y.: Doubleday, 1978), 184. See also Phoebe B. Stanton, *The Gothic Revival and American Church Architecture: An Episode in Taste* (Baltimore, Md.: Johns Hopkins Press, 1968), 91–115.

7. *Upjohn's Rural Architecture* (1852) inspired churches across a wide swath of denominations throughout rural America in the mid-nineteenth century. On Upjohn, see Pierson, *American Buildings*, part III ("Richard Upjohn and the Ecclesiological Movement in America") and chapter 8 ("The Board and Batten and the Gothic Revival Church"). See also Everard M. Upjohn, *Richard Upjohn: Architect and Churchman* (New York: Columbia University Press, 1939).

8. Trinity's history is discussed at greater length in chapter 4.

9. Pierson, *American Buildings*, 159; Edward F. Bergman, *The Spiritual Traveler: New York City* (Mahwah, N.J.: Hidden Spring, 2001), 84–87. See also Dena Merriam, *Trinity: A Church, A Parish, A People* (New York: Cross River Press, 1996), for its lavish illustrations of Trinity, past and present.

10. Betty Hughes Morris, *A History of the Church of the Advent* (Boston: Church of the Advent, 1995); Susan Southworth and Michael Southworth, *A.I.A. Guide to Boston* (Chester, Conn.: Globe Pequot Press, 1987), 182–83; Douglass Shand-Tucci, *Built in Boston: City and Suburb* (Boston: New York Graphic Society, 1978), 156, 158.

11. Shand-Tucci, *Built in Boston*, 158.

12. After Sturgis's death in 1888, work on Advent was taken over by his even more eminent nephew, Russell Sturgis, who in 1863 had been a founder of the Society for the Advancement of Truth in Art, the objective of which was the advocacy of the aesthetic principles of John Ruskin.

13. Morris, *Advent*, 133–37.

14. Ibid., 138.

15. Ibid., 138–43, 159.

16. Ibid., 146, 151. On Vaughan, see William Morgan, *The Almighty Wall: The Architecture of Henry Vaughan* (Cambridge, Mass.: Architectural History Foundation and MIT Press, 1983) and references in chapter 5.

17. Morris, *Advent*, 151–57.

18. Ibid., 159–69.

19. On Ruskin's influence in the United States, see Roger B. Stein, *John Ruskin and Aesthetic Thought in America, 1840–1900* (Cambridge, Mass.: Harvard University Press, 1967).

20. On the influence of both Morris and Ruskin in America, see Eileen Boris, *Art and Labor: Ruskin, Morris, and the Craftsman Ideal in America* (Philadelphia: Temple University Press, 1986).

21. See Kermit Vanderbilt, *Charles Eliot Norton: Apostle of Culture in a Democracy* (Cambridge, Mass.: Belknap Press of Harvard University Press, 1959); James Turner, *The Liberal Education of Charles Eliot Norton* (Baltimore, Md.: Johns Hopkins University Press, 1999); and Linda C. Dowling, *Charles Eliot Norton: The Art of Reform* (Durham, N.H.: University of New Hampshire Press and University Press of New England, 2007).

22. See Wendy Kaplan et al., *"The Art That Is Life": The Arts & Crafts Movement in America, 1875–1920* (Boston: Museum of Fine Arts, 1987); and Marilee Boyd Meyer et al., *Inspiring Reform: Boston's Arts and Crafts Movement* (Wellesley, Mass.: Davis Museum and Cultural Center, 1997), 19.

23. For brief sketches and appraisals of Cram's life, see the elegant essay by Walter Muir Whitehill in *Dictionary of American Biography, Supplement 3, 1941–1945* (New York: Scribner, c. 1973), 194–97, and that of Peter W. Williams in *American National Biography Online* (New York: Oxford University Press, 2000), with bibliography. A full-scale study is Douglass Shand-Tucci, *Ralph Adams Cram: Life and Architecture*, published in two volumes: *Boston Bohemia 1891–1900* (Amherst: University of Massachusetts Press, 1995) and *An Architect's Four Quests: Medieval, Modernist, American, Ecumenical* (Amherst: University of Massachusetts Press, 2005). See also Robert Muccigrosso, *American Gothic: The Mind and Art of Ralph Adams Cram* (Washington, D.C.: University Press of America, 1980); and Cram's autobiographical *My Life in Architecture* (Boston: Little, Brown, 1936).

24. Cram, *My Life*, 58–60.

25. See chapter 4 for a more extended treatment of Bliss. On Cram's early religious involvements, see Shand-Tucci, *Boston Bohemia*, 68.

26. On the Princeton Chapel, see Richard Stillwell, *The Chapel of Princeton University* (Princeton, N.J.: Princeton University Press, 1971); and Margaret M. Grubiak, *White Elephants on Campus: The Decline of the University Chapel in America, 1920–1960* (Notre Dame, Ind.: University of Notre Dame Press, 2013).

27. See Shand-Tucci, *Built in Boston*, 158.

28. Douglass Shand-Tucci, *All Saints Ashmont, Dorchester, Boston: A Centennial History of the Parish* (Boston: All Saints Parish, 1975), 11.

29. Ibid, 21–22; Shand-Tucci, *Built in Boston*, 160; Muccigrosso, *American Gothic*, 73. My colleague Robert A. Benson provided invaluable observations on All Saints's context in architectural history.

30. Shand-Tucci, *Built in Boston*, 162; *All Saints Ashmont*, 20, 24.

31. On Cram's and Goodhue's involvement, see Meyer, *Inspiring Reform*, esp. 17.

32. See ibid., esp. 22; and F. Shirley Prouty, *Master Carver Johannes Kirchmayer, 1860–1930* (Portsmouth, N.H.: Peter Randall, 2007).

33. Shand-Tucci, *All Saints Ashmont*, 31. All Saints's website is a useful and well-illustrated guide to the church: http://www.allsaints.net.

34. Shand-Tucci, *All Saints Ashmont*, 39; Ryan K. Smith, *Gothic Arches*, chap. 3.

35. J. Robert Wright, *St. Thomas Church Fifth Avenue* (Grand Rapids, Mich.: Eerdmans and St. Thomas Church, 2001), 9, 19, 51, 66, 68, 69, 73–75; Upjohn, *Richard Upjohn*, 178–80.

36. See the beginning of this work's Introduction.

37. Bergman, *Spiritual Traveler*, 190.

38. Glenn Collins, "Let There Be Light, and Color, on Fifth Avenue," *New York Times*, May 24, 2009. The article deals with the twenty million dollar restoration project then being undertaken on the church's windows.

39. Bergman, *Spiritual Traveler*, 190–92; "A Walking Tour of St. Thomas" (pamphlet) (n.p.: n.p., n.d.); "St. Thomas Church" (New York: St. Thomas Church, 1965); St. Thomas Church website: http://www.saintthomaschurch.org/building.

40. "'J.P.M.' Money Bags Adorn St. Thomas's," *New York Times*, August 9, 1921. The article also mentions a dollar sign appearing on the "Brides' Door" portal. Yale's Gothic revival Sterling Library and Law School also feature such playful iconography, which had been a feature of medieval Gothic carving. The Darth Vader gargoyle atop Washington's National Cathedral is a still more recent nod to the tradition.

41. The term "Art Deco" derives from the *Exposition Internationale des Arts Décoratifs et Industriels Modernes* held in Paris in 1925. It encompasses a variety of approaches to architectural, industrial, and other ornamental design ranging from the highly ornate to a streamlined classicism reflecting the geometry of the "Machine Age."

42. Muccigrosso, *American Gothic*, 74–75.

43. Ralph Adams Cram, "Radio City—And After," in *Convictions and Controversies* (Boston: Marshall Jones, 1935), 33–44.

44. See, for example, *The Gothic Quest* (New York: Baker and Taylor, 1907), as well as the earlier cited *Convictions and Controversies* of 1935.

45. On the fascination of Americans of Protestant background, including Cram, with the Middle Ages as a *gemeinschaftlich* counterpoint to their own intensely *gesellschaftlich* society, see Peter W. Williams, "A Mirror for Unitarians: Catholicism and Culture in Nineteenth Century New England Literature" (Ph.D. diss., Yale University, 1970); and T. J. Jackson Lears, *No Place of Grace: Antimodernism and the Transformation of American Culture* (New York: Pantheon, 1981).

46. Cram, *Convictions and Controversies*, 80.

47. Twelve Southerners, *I'll Take My Stand: The South and the Agrarian Tradition* (New York: Harper and Brothers, 1930; Harper Torchbook ed. 1962). See especially John Donald Wade, "The Life and Death of Cousin Lucius," 265–301.

48. Lears, *No Place of Grace*, 207–8; Muccigrosso, *American Gothic*, 40, 231.

49. Muccigrosso, *American Gothic*, 117; Lears, *No Place of Grace*, 205.

50. Ralph Adams Cram, *Walled Towns* (Boston: Marshall Jones, 1919), 56.

51. Lears, *No Place of Grace*, 209.

52. E. Clowes Chorley, *The Centennial History of St. Bartholomew's Church* (New York: St. Bartholomew's, 1935), 32, 35, 102, 112, 137, 159, 166, 169, 173.

53. Chorley, *Centennial History*, 251–54; Adrienne Fried Bloch, *Amy Beach, Passionate Victorian: The Life and Work of an American Composer 1867–1944* (Oxford: Oxford University Press, 1998), 257–59.

54. Chorley, *Centennial History*, 190, 215.

55. For an extended account, see Brent C. Brolin, *The Battle of St. Bart's: A Tale of the Material and the Spiritual* (New York: William Morrow, 1988).

56. Chorley, *Centennial History*, 235; Leighton Parks's obituary, *New York Times*, March 22, 1938; Christine Smith, *St. Bartholomew's Church in the City of New York* (New York: Oxford University Press, 1988), 28.

57. Christine Smith, *St. Bartholomew's*, 15.

58. Ibid., 17.

59. Ibid., 19–23.

60. Richard Oliver, *Bertram Grosvenor Goodhue* (New York: Architectural History Foundation and MIT Press, 1983), 1, 145; Christine Smith, *St. Bartholomew's*, 34.

61. Christine Smith, *St. Bartholomew's*, 17.

62. Bergman, *Spiritual Traveler*, 153–55.

63. London's newer (1895–1902) Roman Catholic Westminster Cathedral was also built in the Byzantine style, and influenced Goodhue's design. It was strongly influenced by Istanbul's great church-turned-mosque, Hagia Sophia. Oliver, *Goodhue*, 146.

64. Catherine Coleman Brawer, *Walls Speak: The Decorative Art of Hildreth Meière* (St. Bonaventure, N.Y.: St. Bonaventure University Press, 2009), 46–53. Meière contributed to a variety of churches and synagogues as well as secular structures such as Cram's bête noire, Radio City Music Hall.

65. Christine Smith, *St. Bartholomew's*, 6–7, 42–44, 142; Oliver, *Goodhue*, 146–47. Goodhue's plan for a much higher tower was also abandoned after his death.

66. Christine Smith, *St. Bartholomew's*, 7.

67. See T. S. Eliot's "Little Gidding."

68. Ingrid A. Steffenson-Bruce, *Marble Palaces, Temples of Art: Art Museums, Architecture, and American Culture, 1890–1930* (Lewisburg, Pa.: Bucknell University Press and Associated University Presses, 1998), 129. See also Jeanne Halgren Kilde, *When Church Became Theatre: The Transformation of Evangelical Architecture and Worship in Nineteenth Century America* (Oxford: Oxford University Press, 2002); Grubiak, *White Elephants*, chap. 4 ("New Cathedrals for the Modern University"); and Lawrence W. Levine, *Highbrow/Lowbrow: The Emergence of Cultural Hierarchy in America* (Cambridge, Mass.: Harvard University Press, 1988).

Chapter Three

1. James Elliott Lindsley, *This Planted Vine: A Narrative History of the Episcopal Diocese of New York* (New York: Harper & Row, 1984), 202; Edward Hagaman Hall (original complier), *A Guide to the Cathedral Church of St. John the Divine in the City of New York* (New York: The Dean and Chapter of the Cathedral Church, 1965), 6.

2. Robert Prichard, *A History of the Episcopal Church* (Harrisburg, Pa.: Morehouse, 1999), 192–93.

3. William Lawrence, *Memories of a Happy Life* (Boston: Houghton Mifflin, 1926), 34. This account of the establishment of St. Paul's Cathedral in Boston is based on chapter 25, "Founding the Cathedral, 1902–1912." Phillips Brooks, Lawrence's predecessor as bishop of Massachusetts, had shared Lawrence's sense that centralized episcopal authority and clerical unity were missing in the diocese while he was still rector at Trinity Church. See Raymond W. Albright, *Focus on Infinity: A Life of Phillips Brooks* (New York: Macmillan, 1961), 193.

4. Lawrence, *Memories*, 311–12.

5. Ibid., 312–14; David A. Kalvelage, *Cathedrals in the Episcopal Church in the U.S.A.* (Cincinnati: Forward Movement Publications, 1993), 25. Lawrence notes that William Reed Huntington had suggested a replica of St. Botolph's Tower in Boston, England, be located on the current site of MIT.

6. Kalvelage, *Cathedrals*, 25. In 1927, the interior was remodeled by Ralph Adams Cram, accommodating classical style to more Anglo-Catholic ritual uses, foreshadowing nearby Trinity's remodeling the following decade.

7. Lawrence, *Memories*, 315.

8. Lawrence, *The Cathedral* (1904 diocesan convention address), quoted in *Memories*, 316. (Later published by the Merrymount Press, Boston, 1915.)

9. Lawrence, *Memories*, 319–20.

10. Thomas F. Rzeznik, " 'Representatives of All That Is Noble': The Rise of the Episcopal Establishment in Early Twentieth-Century Philadelphia," *Religion and American Culture* 19, no. 1 (Winter 2009): 72–80.

11. In the Michigan diocese, for example, the new cathedral, though bearing that title, continued to operate as a parish church. It was only some years later that a cathedral

chapter—a formal staff, meeting regularly and charged with the governance and operations of the cathedral itself—was organized, and a new building erected to house the operations both of the chapter and the diocesan staff. The addition of adjoining facilities to house such operations as a cathedral school eventually created a U-shaped complex that was given the traditional English name of "cathedral close," that is, an open space enclosed by the surrounding buildings. See *"Through the Years" 1834–1988: A History of the Episcopal Diocese of Michigan* (Detroit, Mich.: Chapter of the Cathedral Church of St. Paul, 1989), xiv, 134.

12. Andrew S. Dolkart, *Morningside Heights: A History of Its Architecture and Development* (New York: Columbia University Press, 1998), 37. Chapter 2, "Buildings for the Spirit," contains excellent and detailed architectural histories of both St. John the Divine and Riverside Church.

13. Dolkart, *Morningside Heights*, 38.

14. Ibid., 39.

15. Ibid.

16. Ibid., 40.

17. Ralph Adams Cram, who would later take over the cathedral project, characterized it as "a free rendering of Romanesque and Norman motives, conceived on a large and powerful scale both in plan and superstructure, while it had the great central 'preaching space,' at that time, before the sacramental aspect of the Christian Faith had recovered its position of primacy, held by the authorities to be a desideratum." *My Life in Architecture* (Boston: Little, Brown, 1936), 169.

18. Dolkart, *Morningside Heights*, 40–48.

19. Guastavino vaults were also employed at Grand Central Terminal, Ellis Island, St. Bartholomew's Church, and numerous other monumental structures in Manhattan and elsewhere.

20. Dolkart, *Morningside Heights*, 54–58.

21. Cram, *My Life*, 171–72.

22. Ibid., 177; Dolkart, *Morningside Heights*, 60.

23. Dolkart, *Morningside Heights*, 60–64; Cram, *My Life*, esp. 179. See also Cram's *Walled Towns* (Boston: Marshall Jones, 1919), discussed in the preceding chapter, for an elaboration of some of his ideas advocating a revival of medieval cultural and social forms.

24. Dolkart, *Morningside Heights*, 64, 66–67.

25. Other major donors to the cathedral besides J. P. Morgan and the Stuyvesants included prominent members of the Astor, Belmont, and Vanderbilt families. Sheryl A. Kujawa-Holbrook, *By Grace Came the Incarnation* (New York: Church of the Incarnation, 2004), 95.

26. Others among the many prominent members of the Committee for Completing the Cathedral of St. John the Divine included Nicholas Murray Butler, president of Columbia University; Elihu Root, secretary of War and State and U.S. senator; George W. Wickersham, the eponymous chair of the commission to review Prohibition

under Herbert Hoover; and General George W. Goethals, of Panama Canal fame. The Cathedral of St. John the Divine, *A New Cathedral in a New World* (New York, 1925[?]), unpaginated.

27. Dollart, *Morningside Heights*, 67–68.

28. Henry Codman Potter, "The Cathedral and Its Uses" (Albany, N.Y.: Weed, Parsons and Company, 1888).

29. Ibid., 2–3.

30. Ibid., 8–11.

31. Ibid., 11–13.

32. Ibid., 13–14.

33. Ibid., 16–17.

34. Henry Codman Potter, "An American Cathedral," *Munsey's Magazine*, May 1898, 243. See also Potter, "The Significance of the American Cathedral," *The Forum*, May 1892, 351–59.

35. Potter, "An American Cathedral," 244.

36. Ibid., 245.

37. Ibid., 248–49.

38. Ibid., 249.

39. Hall, *Guide to the Cathedral Church*, 146–82; Michael Bourgeois, *All Things Human: Henry Codman Potter and the Social Gospel in the Episcopal Church* (Urbana: University of Illinois Press, 2004), 73, 78.

40. Although he opposed immigration restriction, Potter nevertheless clung to the idea of Anglo-Saxon superiority. Bourgeois, *All Things*, 212.

41. Hall, *Guide to the Cathedral Church*, 151–52.

42. Charles Lewis Slattery, *David Hummell Greer, Eighth Bishop of New York* (New York: Longmans, Green, 1921), 238–39.

43. Quoted in ibid., 236–37.

44. Ibid., 313.

45. Ibid., 304–7.

46. Quoted in ibid., 308–11.

47. Thomas P. Miller, "Magnificent Obsession: Bishop Manning's Campaign to Build the Cathedral of St. John the Divine" (M.S.T. thesis, General Theological Seminary, New York, 1997), 8, 14. For an entertaining contemporary portrait of Manning, see Alva Johnston, "The First Churchman," in *Profiles from the New Yorker* (New York: Knopf, 1938), 154–64.

48. Miller, "Magnificent Obsession," 19, 23, 26, 29–30, 43.

49. Manning in 1923 engaged the public relations firm of Tamblyn and Brown to help manage his fund-raising campaign, thus employing some of the new agencies of commercial persuasion that were characteristic of this business-oriented decade. Ibid., 30.

50. Dollart, *Morningside Heights*, 70.

51. It is possible that George Washington may actually have first conceived the idea of a national church. See David R. Bains, " 'America's Westminster Abbey': Establish-

ing the National Status of the National Cathedral," presentation, annual meeting of the American Society of Church History, Washington, D.C., January 6, 2008. Bains cites C. M. Harris, "Washington's Gamble, L'Enfant's Dream: Politics, Design, and the Founding of the National Capital," *William and Mary Quarterly* 3rd ser. 56 (July 1999): 542, 544–45.

52. Christopher Dean Hamilton Row, "World without End: Philip Hubert Frohman and the Washington National Cathedral" (Ph.D. dissertation, Harvard University, 1999), 6; Richard T. Feller and Marshall Fishwick, *For Thy Great Glory* (Culpepper, Va.: Community Press, 1965), 3.

53. Feller and Fishwick, *For Thy Great Glory*, 4; Richard Greening Hewlett, *The Foundation Stone: Henry Yates Satterlee and the Creation of the Washington National Cathedral* (Rockville, Md.: Montrose Press, 2007), 49.

54. Hewlett, *Foundation Stone*, 43.

55. Ibid., 7–12.

56. Ibid., 15–17.

57. Ibid, 22–30. St. George's and the "institutional church" phenomenon are discussed at greater length in chapter 4. Although Satterlee, like Henry Codman Potter, might be characterized as an advocate of the Social Gospel, he kept his distance from the movement, disliking what he regarded as excessive reliance on the social sciences at the expense of the establishment of a "sacred community" (32–33).

58. Ibid., 65.

59. An earlier Renaissance-inspired scheme by Ernest Flagg had been solicited by the cathedral board and then rejected as too expensive. Ibid., 56–58.

60. Their firms were, respectively, Burnham and Root and McKim, Mead and White.

61. See Richard Guy Wilson, Dianne Pilgrim, and Richard N. Murray, *The American Renaissance, 1876–1917* (New York: Brooklyn Museum/Pantheon Books, 1979). American Renaissance refers to a resurgence of architecture and allied arts and should not be confused with the same phrase that has been used to describe the literary revival of the antebellum era.

62. Hewlett, *Foundation Stone*, 74–78. For a more detailed discussion of the views of the committee's members, see Row, "World without End," 31.

63. Cram was for a time engaged as a consultant, but did not get along with Frohman and was dismissed in 1927. Row, "World without End," 155, 159, 200, 202, 208, Apps. F and G.

64. Although the term "National Cathedral" has been used, both formally and informally, since the time of Satterlee, the official name of the institution is the Cathedral Church of St. Peter and St. Paul. "Washington Cathedral" and "Washington National Cathedral" are other variations. See Bains, "America's Westminster," note 3.

65. *Lux Mundi*, a collection of essays edited by Gore, was first published in 1889.

66. Row, "World without End," 9–10; Hewlett, *Foundation Stone*, 33.

67. Frank E. Sugeno, "The Establishmentarian Ideal and the Mission of the Episcopal Church," *Historical Magazine of the Protestant Episcopal Church* 53, no. 4 (December,

1984): 285–92. See also Ian T. Douglas, *Fling Out the Banner! The National Church Ideal and the Foreign Missions of the Episcopal Church* (New York: Church Hymnal Corporation, 1996).

68. Huntington's major expressions of this idea were his books *The Church Idea: An Essay toward Unity*, of 1870, and *A National Church*, of 1898. His sermon, "The Talisman of Unity," which was preached in the then recently completed crypt of St. John the Divine in 1899, relates this theme to the cathedral idea (New York: Thomas Whittaker, 1899).

69. The four points of the Quadrilateral were scripture, the creeds of the early church, the two "dominically instituted" sacraments (Baptism and the Eucharist), and the "historic episcopate," that is, the apostolic succession of bishops. This last point has often proven a major barrier to union with denominations that espouse other forms of polity.

70. David R. Bains, "A National Cathedral? Protestants' Reception of Washington Cathedral," presented at the "Legacies and Promise" conference of the Historical Society of the Episcopal Church et al., Williamsburg, Va., June 25, 2007, 5–6. In 1930, economic constraints necessitated the sale of this site and a removal of its memorials to a new "National Church" near the American University campus.

71. Ibid., 6; Thomas A. Tweed, *America's Church: The National Shrine and Catholic Presence in the Nation's Capital* (New York: Oxford University Press, 2011).

72. Bains, "National Cathedral?," 7–8.

73. Hewlett, *Foundation Stone*, 65–67.

74. Ibid., 137–38.

75. Ibid., 166.

76. Bains, "America's Westminster," 5.

77. Ibid., 6–7 and note 16. Wilson's body was not actually transferred from the crypt to the sarcophagus in the nave until 1956 (12). Wilson's grandson, Francis B. Sayre Jr., later served as dean of the cathedral and was a powerful public voice on social issues such as civil rights.

78. Ibid., 9–10.

79. Michael Lampen, "Tales from the Crypt," Grace Cathedral website, available at https://web.archive.org/web/20021006121630/http://www.gracecathedral.org /enrichment/crypt/cry_19970919.shtml.

80. Ibid.; Ruth Hendricks Willard and Carol Green Wilson, *Sacred Places of San Francisco* (Novato, Calif.: Presidio Press, 1985), 37–39.

81. D. O. Kelley, *History of the Diocese of California from 1849 to 1914* (San Francisco: Bureau of Information and Supply, 1915), App. E.

82. St. John the Divine measures 601' x 124' and is 232' tall; the National Cathedral, 517' x 142' x 234'; Grace, 329' x 162' x 176'. (Dimensions vary according to whether towers are included and other criteria.)

83. Though medieval in origin, labyrinths are a fairly new feature in American churches of a variety of denominations, and are used as a means to achieve focus during private meditation. Grace Cathedral has two, one inside and the other in the close.

84. Hewlett, *Foundation Stone*, 55–56. Phoebe Hearst was raised in the Cumberland Presbyterian Church and later converted to Baha'i. The Hearsts' son, William Randolph, became one of the most successful and controversial journalists of his era.

85. St. Albans was endowed by Harriet Lane Johnston, who was James Buchanan's niece and served as First Lady during his administration. She later became a serious collector of European art, which she left to the Smithsonian, earning the honorific "First Lady of the National Collection of Fine Arts." She also endowed a major clinic for children at Johns Hopkins University. Bishop Satterlee conducted her funeral at the National Cathedral in 1903. Hewlett, *Foundation Stone*, 85, 134.

86. The school began to admit nonsingers in 1964, and became coeducational a decade later.

87. Marjorie Hunt, *The Stone Carvers: Master Craftsmen of Washington National Cathedral* (Washington, D.C.: Smithsonian, 1999); Robert E. Kendig, *The Washington National Cathedral: The Bible in Stone* (McLean, Va.: EPM Publications, 1995).

88. See, e.g., Kitty Yang, "A Musical History of the Washington National Cathedral, 1893–1998" (DMA thesis, Johns Hopkins University, Baltimore, Md., 1998).

89. An interesting parallel is the "sacred history" of Quebec embodied in the murals of the Notre-Dame Basilica in Montreal.

90. Hall, *Guide to the Cathedral Church*, 44–46. Other bays include those dedicated to the arts, crusaders (broadly defined to include figures such as yellow fever fighter Walter Reed), education, lawyers, "ecclesiastical origins," historical and patriotic societies, fatherhood, all souls, missionaries, labour [*sic*], the press, medicine, the religious life, the armed forces, and pilgrims (44–103). These tributes are inclusive, including figures ranging from medieval saints to contemporary secular figures such as Oliver Wendell Holmes Jr. and Henry Adams (both depicted in the Historical and Patriotic Societies Bay) (63).

91. Horatio Potter's tomb lies behind the high altar of St. John's, the traditional place for the burial of a cathedral's founder. Hall, *Guide to the Cathedral Church*, 62, 138, 151–52. On Satterlee, Hewlett, *Foundation Stone*, 82.

92. Dewey's disinterment from Arlington Cemetery and the transfer of his remains at the request of his widow to the Cathedral aroused considerable controversy among veterans. Bains, "America's Westminster," 8.

93. Ibid., 7.

94. Michael D. Lampen, *The Doors of Paradise* (San Francisco, Calif.: Grace Cathedral, 1979).

95. Feller and Fishwick, *For Thy Great Glory*, 8; Hewlett, *Foundation Stone*, 70.

96. Bains, "American's Westminster," 7.

97. Bains, "National Cathedral?," 9. It was not until the 1930s that the National Cathedral began actively to involve non-Episcopalians in its governance and worship.

98. Bains, "America's Westminster," 14.

99. For an informed discussion of this notion, see Jeffrey F. Meyer, *Myths in Stone: Religious Dimensions of Washington, D.C.* (Berkeley: University of California Press, 2001).

100. It is worth noting that the Woolworth Building (1913), one of New York's earliest and most dramatic skyscrapers, was Gothic in its ornamental scheme (though certainly not in its structural principles).

101. See Jeanne Halgren Kilde, *When Church Became Theatre: The Transformation of Evangelical Architecture and Worship in Nineteenth Century America* (Oxford: Oxford University Press, 2002).

Chapter Four

1. Epigraph source: Vida Dutton Scudder, *On Journey*, New York: E. P. Dutton, 1937, 176.

2. In 1891 the *Christian Union* magazine commented on the apparent paradox that "the Episcopal Church—the church of wealth, culture, and aristocratic lineage—is leading the way" in social action." Quoted in Henry F. May, *The Protestant Churches and Industrial America*, rev. ed. (c. 1949; repr. New York: Harper and Row Torchbook, 1967), 185. For overviews of the Social Gospel movement, see Charles H. Lippy, "Social Christianity," in *Encyclopedia of the American Religious Experience*, ed. Charles H. Lippy and Peter W. Williams (New York: Charles Scribner's Sons, 1988), 2:917–31; and Eugene Y. Lowe Jr., "Social Gospel," in *Encyclopedia of Religion in America*, ed. Charles H. Lippy and Peter W. Williams (Washington, D.C.: CQ Press, 2010), 4:2089–96. For a brief survey of the Social Gospel among Episcopalians, see David L. Holmes, *A Brief History of the Episcopal Church* (Valley Forge, Pa.: Trinity Press International, 1993), 126–31.

3. The ordination of Charles Augustus Briggs as an Episcopal priest by New York Bishop Henry Codman Potter in 1899 is a case in point. Briggs had been suspended from his ministry by the Presbyterian Church after his inaugural lecture endorsing modern biblical criticism at New York's Union Theological Seminary.

4. Bernard M. G. Reardon, *Religious Thought in the Victorian Age: A Survey from Coleridge to Gore* (London: Longman, 1995), 150; K. S. Inglis, "Introduction," in *Churches and the Working Class in Victorian England* (London: Routledge and Kegan Paul and University of Toronto Press, 1963); Bernard Kent Markwell, *The Anglican Left: Radical Social Reformers in the Church of England and the Protestant Episcopal Church, 1846–1954* (Brooklyn, N.Y.: Carlson, 1991), 32–33.

5. Reardon, *Religious Thought*, chap. 5; Clyde Griffin, "An Urban Church in Ferment: The Episcopal Church in New York City, 1880–1900" (Ph.D. diss., Columbia University, 1960), 122–23.

6. Reardon, *Religious Thought*, chap. 6; Griffin, "Urban Church," 151–52.

7. May, *Protestant Churches*, 12–15.

8. Robert C. Bannister, "William Graham Sumner," in *American National Biography Online*, Oxford University Press, 2000, www.anb.org.

9. May, *Protestant Churches*, 64–67.

10. Sharon Otterman, "Trinity Church Split on How to Manage a $2 Billion Legacy of a Queen," *New York Times*, April 15, 2013. The title of the article refers to a 2011 estimate

of the parish's assets, which includes 5,500,000 square feet of commercial real estate. Its holdings derive from a 1705 bequest of 215 acres of farmland from Queen Anne.

11. Eric Homberger, *Mrs. Astor's New York: Money and Social Power in the Gilded Age* (New Haven, Conn.: Yale University Press, 2002), 81–82; Ray Stannard Baker, "A Study of Trinity—the Richest Church in America, 1910," in *The Church and the City 1865–1910*, ed. Robert D. Cross (Indianapolis: Bobbs-Merrill, 1967), 69–95. See also Morgan Dix's "Address at Trinity Church, New York, Ascension Day, 1871," in Cross, *Church and the City*, 55–68; Griffin, "Urban Church," 302–3.

12. Dena Merriam and David Finn, *Trinity: A Church, A Parish, A People* (New York: Cross River Press, 1996), 35–36; Griffin, "Urban Church," 303–4.

13. Griffin, "Urban Church," 314–21.

14. Aaron Ignatius Abell, *The Urban Impact on American Protestantism 1865–1900* (Cambridge, Mass.: Harvard University Press, 1943; repr. Hamden, Conn.: Archon Books, 1962), 29–30; Alvin W. Skardon, *Church Leader in the Cities: William Augustus Muhlenberg* (Philadelphia: University of Pennsylvania Press, 1971), chap. 4. Muhlenberg also makes an appearance in the following chapter in his role as educational leader. By 1900, 40 percent of Manhattan's Episcopalians attended "free churches"—those that charged no pew rent—or "poor chapels," missions established by wealthier parishes in poorer neighborhoods. Griffin, "Urban Church," 12–14.

15. Skardon, *Church Leader*, chaps. 4 and 5.

16. The term is usually attributed to William Jewett Tucker, a Congregationalist who taught social ethics at Andover Theological Seminary and later served as president of Dartmouth College. Tucker also helped found the South End House, one of Boston's first settlement houses. Abell, *Urban Impact*, 137; Jacob Andrew Dorn, "'Our Best Gospel Appliances': Institutional Churches and the Emergence of Social Christianity in the South End of Boston, 1880–1920" (Ph.D. diss., Harvard University, 1994), 40.

17. Dorn, "Our Best Gospel Appliances," 6, 12, 14, 18.

18. Ibid., chap. 4.

19. Brent would later serve as missionary bishop of the Philippines and bishop of Western New York, and eventually as one of the organizers of the first World Conference on Faith and Order, an influential international ecumenical meeting in Lausanne, Switzerland, in 1927.

20. Dorn, "Our Best Gospel Appliances," chap. 4.

21. Ibid.

22. Ibid., 101–4. Dorn discusses the subsequent development of St. Stephen's as well as the story of another Boston Episcopal institutional church, Ascension, and their Congregationalist counterparts, in other chapters.

23. Elizabeth Moulton, *St. George's Church, New York* (New York: St. George's Church, 1964), 39.

24. Ibid., 1, and chap. 5.

25. W. S. Rainsford, *The Story of a Varied Life: An Autobiography* (Garden City, N.Y.: Doubleday, Page, 1922), 13–15, 21–22, 32, 45, 61–63, 109.

26. Ibid., 71, 126, 151, 400.

27. Ibid., 200–4. Morgan's role as a leading Episcopal layman, locally and nationally, is discussed at some length in chapter 6.

28. Rainsford writes of calling on the mother of political boss Richard Croker to shame him into supporting this project. Ibid., 210.

29. Ibid., 213, 267.

30. See, for example, Craig G. Townsend, *Faith in Their Own Color: Black Episcopalians in Antebellum New York* (New York: Columbia University Press, 2005), a history of St. Philip's. See also Griffin, "Urban Church," 32–33. Racial integration was not high on the agenda of most Social Gospel advocates. On Burleigh, see Moulton, *Saint George's*, 87–88.

31. Rainsford, *Story of a Varied Life*, 215–18, 235.

32. New York: Harper and Brothers, 1906. The coauthor, George Hodges, by then had become the dean of the Episcopal Theological School in Cambridge. Rainsford, Theodore Roosevelt, and Bishop Henry Codman Potter all contributed introductory essays. See also Rainsford, *Story of a Varied Life*, 273.

33. Rainsford, *Story of a Varied Life*, 211, 219–20, 224, 227–28, 240–41, 243, 249, 267, 282, 302. On Nelson, see Warren C. Herrick, *Frank H. Nelson of Cincinnati* (Louisville, Ky.: The Cloister Press, 1945).

34. Rainsford, *Story of a Varied Life*, 323; Moulton, *St. George's*, 81, 89–90.

35. Moulton, *St. George's*, 70–71; Augustus Cerillo, "Seth Low," *American National Biography Online*, Oxford University Press, 2000, www.anb.org.

36. Calvary's Presbyterian counterparts, Shadyside and East Liberty, were undergoing a similar musical transformation. Thomas C. Couvares, *The Remaking of Pittsburgh: Class and Culture in an Industrializing City 1877–1919* (Albany, N.Y.: SUNY Press, 1984), 98.

37. Julia Shelley Hodges, *George Hodges* (New York: The Century Co., 1926), 102–3.

38. Hodges, *George Hodges*, 108.; Keith A. Zahniser, *Steel City Gospel: Protestant Laity and Reform in Progressive-Era Pittsburgh* (New York: Routledge, 2005), 65.

39. Hodges, *George Hodges*, 133. The Episcopal Theological School, which had been founded in 1867, merged in 1974 with the Philadelphia Divinity School (founded 1857). The combined institutions, located in Cambridge, assumed the name of the Episcopal Divinity School. This was among the first of a number of accommodations that Episcopal seminaries have been forced into by financial pressures in recent decades.

40. Zahniser, *Steel City Gospel*, 1–2, 10, 103, 114.

41. Hodges, *George Hodges*, 99.

42. In an 1892 letter to his mother, Ely suggested that "the great misfortune of the Episcopal Church has been its eminent respectability—its exclusiveness—its coldness. Many are trying to change this and to bring something of the Methodist zeal into it." Quoted in Eugene Y. Lowe, Jr., "Richard T. Ely: Herald of a Positive State" (Ph.D. diss., Union Theological Seminary, 1986), 182. He was also a lay leader,

warden, and vestryman at Grace Church, very near the state capitol in Madison, Wisconsin (251).

43. Robert T. Handy, *The Social Gospel in America: Gladden, Ely, Rauschenbusch* (New York: Oxford University Press, 1966), 173; Lowe, "Ely," 36; Richard T. Ely, *Ground Under Our Feet: An Autobiography* (New York: Macmillan, 1938).

44. Ely, *Ground*, 137; Lowe, "Ely," 112.

45. Founded at Chautauqua Lake in upstate New York in 1874 by businessman Lewis Miller and Methodist minister (and later bishop) John Heyl Vincent, "mother Chautauqua" and its many "daughters" across North America were assemblies that promoted what now might be called "continuing education," featuring short courses, popular orators such as William Jennings Bryan and Russell Conwell, and musical performances. Ely was also influenced by other Anglican thinkers such as W. H. Fremantle, who promoted the role of the church in the transformation of the entire life of humanity. Lowe, "Ely," 151.

46. Lowe, "Ely," 1, 166; Handy, *Social Gospel*, 175.

47. Lowe, "Ely," 91, 165, 232.

48. Ely, *Ground*, 218.

49. Potter's father Alonzo served as bishop of Pennsylvania from 1845 to 1865.

50. Michael Bourgeois, *All Things Human: Henry Codman Potter and the Social Gospel* (Urbana: University of Illinois Press, 2004), 43.

51. Quoted in Bourgeois, *All Things Human*, 49. Samuel "Soapy" Wilberforce was the son of antislavery reformer William Wilberforce and was bishop of Oxford. He gained notoriety as Thomas Henry Huxley's opponent in an 1860 debate over evolution.

52. See the opening to the introduction of this volume.

53. Bourgeois, *All Things Human*, 49, 53.

54. Ibid., 51, 110.

55. Josiah Strong, *Our Country: Its Possible Future and Its Present Crisis*, ed. Jurgen Herbst (Cambridge, Mass.: Belknap Press of Harvard University Press, 1963).

56. Bourgeois, *All Things Human*, 73.

57. Ibid., chap. 5 ("Reconciling Labor and Capital").

58. Ibid., 133.

59. New York: Thomas Whittaker, 1910.

60. Mary Sudman Donovan, *A Different Call: Women's Ministries in the Episcopal Church* (Wilton, Conn.: Morehouse-Barlow, 1986), 6–12.

61. Ibid., 31.

62. Holmes, *Brief History*, 133–35; Donovan, *Different Call*, 89.

63. Allen F. Davis, *Spearheads for Reform: The Social Settlements and the Progressive Movement 1890–1914* (New Brunswick, N.J.: Rutgers University Press, 1994), 3.

64. Ibid., 8., 27.

65. Jennifer L. Bosch, "The Life of Ellen Starr Gates" (Ph.D. diss., Miami University, 1990), 33; Jill Ker Conway, quoted in Eleanor J. Stebner, *The Women of Hull House: A Study in Spirituality* (Albany, N.Y.: SUNY Press, 1997), 2–4, 12.

66. Bosch, "Gates," 87, 105, 109–10.

67. Ibid., 50; Eileen Boris, *Art and Labor: Ruskin, Morris, and the Craftsman Ideal in America* (Philadelphia: Temple University Press, 1986), 180–83; Stebner, *Women of Hull House*, 83.

68. Bosch, "Gates," 132; Miriam U. Chrisman, *"To Bind Together": A Brief History of the Society of the Companions of the Holy Cross* (n.p.: n.p., n.d.), 16.

69. Bosch, "Gates," 125. On Gates's aunt, see "Eliza Allen Starr" in Rima Lunin Schultz and Adele Hast, *Women Building Chicago 1790–1990* (Bloomington: Indiana University Press, 2001), 836–38.

70. Vida Dutton Scudder, *On Journey* (New York: E.P. Dutton, 1937), 184.

71. Markwell, *Anglican Left*, 139; Scudder, *On Journey*. See also Theresa Corcoran, SC, *Vida Dutton Scudder* (Boston: Twayne, 1982).

72. Markwell, *Anglican Left*, 167; Scudder, *On Journey*, 109.

73. Davis, *Spearheads*, 89–90.

74. Scudder, *On Journey*, 142, 147, 253; Corcoran, *Scudder*, 41. See also Heather M. Capitano, "Denison House: Women's Use of Space in the Boston Settlement" (M.F.A. thesis, University of Massachusetts at Boston, 2010).

75. Markwell, *Anglican Left*, 206, 218, 23; Scudder, *On Journey*, 162, 165, 184.

76. Scudder, *On Journey*, 43, 241, 243; Chrisman, *To Bind Together*, 7, 19.

77. William Reed Huntington (1838–1909), rector of Grace Church in Manhattan and author of *The Church Idea* (1870), the primary inspiration for the Chicago-Lambeth Quadrilateral (1886–88), was a distant cousin.

78. Sources on Huntington include Frank Sugeno, "James Otis Sargent Huntington," *American National Biography Online*, Oxford University Press, 2000, www.anb.org; D. G. Paz, "Monasticism and Social Reform in Late Nineteenth-Century America: The Case of Father Huntington," *Historical Magazine of the Protestant Episcopal Church* 48 (1979): 45–66; Vida Dutton Scudder, *Father Huntington: Founder of the Order of the Holy Cross* (New York: E. P. Dutton, 1940); Markwell, *Anglican Left*, chap. 4 ("James O. S. Huntington: Ritualist Slum Priest, Religious Founder, and Single Tax Radical").

79. Saint Clement's maintains, among other things, a shrine to King Charles the Martyr. Charles I (Stuart) was beheaded by Parliament in 1649 during the course of the English Civil War and is venerated as a martyr by some Anglo-Catholics.

80. Scudder, *Huntington*, 73, 91–92.

81. "The Protestant Episcopal Church" was standard usage until 1967, when "The Episcopal Church" was recognized by the General Convention as an alternative. The latter form is almost universally used today.

82. George expounded this theory in his influential *Progress and Poverty* (1879). He ran unsuccessfully for mayor of New York in 1886, losing to the Tammany Hall candidate. Paz, "Monasticism," 53.

83. Scudder, *Huntington*, 97; Markwell, *Anglican Left*, 99, 103.

84. Paz, "Monasticism," 56–57; Scudder, *Huntington*, 170. See chapter 5 for a lengthier discussion of the order's boarding schools.

85. Bellamy's *Looking Backward: 2000–1887*, one of the best-selling novels of the nineteenth century, was published in 1887. On Bliss's career, see Markwell, *Anglican Left*, 109; Christopher L. Webber, "William Dwight Porter Bliss (1856–1926) Priest and Socialist," *Historical Magazine of the Protestant Episcopal Church* 28, no. 1 (1959): 9–39; Jacob H. Dorn, "William Dwight Porter Bliss," *American National Biography Online*, Oxford University Press, 2000, www.anb.org; Richard B. Dressner, "William Dwight Porter Bliss's Christian Socialism," *Church History* 47 (March 1978): 66–82.

86. Markwell, *Anglican Left*, 114–16, 124; Webber, "Bliss," 16–18.

87. Webber, "Bliss," 19–22; Scudder, *On Journey*, 165.

Chapter Five

1. Louis Auchincloss, one of the most eminent chroniclers of the WASP establishment, published *The Rector of Justin* in 1964. It focuses not on students but rather on a headmaster, who may be based in considerable part on Groton's Endicott Peabody.

2. The term "private family boarding school" was introduced by James McLachlan in what is still the authoritative history of the subject, *American Boarding Schools: A Historical Study* (New York: Scribner's, 1970), 194.

3. The classic study of the emergence of a self-conscious urban elite during this era is E. Digby Baltzell, *The Protestant Establishment: Aristocracy and Caste in America* (New York: Random House/Vintage Books, 1964). Baltzell's work helped to popularize the acronym WASP (White Anglo-Saxon Protestant).

4. On Anglophilia, see McLachlan, *American Boarding Schools*, 27–30 and 253–54. On its background, see Ronald Story, *The Forging of an Aristocracy: Harvard and the Boston Upper Class, 1800–1870* (Middletown, Conn.: Wesleyan University Press, 1980), 124; and Elisa Tamarkin, *Anglophilia: Deference, Devotion, and Antebellum America* (Chicago: University of Chicago Press, 2008).

5. Clifford Putney, "Introduction," in *Muscular Christianity: Manhood and Sports in Protestant America, 1880–1920* (Cambridge, Mass.: Harvard University Press, 2001).

6. On Boston Unitarian philanthropy and elite cultural formation, see Story, *Forging of an Aristocracy*.

7. This section on Round Hill is based on McLachlan, *American Boarding Schools*, 49–100.

8. Ibid., 59–61, 79–81.

9. Ibid., 89, 93.

10. Ibid., 87–88. On Erving Goffman's concept of the "total institution" as applied to boarding schools, see Peter W. Cookson Jr., "Education: Boarding Schools," in *Encyclopedia of Religion in America*, ed. Charles H. Lippy and Peter W. Williams (Washington, D.C.: CQ Press, 2010), 2:620.

11. McLachlan, *American Boarding Schools*, 107–8, 111; Alvin W. Skardon, *Church Leader in the Cities: William Augustus Muhlenberg* (Philadelphia: University of Pennsylvania Press, 1971), chap. 2.

12. McLachlan, *American Boarding Schools*, 114, 125–28, 117–19; Skardon, *Church Leader*, 63, 66–67.

13. McLachlan, *American Boarding Schools*, 81, 83.

14. Ibid., 110, 112, 128–30.

15. Ibid., 132; Skardon, *Church Leader*, 84–90; St. James School website, http://www.stjames.edu/RelId/33637/ISvars/default/Home.htm.

16. McLachlan argues for the latter option as a major thesis of his *American Boarding Schools*.

17. Betty Hughes Morris, *A History of the Church of the Advent* (Boston: Church of the Advent, 1995), 2.

18. August Heckscher, *St. Paul's: The Life of a School* (New York: Charles Scribner's Sons, 1980), 2, 8–9; McLachlan, *American Boarding Schools*, 137, 143–44, 148, 150.

19. Quoted in Heckscher, *St. Paul's*, 10.

20. Ibid., 98; David Hein, "Henry Augustus Coit," in *American National Biography Online*, Oxford University Press, 2000, www.anb.org; McLachlan, *American Boarding Schools*, 156, 161.

21. Heckscher, *St. Paul's*, 14, 34–35, 58, 102, 103; McLachlan, *American Boarding Schools*, 173; James P. Conover, *Memories of a Great Schoolmaster* (Boston: Houghton, Mifflin, 1906), 111.

22. Quoted in William Morgan, *The Almighty Wall: The Architecture of Henry Vaughan* (New York: Architectural History Foundation and MIT Press, 1983), 89. On "instant tradition," see McLachlan, *American Boarding Schools*, 274; and Eric Hobsbawm and Terence Ranger, *The Invention of Tradition* (Cambridge: Cambridge University Press, 1983).

23. Alan N. Hall, "Walking Tour," (leaflet) (n.p.: n.p., n.d.), 9–10; Morgan, *Almighty Wall*, 100 and chap. 4.

24. The Episcopal Church was not nearly as active as other major denominations in the area of higher education, although it was involved in the founding of Columbia, Penn, and William & Mary during the colonial era. It also sponsored Bard, Hobart and William Smith, Kenyon, and the University of the South (Sewanee), which have retained their affiliations with the church to the present; three primarily African American schools in the South; and a handful of others, including Trinity, which have since dropped any church affiliation. (David L. Holmes, *A Brief History of the Episcopal Church* [Valley Forge, Pa.; Trinity Press International, 1993], 138–40.)

25. Heckscher, *St. Paul's*, 57; McLachlan, *American Boarding Schools*, 169.

26. The cause of cricket was promoted especially by Richard Henry Dana III. The first Richard Henry Dana was also the first senior warden of the Church of the Advent; the second, also a founder of Advent and the author of *Two Years before the Mast*, was a trustee of St. Paul's. Morris, *History of the Church of the Advent*, 9; Heckscher, *St. Paul's*, 60.

27. McLachlan, *American Boarding Schools*, 171; Axel Bundgaard, *Muscle and Manliness: The Rise of Sport in American Boarding Schools* (Syracuse, N.Y.: Syracuse University Press, 2005), 49, 62–65, 86, 90.

28. Heckscher, *St. Paul's*, 93; McLachlan, *American Boarding Schools*, 176.

29. McLachlan, *American Boarding Schools*, 161.

30. Ibid., 179, 181.

31. Frank D. Ashburn, *Peabody of Groton: A Portrait* (New York: Coward McCann, 1944). For a popular history of the Peabody family over several generations, see Edwin P. Hoyt, *The Peabody Influence: How a Great New England Family Helped to Build America* (New York: Dodd, Mead, 1968).

32. McLachlan, *American Boarding Schools*, 151–52.

33. Ibid., 152–53; Ashburn, *Peabody*, 24–25. *Tom Brown's School Days* has been adapted to the screen several times, with Arnold being played by actors as different as Sir Cedric Hardwicke (1940) and Stephen Fry (2005).

34. An odd American footnote to the story of Arnold and Rugby is the attempt by Hughes in 1880 to establish a community on Tennessee's Cumberland Plateau to provide employment for the younger sons of upper-class English families whom English law had deprived of an inheritance. The colony was named "Rugby," and featured a library, an Episcopal church, and an Arnold School, among other amenities. Rugby, not surprisingly, failed, but some of its fabric is preserved, and the church still holds services. John Egerton, *Visions of Utopia: Nashoba, Rugby, Ruskin, and the "New Communities" in Tennessee's Past* (Knoxville: University of Tennessee Press, 1977), 36–63.

35. McLachlan, *American Boarding Schools*, 153–54; Ashburn, *Peabody*, 27–29.

36. Ashburn, *Peabody*, 30–33; McLachlan, *American Boarding Schools*, 247. See also Paul T. Phillips, *A Kingdom on Earth: Anglo-American Social Christianity, 1880–1940* (University Park: Pennsylvania State University Press, 1996), 120–23; and Alice Chandler, *A Dream of Order: The Medieval Ideal in Nineteenth-Century English Literature* (Lincoln: University of Nebraska Press, 1970).

37. Ashburn, *Peabody*, 34–37, 45; McLachlan, *American Boarding Schools*, 249.

38. Ashburn, *Peabody*, 65–67; McLachlan, *American Boarding Schools*, 251. On St. Mark's, see Albert Emerson Benson, *History of St. Mark's School* (Alumni Association, 1925); Edward Tuck Hall, *St. Mark's School: A Centennial History* (Lunenberg, Vt.: Stinehour Press, 1967).

39. Ashburn, *Peabody*, 67.

40. Peabody once observed that "one of the fundamental errors of the [Anglo-] Catholic party lies in their belief that there is a life higher than the family life," referring to the celibacy practiced by the monastic orders. Further, he characterized the movement as erroneously regarding sacraments as ends in themselves rather than as a means to holiness. Ibid., 187–88.

41. Peabody, "The Aim of Groton School," *Church Militant* 3, no. 3 (April 1900): 3.

42. St. John's Chapel (1899–1900), like its predecessor (also by Vaughan), was the gift of William Amory Gardner, one of the first Groton masters and nephew of Isabella Stewart Gardner, who helped raise him and his brothers after their parents' death. (Morgan, *Almighty Wall*, 111–15.) Morgan's title for his study of Vaughan is taken from Thring's phrase emphasizing the importance of the built environment for an institution's

character. Gardner's *Groton Myths and Memories* (Groton, Mass.: Rumford Press, 1928) is an interesting resource for Groton's early years. See also Ashburn, *Peabody*, 155–56.

43. Bundgaard, *Muscle*, chap. 7. "56 Years of Whip-Cracking End with Dr. Peabody's Retirement," *Newsweek*, July 1, 1940, quoted in Bundgaard, 119; Ashburn, *Peabody*, 100, 260. See also McLachlan, *American Boarding Schools*, 283.

44. The term "Ivy League" originated among sports writers in the 1930s, and was not formally adopted as an official NCAA conference name until 1954.

45. Ashburn, *Peabody*, 118. See also Jerome Karabel, *The Chosen: The Hidden History of Admission and Exclusion at Harvard, Yale, and Princeton* (Boston: Houghton Mifflin, 2005), 26–38, for the role of Peabody and Groton in the evolution of Ivy League admissions policies.

46. McLachlan, *American Boarding Schools*, 261–65.

47. Ashburn, *Peabody*, 118.

48. Baltzell, *Protestant Establishment*, 128; Ashburn, *Peabody*, 98, 199, 217–20. John F. Kennedy (Choate '35) was something of an exception.

49. McLachlan, *American Boarding Schools*, 287–88, 290–92, 297; Ashburn, *Peabody*, 340, 404; John Woolverton, *The Religion of Franklin D. Roosevelt* (unpublished manuscript), chaps. 3 and 4; Peabody, "Consumers Leagues," Endicott Peabody Papers, Groton School Archives, November 30, 1997 (typescript courtesy of John Woolverton).

50. Ashburn, *Peabody*, 88, 177, 251.

51. Roman Catholic religious orders operated many schools, but few were of the boarding variety. A rule-proving exception is Portsmouth Abbey School in Newport, Rhode Island, founded as Portsmouth Priory in 1926 on the "English" model by John Hugh Diman. Diman was a Dominican priest who had converted from the Episcopal Church and had earlier founded the forerunner of what became St. George's School—part of the "St. Grottlesex" conflation—near Newport.

52. Adam Dunbar McCoy, OHC, *Holy Cross: A Century of Anglican Monasticism* (Wilton, Conn.: Morehouse-Barlow, 1987), provides a comprehensive history of the order.

53. McCoy, *Holy Cross*, 94–95, 171, 211; "A Brief History of Secondary Education on the Mountain," *St. Andrew's-Sewanee School News*, Winter 1991, http://www.sasweb .org/page.cfm?p=723.

54. James Gould Cozzens, "FHS: A Faith That Did Not Fail," in Joan M. Beattie, *Kent: One Hundred Years* (Kent, Conn.: Kent School, 2007), 55–57. Cozzens, whose 1936 novel *Men and Brethren* included a character based on a Holy Cross priest, was also the author of a 1930 series of stories about "Dr. Holt" of the "Durham School," which were fictionalized versions of Sill and Kent (McCoy, *Holy Cross*, 158). Endicott Peabody was more problematically a source for the 1964 novel *The Rector of Justin* by Louis Auchincloss (Groton '35), another chronicler of WASP life in fiction, who also wrote of his experience at Groton in *A Writer's Capital* (1979). See http://www .americanlegends.com/Interviews/rector_of_justin.html.

55. McCoy, *Holy Cross*, 97–98, 173; Beattie, *Kent*, chap. 1. The order ended its connection with the school in 1943, but Kent has retained its Episcopal affiliation.

56. McCoy, *Holy Cross*, 97–98; Beattie, *Kent.*

57. Annie Wright Schools website, http://www.aw.org/Page/About-Us/About
-Annie-Wright-Schools/History-of-Annie-Wright-Schools.

58. In 1971 the two institutions began a process of merger to form what is now Choate
Rosemary Hall. Like Rosemary Hall, Choate was a family-founded school that maintained a relationship with the Episcopal Church; two of its most notable headmasters,
George St.-John and his son Seymour, were Episcopal priests. The chapel was designed
in neocolonial style by Ralph Adams Cram.

59. Tom Generous and Charles T. Wilson Jr., "The Beginnings" (2–17) and "A Woman
and Her School" (38–63) in *Choate Rosemary Hall: A History of the School* (Wallingford, Conn.: Choate Rosemary Hall, 1997); Caroline Ruutz-Rees, *Letters to Rosemary
1905–1906* (Wallingford, Conn.: Choate Rosemary Hall, 2006), 2, 16.

Chapter Six

1. Robert H. Bremner, *American Philanthropy* (Chicago: University of Chicago Press,
1960), 105–10.

2. For an historical overview of these developments, see Ralph F. Bogardus, "Urban
Cultural Institutions," in *The Encyclopedia of American Social History*, ed. Mary Kupiec
Cayton, Elliott J. Gorn, and Peter W. Williams (New York: Scribner's, 1993), 3:2475–91.

3. On these phenomena, see Lawrence W. Levine, *Highbrow, Lowbrow: The Emergence
of Cultural Hierarchy in America* (Cambridge, Mass.: Harvard University Press, 1988);
and Helen Lefkowitz Horowitz, *Culture and the City: Cultural Philanthropy in Chicago
from the 1880s to 1917* (Chicago: University of Chicago Press, 1989 [orig. pub. 1976]).

4. Kit and Frederica Konolige, *The Power of Their Glory: America's Ruling Class: The
Episcopalians* (New York: Wyden, 1978), 76, 178–79. This not always accurate study of
"Episcocrat" culture does contain some useful information and insight.

5. Benjamin Rowland, "Introduction" to James Jackson Jarves, *The Art-Idea*
(Cambridge, Mass.: Belknap Press of Harvard University Press, 1960), xii–xiii.

6. See Sally Promey, "Visible Liberalism: Liberal Protestant Taste Evangelism, 1850
and 1950," in *American Religious Liberalism*, ed. Leigh E. Schmidt and Sally M. Promey
(Bloomington: Indiana University Press, 2012), 76–96, on this transition in the broader
American Protestant realm.

7. Articles on Procter in the *Dictionary of American Biography* (hereafter DAB) and
American National Biography (hereafter ANB) provide basic biographical information,
as they do for all subsequent subjects except Booth and Goodwin. See *The Letters of
William Cooper Procter* (Cincinnati, Ohio: McDonald Printing Co., 1957) (privately
printed by his niece, Mary E. Johnston), 97 and 100–101, for his views on labor.

8. *High on a Hill: The Story of Christ Church, Glendale, 1865–1965* (Glendale, Ohio:
privately printed, 1965), 21.

9. On Glendale, see John Clubbe, *Cincinnati Observed: Architecture and History*
(Columbus: Ohio State University Press, 1992), 432. On Christ Church, see Clubbe,

445–46; on "Ivorydale," the Procter and Gamble plant, sited on a model industrial campus, 429–32.

10. The Benedicts departed for Sewanee, Tennessee, in 1910, when the sometime rector accepted a call to be dean of the seminary. *High on a Hill*, 115–16.

11. Ibid., 106–9. Two Matthews nieces, daughters of brother Mortimer, would also join the community. The community's chapel is a Gothic gem designed by Ralph Adams Cram. For the history of both the order and the chapel, see *Chapel of the Transfiguration* (Cincinnati, Ohio: Community of the Transfiguration, 2002).

12. *High on a Hill*, 73, 112, 123, 151, 152, 183–84, 272, 275, 276. See also *Letters*, 22, on the 1910 General Convention.

13. Procter, *Letters*, 13.

14. Ibid., 26.

15. Ibid., 20, 35–37, 130–31. Procter also received an honorary degree from Episcopal-related Kenyon College.

16. DAB entry, Supplements 1–2.

17. Procter, *Letters*, 55 (March 4, 1915).

18. Ibid., 49.

19. Mark Schorer, *Sinclair Lewis: An American Life* (New York: McGraw-Hill, 1961), 302–4.

20. Procter, *Letters*, 51 (February 7, 1914).

21. Ibid., 158 (August 5, 1925).

22. Ibid., 147–48 (December 22, 1922).

23. Jean Strouse, *Morgan: American Financier* (New York: Random House, 1999), 685.

24. Ibid., 17.

25. Ibid., 24–25; Herbert W. Satterlee, *J. Pierpont Morgan: An Intimate Portrait* (New York: Macmillan, 1939), 5. Satterlee was Morgan's son-in-law and a cousin of the Washington, D.C., bishop who founded the National Cathedral. Satterlee's account of Morgan's life is neither as full nor as candid as Strouse's, but is replete with details of his church involvements.

26. Satterlee, *Pierpont Morgan*, 31; basic narrative in *Dictionary of American Biography*.

27. Strouse, *Morgan*, 217. Although his family had been both wealthy and cosmopolitan for some time, Morgan's amassing his own fortune during the age of the Robber Barons qualified him for membership in ranks of the nouveaux as well as the anciens.

28. Ibid., 79, 81, 126.

29. Ibid., 218–19.

30. Satterlee, *Pierpont Morgan*, 246–47.

31. Ibid., 312.

32. Ibid., 236, 242–43; Strouse, *Morgan*, 275.

33. Strouse, *Morgan*, 290.

34. Ibid., 217, 236.

35. Satterlee, *Pierpont Morgan*, 130, 154.

36. Ibid., 153, 185, 206–7.

37. Ibid., 239.

38. Ibid., 262–63.

39. Strouse, *Morgan*, 274.

40. Satterlee, *Pierpont Morgan* 239, 251, 262, 304–5, 363, 450, 523. Bishops Doane, Greer, and Lawrence were among those favored.

41. Ibid., 453.

42. Ibid., 125.

43. Ibid., 169.

44. Ibid., 156.

45. Ibid., 501, 517, 533.

46. Strouse, *Morgan*, 221.

47. Satterlee, *Pierpont Morgan*, 145–46.

48. Aline B. Saarinen, *The Proud Possessors: The Lives, Times, and Tastes of Some Adventurous American Art Collectors* (New York: Random House, 1958), 57.

49. Strouse, *Morgan*, 7.

50. Ibid., 205, 379. On Morgan's medieval collections and their legitimation and stimulation of a broader American interest in medieval art, see R. Aaron Rottner, "J. P. Morgan and the Middle Ages," in *Medieval Art in America: Patterns of Collecting 1800–1940*, ed. Elizabeth Bradford Smith (University Park, Pa.: Palmer Museum of Art, Pennsylvania State University, 1996).

51. Quoted in Francis Henry Taylor, *Pierpont Morgan as Collector and Patron, 1837–1913* (New York: Pierpont Morgan Library, 1957), 21, 25. Lawrence's unpublished manuscript is in the Morgan Library's collection.

52. Wayne Andrews, *Mr. Morgan and His Architect* (New York: Pierpont Morgan Library, 1957), 2–3, 5, 9.

53. Satterlee, *Pierpont Morgan*, 130, 147.

54. Saarinen, *Proud Possessors*, 72. See also Strouse, *Morgan*, 378 and 486.

55. Strouse, *Morgan*, 496–97.

56. Ibid., 377.

57. Taylor, *Pierpont Morgan as Collector*, 36.

58. Saarinen, *Proud Possessors*, 91.

59. Taylor, *Pierpont Morgan as Collector*, 4–5.

60. Basic biographical information from DAB. Of the three Gardner biographies, the most extensive, reliable, and suggestive is Douglass Shand-Tucci's *The Art of Scandal: The Life and Times of Isabella Stewart Gardner* (New York: HarperCollins, 1997).

61. Shand-Tucci, *Art of Scandal*, 5.

62. Ibid., 31–32, 126–27, 133.

63. This story appears, among other places, in an earlier Gardner biography: Louise Hall Tharp, *Mrs. Jack: A Biography of Isabella Stewart Gardner* (Boston: Little, Brown, 1965; Fawcett Crest paperback reprint, 1968), 143.

64. Betty Hughes Morris, *A History of the Church of the Advent* (Church of the Advent: Boston, 1995), 201.

65. Shand-Tucci, *Art of Scandal*, 117, 167.

66. Berenson also became a Roman Catholic for a period. Ernest Samuels, *Bernard Berenson: The Making of a Connoisseur* (Cambridge, Mass.: Belknap Press of Harvard University Press, 1979), 38–39, 136, 140. See also Shand-Tucci, *Art of Scandal*, 118.

67. Anne Higonnet, "Private Museums, Public Leadership: Isabella Stewart Gardner and the Art of Cultural Authority," in *Cultural Leadership in America: Art Matronage and Patronage, Fenway Court*, vol. 27 (Boston: Isabella Stewart Gardner Museum, 1997), 81.

68. Hilliard T. Goldfarb, *The Isabella Stewart Gardner Museum: A Companion Guide and History* (New Haven, Conn.: Yale University Press, 1995), 3. An exhaustive listing of these contents can be found in Gilbert Wendel Longstreet, compiler, *The Isabella Stewart Gardner Museum Fenway Court General Catalogue* (Boston: Isabella Stewart Gardner Museum, 1935).

69. Shand-Tucci, *Art of Scandal*, 240.

70. Ibid., 91, 110, 124.

71. Ibid., 216; Goldfarb, *Gardner Museum*, 42, 45.

72. Goldfarb, *Gardner Museum*, 41.

73. Saarinen, *Proud Possessors*, 51.

74. Goldfarb, *Gardner Museum*, 133; Shand-Tucci, *Art of Scandal*, 236. Adams once told Gardner in a letter that "You are a creator. You stand alone." (Quoted in Shand-Tucci, 236–37.)

75. Goldfarb, *Gardner Museum*, 133.

76. Henry James, *The American Scene* (New York: Charles Scribner's Sons, 1946), 249–50. James is here using the term to contrast European libraries with their more democratically open American counterparts, such as Boston's. James was also a member of Gardner's circle of notables.

77. Goldfarb, *Gardner Museum*, 135.

78. Ibid., 141. For "Madame X," see Deborah Davis, *Strapless: John Singer Sargent and the Fall of Madame X* (New York: Tarcher Penguin, 2003).

79. Goldfarb, *Gardner Museum*, 145.

80. Higonnet, "Private Museums," 84; Goldfarb, *Gardner Museum*, 145–47.

81. Higonnet, "Private Museums," 84.

82. Tharp, *Mrs. Jack*, 317.

83. Norton had carried on an extensive correspondence with John Ruskin. Shand-Tucci, *Art of Scandal*, 167.

84. Higonnet, "Private Museums," 80–81, 79.

85. Arthur Pound, *The Only Thing Worth Finding: The Life and Legacies of George Gough Booth* (Detroit, Mich.: Wayne State University Press, 1964), 19–25, 60, 108, 115–16.

86. Leonard Lanson Cline, quoted in Neil Harris, "North by Midwest," in *Design in America: The Cranbrook Vision 1925–1965* (exhibition catalogue) (Detroit and New York: Detroit Institute of Arts and Metropolitan Museum of Art, 1983), 18.

87. Pound, *Only Thing*, 251–55.

88. Ibid., 271, 273; Kathryn Bishop Eckert, *The Campus Guide: Cranbrook* (New York: Princeton Architectural Press, 2001), 1.

89. Eckert, *Cranbrook*, 18–21.

90. Ibid., 24.

91. Pound, *Only Thing*, 330.

92. Eckert, *Cranbrook*, 6.

93. Pound, *Only Thing*, 304–6.

94. Harris, "North by Midwest," 15–16.

95. Eckert, *Cranbrook*, vii.

96. Ibid., 96–103, 140–42.

97. Jervis Bell McMechan, *Christ Church Cranbrook: A History of the Parish to Commemorate the 50th Anniversary of the Consecration of the Church, 1928–1978* (Bloomfield Hills, Mich.: Christ Church Cranbrook, 1979), 37–38, 46.

98. McMechan, *Christ Church*, 40–41; Eckert, *Cranbrook*, 56.

99. Keith N. Morgan, "Introduction," in *The Makers of Trinity Church in the City of Boston*, ed. James F. O'Gorman (Amherst: University of Massachusetts Press, 2004), 7; Richard Guy Wilson, "Architecture, Landscape, and City Planning," in *The American Renaissance 1876–1917* (exhibition catalog) (New York: Brooklyn Museum, Pantheon, 1979), 112.

100. Eckert, *Cranbrook*, 56.

101. Ibid., 57–58, 64, 65.

102. Ibid., 62, 64.

103. "On the High Duty of Architects," in Pound, *Only Thing*, 487.

104. See ANB article for basic narrative.

105. Ford R. Bryan, *Clara: Mrs. Henry Ford* (Dearborn, Mich.: Ford Books, 2001), 144.

106. Ibid., 16, 27.

107. Ibid., 297.

108. Robert Lacey, *Ford: The Men and the Machine* (Boston: Little, Brown, 1986), 7.

109. Lacey, *Ford*, 7.

110. Ibid., 114. Burroughs was the enthusiastic, if somewhat unlikely, traveling companion of Ford and his more likely friends, Thomas Edison and Harvey Firestone. For several summers, the four assembled a small caravan and toured the country, attracting both humble and presidential visitors during their stops. See Harvey S. Firestone, *Men and Rubber: The Story of a Business* (Garden City, N.Y.: Doubleday, Page, 1926), 228. Firestone was senior warden of St. Paul's Episcopal Church, Akron, during the rectorship of Walter Tunks, who played a role in the founding of Alcoholics Anonymous because of the problems of one of the younger Firestones. For this connection, see "AA History," http://www.rewritables.net/cybriety/aa_and_the_oxford_group.htm.

111. Lacey, *Ford*, 57–58.

112. Ibid. 409–10.

113. See Neil Baldwin, *Henry Ford and the Jews: The Mass Production of Hate* (New York: Public Affairs, 2001).

114. Samuel S. Marquis, *Henry Ford: An Interpretation* (Boston: Little, Brown, 1923), 147, 154.

115. Ibid., 96–97. Marquis staunchly defended this enterprise against charges of paternalism, claiming that the only liberties Ford employees were deprived of were those of getting drunk, abusing their families, and the like (98–99).

116. Bryan, *Clara*, 144; Douglas Brinkley, *Wheels for the World: Henry Ford, His Company, and A Century of Progress 1903–2003* (New York: Viking, 2003), 276.

117. Marquis, *Henry Ford*, 140.

118. Ibid., 104.

119. Ibid., 109.

120. Ibid., 90.

121. Ibid., 57, 127.

122. Ibid., 142.

123. Ibid., chap. 16.

124. Ibid., 164.

125. Ibid., 97–98.

126. Lacey, *Ford*, 224–27. During his lifetime, Ford donated a total of some $37 million dollars to philanthropic causes, including $10.5 million to the hospital. William Greenleaf, DAB Ford biography, supp. 4.

127. Lacey, *Ford*, 313–26. Edsel was a member of Christ Church in Grosse Pointe, from which he was buried in 1943, but it is not clear that his activity as an Episcopalian was any greater than his father's had been. Bryan, *Clara*, 280.

128. Bryan, *Clara*, 233.

129. Lacey, *Ford*, 31; *Henry Ford Museum/Greenfield Village: An Illustrated History* (Santa Barbara, Calif.: Allison Publishing Group, 1993).

130. *Henry Ford Museum*, 17.

131. Franklin Leslie Long and Lucy Bunce Long, *The Henry Ford Era at Richmond Hill, Georgia* (Darien, Ga.: privately printed, 1998), 70–72.

132. Bryan, *Clara*, 310–11, 318, 320.

133. Ibid., 180, 292.

134. Marquis, *Henry Ford*, 55.

135. George Humphrey Yetter, *Williamsburg Before and After: The Rebirth of Virginia's Colonial Capital* (Williamsburg, Va.: Colonial Williamsburg Foundation, 1989), 49. A full biography, lacking annotation, but based on voluminous primary sources left behind by Goodwin, is Dennis Montgomery, *A Link Among the Days: The Life and Times of the Reverend Doctor W.A.R. Goodwin, the Father of Colonial Williamsburg* (Richmond, Va.: Dietz Press, 1998).

136. Montgomery, *Link*, 22, 26.

137. Ibid., 32–33, 36.

138. *History of the Theological Seminary in Virginia and its Historical Background* (2 vols.) (New York: Edwin S. Gorham, 1923).

139. Montgomery, *Link*, 47–48, 52.

140. Anders Greenspan, *Creating Colonial Williamsburg* (Washington, D.C.: Smithsonian Institution Press, 2002), 16–17.

141. Montgomery, *Link*, 65–66.

142. Ibid., 100.

143. Ibid., 88–89.

144. Ibid., 101–2.

145. Ibid., 107, 118, 163.

146. See Montgomery, *Link*, 4, for an account of a radio broadcast of Goodwin's sponsored by the Daughters of the American Revolution.

147. Greenspan, *Creating Colonial Williamsburg*, 8.

148. Yetter, *Williamsburg Before and After*, 51–52.

149. Greenspan, *Creating Colonial Williamsburg*, 9.

150. Yetter, *Williamsburg Before and After*, 49.

151. Quoted in Montgomery, *Link*, xiv.

152. Rev. Wm. A. R. Goodwin, A.M., *Bruton Parish Church Restored and its Historic Environment* (Petersburg, Va.: Franklin Press, 1907), 33, 176, 178.

153. Ibid., 153.

154. Ibid., 45. A bible was given to Bruton Parish Church by King Edward VII on the occasion of its three hundredth anniversary, which was also that of "the establishment of the English Church and English civilization in America" (50–51).

155. Ibid., 162–63.

156. Ibid., 167.

157. For the latter two, see *Centennial Celebration: 1835 + 1935 St. Paul's' Episcopal Church, Akron, Ohio* (Akron, Ohio: St. Paul's, 1935), and Charles A. Silliman, *The Story of Christ Church Christiana Hundred and its People* (Wilmington, Del.: Hambleton Co., 1960), 136.

158. Douglass Shand-Tucci, *Boston Bohemia 1881–1900*, vol. 1 of *Ralph Adams Cram: Life and Architecture* (Amherst: University of Massachusetts Press, 1995).

159. Levine, *Highbrow, Lowbrow*, chap. 2 ("The Sacralization of Culture.") On museums as temples, see Ingrid A. Steffenson-Bruce, *Marble Palaces, Temples of Art: Art Museums, Architecture, and American Culture, 1890–1930* (Lewisburg, Pa.: Bucknell University Press, 1998).

160. Susan M. Pearce, *On Collecting: An Investigation into Collecting in the European Tradition* (London: Routledge, 1995), 374.

161. Ibid., 272, 232.

162. Jeanne Halgren Kilde, *When Church Became Theatre: The Transformation of Evangelical Architecture and Worship in Nineteenth Century America* (Oxford: Oxford University Press, 2002).

163. Shepherd Knapp, *A History of the Brick Presbyterian Church in the City of New York* (New York: Brick Presbyterian Church, 1909), 380–83. See also Promey, "Visible Liberalism."

164. William Leach, "Strategists of Display and the Production of Desire," in *Consuming Visions: Accumulation and Display of Goods in America, 1880–1920*, ed. Simon

J. Bronner (Winterthur, Del., and New York: Winterthur Museum and W.W. Norton, 1989), 103.

165. Ibid., 104.

166. Ibid., 127.

Epilogue

1. "Communicants" are members who have received Communion at least once during a given year. Figures for "baptized members" begin only in 1930, and in that year these members numbered slightly under two million—considerably more than communicants. "Comparative Statistics of the Episcopal Church," *The Episcopal Church Annual 2008* (Wilton, Conn.: Morehouse-Barlow, 2009), 20–21.

2. David L. Homes, *A Brief History of the Episcopal Church* (Valley Forge, Pa.: Trinity Press International, 1993), 150–51. Boarding school histories show little recognition of the Great Depression but give considerable coverage to the years of World War II, during which many of their students and alumni perished. See Holmes, chap. 3, for accounts of cathedral building during this time.

3. Kit and Frederica Konolige, *The Power of Their Glory: America's Ruling Class: The Episcopalians* (New York: Wyden, 1978), 265, 268. Acheson was the son of the bishop of Connecticut; Hull is buried at the National Cathedral.

4. Gardiner H. Shattuck Jr., *Episcopalians and Race: Civil War to Civil Rights* (Lexington: University Press of Kentucky, 2000), 44.

5. See Jerome Karabel, *The Chosen: The Hidden History of Admission and Exclusion at Harvard, Yale, and Princeton* (Boston: Houghton Mifflin, 2005), 2.

6. "Comparative Statistics," 21. The number of communicants for that year was approximately 2.3 million.

7. Shattuck, *Episcopalians and Race*, chap. 7.

8. At this writing (2015), the most recent effort, in South Carolina, is still enmeshed in the courts.

9. Daniel T. Rodgers, *Age of Fracture* (Cambridge, Mass.: Belknap Press of Harvard University Press, 2011).

10. David A. Hollinger, *After Cloven Tongues of Fire: Protestant Liberalism in Modern American History* (Princeton, N.J.: Princeton University Press, 2013), 38.

11. On Ford and the Bushes, see David L. Holmes, *The Faiths of the Postwar Presidents: From Truman to Obama* (Athens: University of Georgia Press, 2012); and Randall L. Balmer, *God in the White House: A History* (New York: HarperCollins, 2008). On McCain, see http://www.nytimes.com/books/first/t/timberg-mccain.html and http://www.christianpost.com/news/mccain-i-m-baptist-not-episcopalian-29334/.

12. One conspiracy-minded website argues, with some plausibility, that twenty of the twenty-four "senior administrators" (presidents, provosts, board chairs) of the eight Ivy League schools at the time were either Jewish or had Jewish spouses.

13. Phillip E. Hammond, *Religion and Personal Autonomy: The Third Disestablishment in America* (Columbia: University of South Carolina Press, 1992). According to Hammond, the first disestablishment resulted from the First Amendment's prohibition of the recognition of any particular religious group by the federal government. The second was the growing popular legitimacy of Catholicism and Judaism and the loss of the informal "establishment" status of Protestantism during the mid-twentieth century.

14. Laurie Goldstein, "Air Force Chaplain Tells of Academy Proselytizing," *New York Times*, June 12, 2005.

15. James D. Davidson and Ralph E. Pyle, *Ranking Faiths: Religious Stratification in America* (Lanham, Md.: Rowman & Littlefield, 2011), 111.

16. For an account of the current state of one such school, see Shamus Rahman Kahn, *Privilege: The Making of an Adolescent Elite at St. Paul's School* (Princeton, N.J.: Princeton University Press, 2011).

17. Hollinger, *After Cloven Tongues*, 13–14, 46.

18. Davidson and Pyle, *Ranking Faiths*, 133–34.

19. For an example, see David Hein, *Noble Powell and the Episcopal Establishment in the Twentieth Century* (Urbana: University of Illinois Press, 2001). A fictional counterpart appears in Edwin O'Connell's novel of Boston politics, *The Last Hurrah* (Boston: Little, Brown, 1956).

Index